F

Also by Eugene A. Sloane

Sloane's Handy Pocket Guide to Bicycle Repair

Sloane's New Bicycle Maintenance Manual

The Complete Book of Bicycling All-New 4th Edition

Sloane's Complete Book of All-Terrain Bicycles

Eugene A. Sloane

A FIRESIDE BOOK

Published by Simon & Schuster

New York   London   Toronto   Sydney   Tokyo   Singapore

Fireside
Simon & Schuster Building
Rockefeller Center
1230 Avenue of the Americas
New York, New York 10020

Copyright © 1985, 1991 by Eugene A. Sloane

First Fireside Edition 1985

FIRESIDE and colophon are registered trademarks
of Simon & Schuster Inc.

Designed by Chris Welch
Manufactured in the United States of America

1 3 5 7 9 10 8 6 4 2

Library of Congress Cataloging in Publication Data

Sloane, Eugene A.
Sloane's complete book of all-terrain bicycles.
p. cm.
"A Fireside book."
Rev. ed. of: Eugene A. Sloane's complete guide to all-terrain
bicycles. ©1985.
Includes bibliographical references (p.) and index.
1. All-terrain bicycles. 2. All-terrain cycling. I. Sloane, Eugene A.
Complete guide to all-terrain bicycles. II. Title. III. Title: Complete
book of all-terrain bicycles.
TL410.S55 1991
629.227′2—dc20   91-7383
                                            CIP
ISBN 0-671-67587-7

Acknowledgments

This book would not have been possible without the wholehearted and enthusiastic support and cooperation of key people in the bicycle industry, friends who run bike shops or who do a lot of ATB riding, and medical health experts who sent along data on helmets and physical well-being.

In particular I want to thank my wife, Carol, who wrote the section on clothing in Chapter 4, and Sara Ballantyne, world champion women's ATB racer, who wrote most of Chapter 10 on ATB racing.

My thanks go to these people in the bicycle industry who furnished much helpful technical information on their products: Robin Parker, Fisher MountainBikes; Jack Moore, The Third Hand (bicycle tools via catalog); Mark Super, United Bicycle Tool Supply, Ltd.; Ted Dishner, Moss, Inc.; Arlene Haislip, Lite-Speed (much good technical data on clothing); Doris Riefling, Yakima Racks, and Peter J. Fell, Thule, makers of excellent bike carriers; John Rossi, Proto Tools, and Howard Hawks, Park Tools; Dave Hostetter, Blackburn Designs (carriers for bikes); Imre J. Barsy, Specialized Bicycle Components; Richard Storino and Patrick S. Clay, Campagnolo USA; Bill Russell, Klein Bicycle Corporation; Richard Goodwin, Mavic USA; Walt Jarvis, Bicycle Dealer's Showcase; Clarke Brooks, Wheelsmith Fabrications, Inc.; Bill Wilkinson, Pro-Bike News and Bicycle Federation of America; John Arrington, Moonstone Manufacturing, Inc.; Rob Templin and Gary Marcus, Shimano American Corporation, for technical data and excellent artwork; Conrad Anderson, Sun Metal Products Company; Sky Yaeger, SunTour USA; Brian Foley and Tom Armstrong, Cannondale Corporation; Paul Chess, Schwinn Bicycle Company.

For much valuable information on health, head injuries and preventive medicine, my thanks to Joanne Fairchild, Emanuel Hospital, Portland, OR; Lisa Rogers, Injury Prevention Department, Harbor View Hospital, Seattle, WA; A. Irving Marshall, Director, Snell Laboratories; Chris Tomaselli, LTI Life Technology, Inc.; Mary Beth Harhen, Giro Sports Design, Inc.; Michael Martindale, Sports Medicine Director, Portland Adventist Medical Center, Portland, OR; and Mark Williams, Bell Helmets, Inc.

My thanks to Garry Snook, Performance Bicycle Shop, and Arnie Nashbar, Bike Nashbar, for permission to use tables from their excellent and exhaustive bicycle catalogs.

Joe Foggia, who operates a very fine all-terrain bicycle shop, in Sandy, OR, and Theo Patterson, Portland, OR, editor of P.U.M.P., an ATB newsletter and ATB enthusiast club, I owe a lot of appreciation for their tips on trail riding based on their years of experience on the mountain trails of Oregon and Washington. And to Diana Fritschner and Andy Bowman, Media Director, United States Cycling Federation, for data on racing.

Greg Siple, of the BikeCentennial, sent along some excellent photos of road and trail scenes. Thanks, Greg.

I just know I have left a lot of people out of this acknowledgment list. You all helped immensely to get this book done, not, perhaps, on time, but at least as complete as I could make it. Thanks again, gang.

Eugene A. Sloane
Vancouver, WA.

Contents

1

The Adventures of All-Terrain Bicycling

Y ou're not just buying one bike when you invest in an all-
terrain bicycle. You're buying at least seven bikes in one.
Here's a two-wheeler that takes you smoothly on paved roads, comfortably on remote mountain trails, reliably through sand, mud, even
snow, and through shallow streams. It's a bike you can commute to work
on one day, ride on a dirt mountain fire trail the next. If your favorite
trout stream is a day's hike over a narrow trail, it will be an hour away
on your ATB. On overnight or longer wilderness trail rides your ATB
will easily carry all your camping gear as well as yourself. You can carry
a child safely and comfortably in a child carrier over the rear wheel or
tow a trailer to carry a child, your camping gear or groceries.

On an ATB you can traverse remote mountain trails so silently that
nearby wild animals may not sense your closeness. I have stopped to
admire the view from a mountainside, watched bald eagles and hawks
soaring on thermals, searching for prey, deer grazing on a hillock across
the valley. On one memorable occasion I rounded a twist in a trail and
was confronted by a rattlesnake straddling the narrow path, coiled in a
pool of sunshine, sunning itself. We met so suddenly I had no choice but
to pull up on the handlebars, hop the front wheel over the snake and
then lean quickly over the handlebars to lift the rear wheel over the
rattler. I'm not sure if the rear wheel did clear, I felt a bump, but a turn
came up quickly and for some reason I felt safer going on rather than
returning to see if the snake was okay. Sorry, SPCA.

You can race ATBs in National Off-Road Bicycle Association (NORBA) trail events and trials events, which are fully described in Chapter 10. Or go solo or convivially with friends on long-distance rides over the highway.

ATBS ARE EASY TO RIDE

It takes very little more effort to pedal an ATB than to pedal a skinny-tire road bike, even on paved roads. On rough mountain trails, a road bike would slither and slide all over the place. Here an ATB would soar past the skinny-tired machine. An interesting year-long ride test by one of the pioneers of ATB design, Joe Breeze of Mill Valley, CA, compared elapsed times over a measured course. Joe rode an ATB one day, a skinny-tired road bike the next. Over the 12 months it took him only 10 percent longer to ride the ATB than the road bike. That extra time is more than made up for by the additional comfort built into the ATB, thanks to its shock-absorbing fat tires and the more comfortable, upright stance from the flat handlebars (Fig. 1-1). My ATB soaks up road shock so well, in fact, that I find myself able to ride longer distances without tiring than on my favorite handmade road bike. I have pedaled long distances, for weeks at a time, across country over paved roads on both road bikes and ATBs. I much prefer the ATB for comfort, greater safety (better brakes, because the fat tires offer more road contact), vastly improved handling and stability when carrying camp-gear-laden panniers fore and aft (Fig. 1-2). The sturdier, heavier-duty components of an ATB, such as brakes, derailleurs, cables, pedals and headset are more reliable than those of a road bike, especially when you're carrying all your gear, such as clothing, tent, sleeping bag, cook stove. Reliability of components is vital on a trail ride, when the nearest bike shop may be miles and days away.

ATBs are great for kids. The sturdier frame and the fat-tire-protected wheels can withstand rough use, so even the less expensive models are ideal for teens and college folk to use between home and class or around the campus. You can hop these bikes over curbs and other obstructions with far less concern (and more safety) than you'd feel for your more fragile skinny-tired wheel and frame.

Fig. 1-1. *The flat handlebars of an ATB have all controls ready to hand, making for a more upright, comfortable riding position than the down-turned bars of a road bike. Note, too, the frame-mounted carriers, fore and aft, and the elliptical tubing of this premier Mountain Goat deluxe machine.*

Fig. 1-2. *When it's loaded down with panniers front and rear and other camp gear, an ATB is far more stable and easier to handle than a similarly equipped road bike. Note that the load is evenly divided front and rear, and that panniers, especially up front, are carried low to the ground for a low center of gravity.*

ATBS PRESERVE NATURE

You'll be cheered by the fact that ATBs, ridden with care on remote trails, are far less damaging to the sensitive ecology of mountain and prairie than horses and certainly noisy, polluting dirt motorcycles. ATBs have no sharp hooves, for example, to pit once-smooth grassy slopes and trails, nor do they create noise and pollution and rip up the trail as do dirt motorcycles.

In fact, one of the major joys of riding an ATB off the road, far from the madding crowd, is the peace, quiet and solitude one experiences. There's nothing but you and your ATB between sky and trail; the vista of distant hills, the nearness of old growth timber, the soothing scent of mountain flowers seem to be for you alone.

One trip—it took only a day, but its memory lingers on—began early one morning. We hit the trailhead near the sparkling blue waters of a small lake. As we climbed back and forth over a switchback trail, we could see the little lake shining through trees from time to time as we ascended higher and higher. We pedaled through the scent and beauty of pine, madrone and buckeye trees. In half an hour we had left the noise and bustle and stress of modern society far behind. The only sounds to be heard were the songs of birds, the chirp of squirrels signaling our presence, the soft push of our tires on the dirt trail. After just one hour we had traveled about five miles, the equivalent of a half-day's journey of a backpack-laden hiker. We felt peace, tranquility and gratitude for the absence of trucks, cars and motorcycles. On this trail the dangers of motor homes controlled by inexpert drivers on narrow highways was, thankfully, absent.

From time to time we came upon equestrians. The tinkle of a bike bell signaled our presence well in advance, so the four-footed animals had plenty of time to single file to give us passing room. In a few hours we had traveled nearly 10 miles and climbed some 1,500 feet. While stopped for lunch, we spotted a blue heron far below near the water (yes, we used binocs), a huge eagle, wings outspread, soaring above, a herd of deer watching us warily from a nearby ridge. Later, the grade began to increase, at times to an estimated 10 percent, which we could handle by shifting our 18 or 21 speeds to the lowest gear. Returning down the trail's sometimes steep incline was no problem. The excellent brakes of our ATBs kept speed well under control. Fat tires and resilient frames absorbed shocks as our wheels sped over bumps, small rocks and even an occasional tree root or small fallen log. Our wide, flat handlebars, together with the ATB's shock-absorbing characteristics, combined to give excellent steering control and stability. Brake and shift levers, right on the handlebar, were within easy, quick reach (Fig 1-1) without having to look down to fumble for shift levers. The aggressive knobby tread pattern of our fat tires gripped the ground going up and helped us maintain accurate steering going down as well as going up.

SAFER ROAD TOURING ON AN ATB

Even on the highway I find an ATB safer to ride than a road bike. For example, there are going to be times, few if you're lucky, when you just *have* to leave the road to escape an erratic driver, or one who is after your skin. It happens. Or sometimes the car coming toward you and the car coming from behind meet just where you are. Why cars can't meet someplace else I'll never know! If you have to get off the road to escape an erratic driver, your deeply treaded fat tires can help keep you upright even if you have to drop an inch or two off the pavement down onto a more slippery surface, such as gravel or grass. And if you have to hit a ditch, chances are much greater on an ATB than on a road bike that you can keep upright until you can safely stop, or even stay upright and veer safely back onto the highway once the hazard has passed. The fat tires, with a more aggressive tread, grip better for hard steering, and the flat wider handlebar gives you greater turning leverage than the narrow downturned handlebar of a road bike. There's a lot more about safe cycling, on and off the road, in Chapter 3, which I urge you read carefully.

PEDAL EXERCISE AND YOUR HEART

Cycling helps make your heart stronger, pump more blood at a slower rate and so work less stressfully even when you're exercising hard, making demands on it. Many racing cyclists, for example, have a resting pulse rate as low as 45 beats per minute. If you have been sitting still while reading this book, stop now and measure your pulse rate. If it's much over 75 beats a minute it's working too hard for this sedentary activity. The higher the pulse rate, the higher your blood pressure (not, of course, the only reason for high blood pressure). A strong, healthy heart *can* pump more blood with less effort than one that's in the chest of a couch potato (not you, not you). Cycling helps your heart in several ways:

1. *Bicycling exercise helps keep your blood pressure at a healthy low level.* It takes muscles to sustain the workout that drives your heartbeat up to your threshold aerobic rate for at least 30 minutes. Your heart should pump blood efficiently and at a high enough rate to reduce the buildup of fatty substances on artery walls (atherosclerosis) that contributes to high blood pressure. It's a good idea to have your blood pressure checked once in a while. As a ballpark figure, a blood pressure of 120/60 is great if you're under 30. If it's much over 160/95, ask your physician to set up an exercise regimen, using your bike, to bring it down. Blood pressure varies with age, so a pressure that's a health hazard at, say, 30 may be perfectly normal at age 50 or above.

2. *There's medical evidence that exercise inhibits or reduces the level of "bad" cholesterol in your bloodstream and builds up the level of the "good" cholesterol which keeps arteries clean.* Exercise doesn't mean that you can consume a high-cholesterol diet such as a breakfast of bacon, ham and eggs, or a dinner of pork chops, though! It's no excuse for a high-cholesterol diet. There really isn't *any* excuse for such a fatty food intake. There are plenty of good books on what's healthy to eat, so my advice is to buy one and follow it. Get your cholesterol level checked at any hospital (for around $7). It takes about 10 minutes to get an answer. If your cholesterol level is much over 200 you need to make some drastic changes in your exercise and diet regimes, again with the advice of your physician. Many hospitals have a special day on which they make these tests and ask that you call for an appointment. Hospitals with departments named "Health Education," "Health Maintenance" or "Sports Medicine" make such cholesterol level checks.

A stress test at your local hospital is an excellent way to assure yourself that you can safely exercise for hours at your threshold aerobic level by bicycle. In a stress test you're hooked up to an electrocardiogram (EKG) monitor. Then you start walking on a treadmill. A trained medical technician watches the EKG readout. The treadmill is gradually sped up until your pace brings your heart rate to your *maximum* aerobic capacity. The EKG chart will spot any abnormalities in your heart as it pumps away at full blast. Once you get a clean bill of health from such a stress test you can pedal away as hard as you wish *provided* you have built up the muscles needed to do it.

3. *Bicycling helps keep calcium deposits from hardening arteries,* a process that begins at birth. Calcium-coated arteries also impede blood

flow, contribute to high blood pressure, even cause cerebral hemorrhage, strokes and death.

4. *Bicycling helps create auxiliary networks of arteries and veins* that carry blood to heart muscles. If one such artery gets blocked, there will be others to take over the task of supplying nutrient-laden blood to the heart and so prevent coronary heart failure.

5. *Exercise relieves stress.* Work, marriage or other personal relationships can, as you know, create stress in your life. One excellent way to relieve the pressure from stress is by exercise—what better way than by commuting to and from work each day by bicycle or pedaling hard for an hour or so in the evening? Stress can be a root cause of hypertension, drug abuse, even cancer. I found cycling the 12 miles each way between my home in a Chicago suburb and my job in downtown Chicago to be a great way to unwind both before and after work. When I got home I was even ready to speak sweetly to everyone. While riding to work along the beautiful bike path along Lake Michigan, I had time to plan what I wanted to get done that day.

Exercise and a long and healthy life are closely related. It is a fact that as the annual sales of bicycles skyrocketed from around 6 million to over 10.8 million between 1970 and 1980, the incidence of hypertension (high blood pressure above 160/95) dropped about 16 percent, the death rate for all males by 21 percent. Certainly a nationwide emphasis on diet and exercise gets a lot of credit here. For men between 25 and 44 the death rate dropped 37 percent during this period, and for men 65 and over it fell by 15.5 percent. I like to think that bicycle sales and health statistics are closely related.

6. *Cycling maintains a higher level of sustained energy all day.* When you're in good physical condition you can keep alert, work harder and more efficiently than a person in poor shape. In the business world you need this alertness, especially after lunch, when around 2:00 P.M. many people (myself included before I began a cycling regimen) tend to lose steam, to slow down, become less alert, make more mistakes.

7. *Cycling saves money.* Commuting to work by bicycle saves wear and tear on your car, cuts fuel costs, ends parking lot fees and train fare. I paid for my good bike in one year by taking my bike to work. Health benefits aside, I found it took very little more time to commute by bike than by car or train. It sure was pleasant to be able to be close to nature enroute to work each day and, above all, to be free of the hassles of rush-hour traffic or crowded trains.

CYCLING MAKES YOU HEALTHIER (MAYBE EVEN WEALTHIER AND WISER)

You can tailor exercise on your bike to match your level of physical fitness. First, find your level of fitness by consulting your doctor. Work your way up from a soft body to one with muscle and energy to spare. If you've just bought a bike but haven't engaged in regular physical exercise, start out by cycling slowly, say, at a pedal cadence of 60 rpm (spinning a pedal 60 times per minute) on the flat. Stay off steep hills. Pedal for 20 or 30 minutes. Don't push it, or you could tear a muscle, which can be painful and keep you off the bike for a couple of weeks. In a half hour you should ride about three to four miles (pretty slow, but you'll be able to sustain more speed as you shape up).

If you've been ill with, say, the flu and have been bedridden or housebound, be aware that even if you *were* in good shape it takes twice as long to get back in shape as it did for you to lose your conditioning. For example, if you were laid up for two weeks it's going to take a month of steadily increasing workouts to get back to your preillness physical condition. Please note, too, that you should *never* stop exercising, no matter what your age. If you stop, you lose body strength fast. That's why there seems so little connection between athletic prowess as a youth, and health and a long life when you get older.

Here's a brief for cycling in old age! Keith Kingbay, one of the most knowledgeable bicycle experts I have ever met, reported in an old issue of the *League of American Wheelmen Journal* about a 117-year-old man in Kuala Lumpur, Malaysia, who cycled 27 miles to "pay the fine of a 40-year-old woman who was imprisoned for living with him out of wedlock." Both Moslems, he had been married 17 times, she was married and so could not marry him, but later did so after a divorce. Way to go, man! There's a moral here, somewhere.

After a few weeks of daily slow and easy pedaling, gradually increase your pedal cadence to 70 rpm and try a few easy hills, say, of no more than 5 percent grade (check your local highway or road department for the grade, if you wish).

Now you're ready for an aerobically significant workout. There are two levels of aerobic activity, the maximum and the threshold level. The maximum level is based on your age (assuming a reasonable level of physical fitness) and is a pulse or heartbeat rate which you should not exceed. Calculate your maximum pulse count by subtracting your age from 220. For example, if you're 30 years old, your maximum pulse rate will be 220 − 30, or 190. Check this with your doctor. The threshold level is a pulse rate you can safely maintain in exercise, and is generally taken to be 75 percent of your maximum rate, although some athletes prefer 85 percent. I'd stick to the lower, 75 percent rate. If your maximum pulse rate for your age is 190 beats per minute, your threshold level would be 190 × .75, which is 142 beats per minute. If you don't reach that level (pulse rate of 142 beats per minute), you are not working hard enough to get the full health benefits from the time you spend exercising. If you're riding a stationary exerciser and reach your aerobic threshold, you should be bathed in sweat and feeling great after a 30-minute workout. I should point out that cycling is a *lot* easier on leg joints, particularly knees, than jogging. A less stressful exercise is swimming, but I can't say that does much for your leg muscles. At least it never has for mine. But if you grip the handlebars, bear down and pull up (slightly) as you ride, you'll strengthen and tone upper body muscles as well as those of legs and thighs. You can buy a bike computer in most bike stores that will give you a readout of pedal cadence, mph, elapsed time, trip and accumulated mileage. Some of these computers can also read your heart rate in beats per minute, although I find the second hand on my watch an easy way to measure heart rate. Just count your pulse for 15 seconds and multiply that rate by 4.

WANT TO LOSE WEIGHT? GET ON YOUR BIKE!

You'll burn around 350 to 500 calories for each hour of vigorous (70 crank rpm or more) cycling. If you eat a low-fat diet of 1,800 to 2,000 calories a day, you'll be a trimmer, leaner, younger-looking you after six months or so of cycling an hour each day. Commuting an hour each way to work by bicycle sure did it for me. In just three months I could take in my belt an inch and a half. I did not lose much weight, because the lard around my middle was replaced by bigger, heavier and stronger muscles in my abdomen, legs, chest and arms. I was happy to make this swap, believe me.

PROTECTS YOUR JOINTS

When I started biking regularly, way back in the olden days of the mid 1960s, my right knee pained a lot. This knee had been injured in a football accident in high school many years before. The pain became so intense I consulted an orthopedic surgeon, who determined, after x-ray and arthroscopic examination, that I had torn a major knee cartilage. My doctor said that if I wanted to avoid becoming a cripple in my old age I should give up cycling. So I did, with great reluctance. I went out and bought a good pair of roller skates, the kind with plastic wheels, and began roller skating to work. He hadn't said anything about not skating.

Each day I skated past the *Chicago Tribune* office. Finally one of my reporter friends spotted this stock exchange executive in a business suit on his skates and ran a short story with a photo about this phenomenon. My orthopod phoned that day and advised that, all things considered, I was, after all, better off on the bike. Those were the days before sports medicine had become a medical specialty and doctors began to realize that strong muscle tissue around bad knees can compensate for such knee damage as mine. So I hung up the skates, got back on the bike and eventually found that by cycling gently, and with more pressure from my good left leg, I had built up supportive muscles around the right knee and the pain had disappeared.

I should also add that cycling leads to balanced muscles, so that one set of weak muscles won't lead to painful tears in a stronger set. For example, I was back on the bike after nearly a month off from a bad case of flu. It was springtime, and I tucked in behind a lovely young woman dressed in cycling togs. She must have seen me, because she began to speed up a bit. No woman was going to leave *me* behind, no sirree. So I stayed with her. The next day was filled with pain, which lasted two weeks and kept me off the bike during that period. What happened was that the adductor muscles which control the twist or turning of the leg were torn by the undue stress of my admittedly chauvinistic behavior. They were not strong enough to compensate for the stronger muscles that pushed my leg up and down. It took over two months to build up all my leg muscles so they were all equally strong.

CYCLING SLOWS AGE-RELATED OSTEOPOROSIS

As you age, calcium tends to leave your bones, so they become more brittle and break easily. Let me tell you what happened to me. I had x-rays taken a few years ago, for a reason I do not recall. Viewing the x-rays, my doctor remarked that I had the hip bone density of a 25-year-old, though I was well over 50 at a time. He felt that my cycling had slowed or even prevented undue calcium loss that would have made these bones less dense, more brittle. So get on a bike for denser bones, and avoid the tragedy of having to have artificial replacement of glass-brittle hip bones.

I won't take bad weather for an excuse not to ride your bike. Even if you live in the so-called Temperate Zone, where the winter temperature can drop well below zero degrees Fahrenheit, you can still get a good workout on a bike exerciser. On the market are excellent machines on which you can mount your bike and pedal away while watching TV. There's even a model with rollers that grip the rim flats of wheels with knobby fat tires so you don't have to change to a smooth-tread fat tire when you mount the bike on this trainer.

Bicycling can really be your route to a longer, healthier and even happier life. In the next chapter I will review the options available to you in an all-terrain bicycle, including selecting the one model that's right for you.

2

Selecting the All-Terrain Bicycle That's Right for You

I n this chapter I will discuss price considerations, bike quality, how to fit the bike to your body, where and how to buy an all-terrain bicycle and how to safety-check a new bike before taking it out of the store. I'll review a few selected ATBs only as samples of what's on the market. There are too many ATB manufacturers, too many styles, prices and qualities of bikes, too many choices to do justice to all of them in one book. For example, by my last count, there were some 78 ATB manufacturers, and each had 2 to 12 models in its line. In this chapter I'll select a few I have used, ridden, tested and dissected, and will try to cover a price range from $200 to $2,500.

If you go on price alone, you may regret the choice later on. If you go on quality alone, you could spend well over $2,000 and still not have the bike that fits your needs. If you want a comfortable, reliable and safe bike to ride to work, you could buy one of the better hybrids, a bike that has some of the ruggedness and all of the comfort of an ATB but at a much more modest price. If you want a bike for all purposes and all seasons, then you need a top-quality *reliable* machine that can take a beating on the trail, yet be comfortable enough for long-distance road trips or for commuting between home and work. The bike that's right for you will combine utility, cost, quality and fit. Here's what to look for in an ATB.

SELECTION CRITERIA

Before deciding on price, I urge you to review the following selection criteria. You'll likely have to spend, in 1990 dollars, *at least* $350 for a safe, reliable all-terrain bicycle. You may be able to do better by buying a used machine for sale in the classified ads.

If you have the time, you could start your search for a good ATB by talking to experienced riders. You can find friendly riders at any ATB race. To find such races check local bike shops or bike clubs, read local or regional bike newsletters, or join the National Off-Road Bicycle Association (NORBA) (see Appendix). Races are held all over the country, even in winter through snow and over ice. You can count on ATB racers for a wealth of information on the sturdiest, most reliable bike for the money. These men and women give their bikes a workout bouncing downhill, taking jumps, riding fast down rough trails and doing other bike-breaking maneuvers. If there's any weakness in a bike's frame, or in any of its components such as derailleurs, brakes or rims, believe me, it will be discovered in a race.

YOUR RIDING NEEDS

If you're going to commute or go on casual day trips on paved roads, consider an ATB that's part mountain bike and part road bike, such as shown in Figure 2-1. If most of your riding will be on paved roads, a moderately priced ATB, around $350 to $500, will get you there in comfort and safety. If you intend to go off into the wilderness, you should get the best bike you can afford, or better, even if you have to eat oatmeal for a while. Count on spending a minimum of $500 for such a machine (Fig. 2-2). You can spend over $2,000 for the very best ATB, however (Fig. 2-3), or even more for a handmade custom bike tailored just for you. Remember, if you ride on trails, you could be miles from the nearest bike shop, so you do need, above all, a reliable bike that can stand up to the rigors of rides over bumpy trails, through mud, sand and even water up to the chain. If you want to compete in "trials" races (see Chapter 10), there's a special trials racing bike with super low gearing (Fig. 2-4) (more about gear selections in Chapter 6) so you can climb over logs, hop over stumps and ride over incredible obstacles most people would not even walk over.

Fig. 2-1. *Typical "city bike" is a cross between an ATB and a conventional road bike. This model, Schwinn's "Neu-Citi," has 1.75-inch × 26-inch tires, 10 speeds, flat handlebars, weighs 33 lb and costs $210.*

Fig. 2-2. *Mid-price ATB, Specialized's "Rockhopper" costs $532, has 21 speeds, is typical of ATBs in this price range.*

Fig. 2-3. *At around $2,000, this "Carbon 14" model by Ibis has a wound carbon fiber frame which offers light weight, responsiveness and durability.*

Fig. 2-4. *A special "trials" racing bike. Note the small chainwheel, the guard under the chainwheel which protects it in climbs over stumps and rocks, the rear-facing axle dropouts to keep the rear wheel aligned, and the sloping top tube which gives the rider more room to exert "body english" when climbing over obstructions. This is a special-purpose trials racing machine by Ibis.*

BUY ONLY IN A BIKE SHOP

Stay away from discount stores, auto parts shops and any other outlet that does not specialize in bikes. First, these oufits almost always carry cheap, poorly made ATBs. These bikes have heavy "clunker" frames, poor brakes, steel rims that don't stop as well as alloy rims, and other inferior components. Even if the discount store, by some miracle, offers a good ATB, you could still have problems. Cut-rate stores almost *never* have a trained mechanic who knows how to safely assemble a bike from the carton. I spend a lot of time working for attorneys as an expert witness on bike accidents, and I have many horror stories in my files of serious injuries suffered by riders on their very first ride out of the discount store. Not only are brakes on cheap bikes not nearly as effective as on more expensive machines, they are all too often improperly and unsafely adjusted by the untrained clerk who assembled the bike. There's also usually no one in the store who can instruct you on how to shift the bike safely or how to ride safely. It's unlikely that the store will have a trained bike mechanic who knows how to check and, if necessary, adjust the transmission system so the chain won't fall off the gears. If the chain falls off the big rear cog, it could get jammed between the spoke protector and the cog, or the spokes and the cog. Such a jam can lock up the rear wheel and the pedals and cause you to lose balance, fall and get hurt. If the chain falls off the small rear cog it can jam between the cog and the chain stay, with the same result. Even expensive bikes may require a lot of makeready before they're safe for you to ride. A trained, experienced mechanic is best qualified for this work.

You can also buy excellent ATBs from the catalog houses listed in the Appendix. If you're good with tools and know how things work, you can assemble the bike. Before you do, I urge you to read the rest of this book and study your owner's manual. Otherwise, I advise you to take the bike, in the carton, to a bike shop and let them assemble it for you. Later in this chapter I'll discuss how to check a new bike for safety before you ride off down the road or trail. Follow these same instructions when you've finished assembling a mail-order bike that's shipped to you.

Fig. 2-5. *Anatomy of an all-terrain bicycle: A, seat post. B, top tube. C, stem. D, steering head tube. E, fork. F, down tube. G, seat tube. H, chain stays. I, seat stays. J, chainwheels. K, crank.*

FITTING THE BIKE TO YOU

A bike too big or too small for you will most likely be hard to handle and for that reason may not be as safe as it should be. If the bike is too big there won't be enough room between the top tube (Fig. 2-5) and you. If you have to come down hard on the top tube for any reason, such as a panic stop, you could be hurt. If the bike is too small you can be hunched over the handlebars at an uncomfortable angle. Or you may not be able to get the saddle up high enough for full leg extension. You should be able to get the saddle up high enough so when the pedal is parallel to the seat tube (Fig. 2-6) your knee is just slightly bent. Too low a saddle can lead to serious knee injury if you pedal hard for a long time over a long distance. The saddle should not be so high that there is little or no clearance for you when you want to stand on the pedals to absorb road shock. If you're going over a speed bump, down a curb or fast downhill on a rough trail, you should use your legs and arms to lift your bottom up off the saddle (there's more on riding techniques in Chapter 3). If you can't lift your body up slightly, say, at least an inch, above the saddle, then the saddle's too high. Try a test ride to check these points.

Fig. 2-6. *To find the initial correct saddle height, sit on the bike with one foot on a pedal and the crank parallel to the seat tube. Adjust the saddle so your knee is slightly bent, as shown by this rider. Fine-tune saddle height as you ride, but pedal at least one hour between adjustments.*

START WITH FRAME SIZE

To find the bike that fits you, start with frame size. The simplest way to find your correct frame size is simply to straddle the bike, with both *stocking* feet on the ground. Stand up straight, over the top tube (Fig. 2-5). Now check the clearance between your crotch and the top tube (Fig. 2-7). Make sure there is at least 2 inches between your body and the top tube. A 1.5-inch clearance is okay for a road bike, but for bounc-

Fig. 2-7. *Stand over the top tube to make sure you have at least 2 inches clearance between you and that tube. The bike is too small if you have less clearance, because you need body room to set a foot on the ground when negotiating rough terrain or coming to a stop.*

ing around on the trail on an ATB you need more body clearance. Another way to determine proper frame size is to measure the distance from the ground to your crotch (inseam measurement) and select the frame size that gives you the minimum 2-inch clearance over the top tube. To get your inseam measurement stand straight up against the wall in your stocking feet, heels to the wall, and measure the distance between crotch and ground. Bicycle frame sizes are determined by the length of the seat tube, to the centerline of the bottom bracket axle (Fig. 2-8). Some makes of ATBs have a sloping top tube (Fig. 2-9 and Fig. 2-10) for greater crotch-to-top-tube clearance for a given frame size. Select such a bike by straddling it about two thirds of the way toward the highest point of the slope, toward the handlebars, to determine safe body-to-top-tube clearance.

All-terrain bicycles need and have a higher bottom bracket clearance than do road bikes (Fig. 2-8). The bottom bracket has to be higher so you can safely go over bumps, small logs and other trail hazards that

Fig. 2-8. *ATB frame size is determined by the length of the seat tube, B. A more accurate frame size specification would be the length of the head tube, D, because that's the same for ATBs as well as road bikes. The saddle can be adjusted fore or aft to lengthen or decrease the distance between the saddle and the handlebars, A. ATBs have a higher bottom bracket clearance, C, than road bikes.*

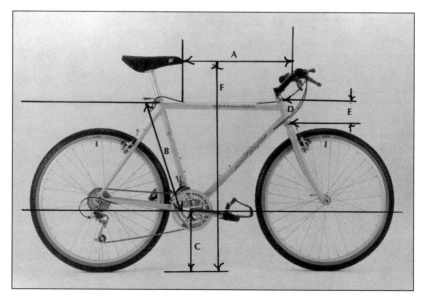

Fig. 2-9. This Schwinn "Essence" model has a sloping top tube, which gives the rider greater clearance between body and bike when maneuvering on rough terrain, for a given frame size B and C.

Fig. 2-10. A less sloping top tube is shown on this Marin Titanium model, which costs $1,500.

would dump a road bike. The higher bottom bracket clearance of an ATB also lets you make sharper turns at higher speeds on narrow trails. There is less danger of the pedal striking the ground as you lean into the turn, with the pedals and cranks parallel to the ground on such turns, as I note in Chapter 3 on trail riding techniques. Road bikes are (or should be) ridden only on smooth surfaces, so their bottom bracket can be closer to the ground.

ATB frame *sizes* are typically smaller than road bike sizes, simply because the seat tube on an ATB is shorter on these bikes. For example, if your road bike frame is 21 inches, an ATB with a top tube the same distance from the ground as your road bike would be around 19 inches. See Table 2-1 for sizing information and road and ATB bike size comparisons. Your inseam measurement is what's important here, not your overall body height, so far as frame size is concerned. People with the same height can have different inseam measurements. If your inseam measurement puts you *between* two frame sizes, select the smaller frame to be sure you have plenty of crotch-to-top-tube clearance. You'll be going a lot slower on the trail than you're used to on the road. Slow speeds, narrow twisting trails, means you have to do a lot of balancing, use a lot of body "english" to keep upright, another reason for lots of clearance between you and the top tube.

ATB and road bike sizes are given, in this country at least, as the length of the seat tube, from where the top of the seat tube intersects the top tube, to the centerline of the bottom bracket (crank) spindle (axle), as I noted earlier. Depending on make, distances from the bottom bracket to the ground may vary from 11 to as high as 13 inches. This, again, affects the length of the seat tube. Also, as noted (Fig. 2-9 and Fig. 2-10), some ATBs have a sloping top tube, therefore the seat tube is shorter for the same frame size than for those ATBs that do *not* have a sloping top tube. The only way I know out of this dilemma is to use the length of the head tube as a basic criterion of frame size (Fig. 2-8 and 2-9). As you can see, the longer the head tube, the greater the distance the top tube is from the ground.

If you have a long torso and short legs and arms, a bike frame size based on a 2-inch or 3-inch clearance between your crotch and the tube would most likely mean the frame would be too small for you. Handlebars would be too close for comfort. There's a limit as to how high you can raise the handlebars, and even then this really does not move the handlebars farther *away from your body*. A moderate crouch position is okay, but not if you have to lean way over and strain to reach the handlebars. If you have to bend way over, or crook your elbows, because the top tube is so short the handlebars are too close, then you have a frame that's going to be uncomfortable on long rides. To find a frame that fits *all* your body dimensions, you may have to try different makes and frame sizes. There is no reliable standard of frame size specification you can rely on, anymore than there is a reliable correlation between torso, leg and arm length of the general population. Bicycle manufacturers design the best combination of top tube height above ground, bottom bracket ground clearance, top tube length, stem length and elevation, to fit as large a percentage of the general population as possible. So bike fit is purely empirical, trial and error. Again, if you simply can't find a stock bike that's comfortable, that fits you, you're a good candidate for a custom-built bike, with frame dimensions tailored to fit just you. There's a list of excellent custom frame builders in the Appendix, and if you write and ask them what body measurements they need to build you a frame, they will tell you what they need and how to measure these dimensions.

Table 2-1   FRAME SIZE COMPARISONS

(All measurements are in inches)

Crotch Height	ATB Frame Size	Road Bike
28.5 to 29.5	16	18
29.5 to 30.5	17	19
30.5 to 31.5	18	20
31.5 to 32.5	19	21
32.5 to 33.5	20	22
33.5 to 34.5	21	23
34.5 to 35.5	22	24
35.5 to 36.5	23	25

A WORD ABOUT CHAIN STAYS

For trail riding, select an ATB with short chain stays (Fig. 2-5), around 18 inches. The short chain stays put your weight over the rear wheel for maximum traction. You need all the traction you can get when climbing steep hills, especially on slippery surfaces such as sand, mud or grass. A bit shorter wheelbase bike lets you stand up on the pedals when climbing steep hills, yet keeps weight over the rear wheel for traction and over the front wheel for ground-gripping steering. *For paved road riding,* chain stays of 19 inches will give a more comfortable ride from a longer wheelbase frame.

I recommend fenders on your ATB (Fig. 2-11), a feature you'll appreciate the first time you go through mud or ride on a rainy day. Fenders should have at least one inch clearance above the tires, because mud, snow, loose grass, etc., can pack up underneath the fenders and make pedaling tough if not hazardous. Make sure fenders do not contact a pedal on a sharp turn (Fig. 2-12). If your foot hits the front fender, you could lose control and dump the bike.

SADDLE ADJUSTMENTS

You can adjust the saddle for tilt, height, and distance from the handlebars (Fig. 2-8), dimensions that are vital to comfort. Chapter 8 has more information on saddle adjustments.

Fig. 2-11. Fenders keep rider and bike clean when on mud or dirt. Make sure you have an inch between tire and fender so dirt, snow or muck can't build up under the fender and jam the wheel.

Fig. 2-12. For safety, make sure your toe won't touch the fender on a sharp turn. The fender shown here is unsafe because the rider's toe can touch the fender.

Saddle height: Sit on the saddle while someone holds the bike upright. Your leg should be slightly bent at the knee when the crank is at the 6 o'clock position (Fig. 2-6). Your elbows should be slightly bent (Fig. 2-7), and you should be able to reach the handlebars from this position without strain. Your knee should be vertically above the pedal spindle when the pedal is at the 9 o'clock position. If the bike feels uncomfortable, you have a poor match between the bike's frame and your own.

If all the measurements of the bike of your choice fit but you can't get the saddle up high enough, you may have a short seat post. Most ATBs these days come with extra-long seat posts (Fig. 2-13). You must have at least 2½ inches of the seat post *inside* the seat tube (Fig. 2-14) to keep the seat tube from snapping off or the seat post cluster from breaking. This is particularly important with aluminum frames, where the stress of a too-high saddle can actually snap off the top of the seat tube (Fig. 2-15) (don't blame this damage on the frame; blame it on whoever raised the saddle beyond the danger mark on the seat post). Have a longer seat post installed if necessary to get the saddle up higher. By the way, the reason for the saddle quick release is so you can quickly adjust saddle height for more efficient and safe riding up and down hills.

Saddle tilt: The saddle nose should point slightly upward. That will keep you from sliding forward on the saddle on steep descents. Some people prefer the saddle flat, horizontal to the ground, and that's okay, too. See Chapter 3 for riding techniques on the road and trail. These adjustments are only initial, you may well want to refine them as your riding experience and comfort dictate.

Fig. 2-13. *Install an extra-long seat post, center, if necessary to move the saddle up. A Breeze "Hite Rite" spring, top left, lets you move the saddle up for normal riding, down for downhill control. A saddle quick release unit is at upper right.*

Fig. 2-14. *Keep at least 2½ inches of the seat post* inside *the seat tube to avoid damage to the seat tube collar or seat post. This is* especially *important on aluminum frame bicycles.*

Fig. 2-15. *The top of the seat tube collar can snap off under the lever stress of a too-high seat post, as shown here. This is rider error.*

HANDLEBAR ADJUSTMENTS

In the normal riding position, with your hands resting on the handlebars, your arm and upper torso length determine how far the handlebars should be from your shoulders. If after adjusting the saddle fore and aft position as noted above, you still have to lean way over to reach the handlebars, you need a *shorter* stem which your bike shop can provide. If you can't lean over to rest your hands on the handlebars, but have to sit virtually upright, you need a *longer* stem. It's also possible, as I noted earlier, that even though the top tube distance above ground gives you ample crotch clearance, the top tube (Fig. 2-5) can be too short or too long for your upper torso or arm length. In this case, keep trying other makes of bike until you find one that fits.

Adjust handlebar height so that when you sit on the saddle, you are just leaning forward slightly. You can make adjustments, for comfort, later on as you ride. The bike shop can make the initial adjustment. See Chapter 8 for instructions on adjusting handlebar height yourself.

TOE CLIPS AND STRAPS

If you've been riding a road bike with *toe clips and straps,* you'll appreciate how much they contribute to pedaling efficiency. Toe clips and straps perform equally as well on an ATB. They help increase pedal efficiency as much as 40 percent because you can pull a pedal up with one foot while pushing the other pedal down. On rough terrain, toe clips and straps contribute to safety. They help keep your feet on the pedals during rough descents or when climbing hills. If a foot slips off the pedal when you're straining hard uphill, you could come down awfully hard on the top tube, or even fall all the way over onto the ground. If you use toe clips, keep them loose on fast, rough descents so you can keep a foot out to stay upright, if necessary. Of course, you should also keep toe straps loose in city riding for the same reason, should you have to make a panic stop. My ATB has modified toe clips without a strap, which let me pull up with one foot while I push down with the other one; and after riding this bike for years without them I can tell you these clips (Fig. 2-16) are a big help on the flats and when going up or down hills.

TIRES

There are dozens of *tire treads* and at least three tire widths available. Please refer to Chapter 3 for tire selection data. In general, you need a smooth tread for paved roads and more aggressive knobby tires for rougher terrain. There are specific treads for good traction in mud, in sand, and on very rough trail surfaces. Stock, off-the-shelf ATBs usually come with a compromise tread, with a smooth center for paved roads and knobby sides for rougher terrain. I like these dual-use tires because

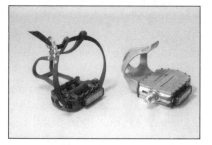

Fig. 2-16. Toe clips and straps, left, or even toe clips alone, right, can keep your feet from bouncing off the pedals on rough terrain. They increase pedal efficiency by letting you apply power on the pedal upstroke as well as on the downstroke.

they can keep you upright if you have to leave the pavement and hit a gravel or dirt shoulder to escape a car or truck. A smoother tire, on the other hand, could let a wheel slip and cause a fall, especially if there's a 1- or 2-inch drop where the pavement hits the gravel. Gravel may not be as slippery as ice, but it can let your wheel slide unless you have a tire tread that can grip the ground on gravel.

Inspect Tires

Look at the *valve stem*. It should be perpendicular to the rim. Turn the wheel slowly and inspect the tire bead where it fits over the rim. The bead wall should show the same amount of sidewall, or close to it, all around both sides of the tire. An improperly mounted tire could come off the rim, even cause a blowout, loss of control and an accident. If you're going to ride on a paved surface, the fat tire can be inflated to around 50 psi. If your ride will take you on a softer surface, inflate to around 30 psi so the tire can get a good grip on the slipperier surface.

LOOK FOR BRAZED-ON FITTINGS

Even a moderately priced ATB should have brazed-on fittings for attaching water bottle cages (Fig. 2-17) (at least one cage, two is better because you can get awfully thirsty on a hot day) and for attaching carriers (Fig. 2-18).

Carriers can be bolted to brazed-on fittings. Without them, carriers must be clamped to the frame. Clamp attachments are less secure and can mar frame finish. If the clamps work loose, a heavily laden carrier can work loose and catch in the wheel.

Fig. 2-17. *Better ATBs have braze-ons so you can bolt water bottle cage on a tube, as shown here.*

Fig. 2-18. *Braze-ons for bolting a car-rier, arrow, are a safety feature be-cause they are more secure than clamps. Clamps also mar frame fin-ish.*

MAKE THESE SAFETY CHECKS BEFORE YOU LEAVE THE STORE

I recommend you run through this checklist on your new ATB before riding it away from the store (this is also an excellent safety check before embarking on a tour).

Brakes

Eyeball *brake shoe clearance* from wheel rims. They should be evenly spaced about one-eighth inch from each side of wheel rim (Fig. 2-19).

If brake shoes are more on one side than the other, the shop should balance shoe clearance for even spacing on both sides. Otherwise brake shoes could rub one side of a rim, reduce braking and make cycling harder. Squeeze brake levers as hard as you can to *check cable stretch.* Cables do stretch, and when they do, brake shoes are farther from the rim, which reduces braking efficiency (see Chapter 5 for more infor-mation). After squeezing both brake levers, again eyeball brake shoe clearances as above and have brakes readjusted as necessary.

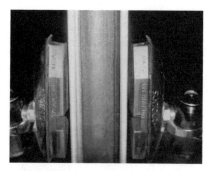

Fig. 2-19. *Make sure brake shoes are about one-eighth inch from the rim flat, evenly spaced on both sides of the rim, for fastest brake response.*

Check brake cable binder bolts for tightness: Grasp each brake lever in turn. Squeeze each lever as hard as you can. Release the brake lever. Did one of the cables slip? If so, it was loose in the binder bolt. Have the shop tighten it. If a cable slips in an emergency stop, you could wind up in the ER ward of the nearest hospital. The cable could slip if the fixing nut in the cable yoke (Fig. 2-20) is too loose. The cable could slip if the crossover cable binder nut (Fig. 2-20) on the brake arm is too loose.

Brake levers should be adjusted so you can reach them comfortably and stop safely. Better levers can be adjusted in two ways. First, they can be positioned up or down from a horizontal position. I find my brake levers at the most comfortable position for me when they are angled about 20° from the horizontal position. You can also adjust brake lever travel, the distance the lever has to move before the brake shoes contact wheel rims. If you have short fingers you may want more travel. Your bike dealer can make this adjustment. I also advise you to study every page of your owner's manual carefully to check these adjustments. Chapter 5 covers all brake adjustments, when it comes time to make them yourself.

Check brake lever tightness: Forcibly try to rotate the brake and shift levers on the handlebar. If brake levers are not clamped tightly to the handlebars they could shift as you grasp them. As the levers move away from your fingers you then may not be able to grip them hard enough to stop in an emergency.

Wheels

With the bike off the ground, spin each wheel to check side-to-side (lateral) and roundness (concentric) alignment. Watch where the rim passes a brake shoe. If the rim goes from side to side, closer to and then

Fig. 2-20. Check cable binder bolts by squeezing each brake lever hard. Cables should not slip out of the main cable carrier binder bolt, A, or the crossover cable binder bolt, B, on the brake arm.

away from a brake shoe as the wheel rotates, the wheel is out of alignment and should be trued up.

Spin the wheel again while you watch the top of the rim or the tire as it passes a brake shoe. If the wheel rotates unevenly up and down, it's out-of-round untrue (not perfectly round, or nearly so), and should be trued. Untrue wheels can affect braking. Have the wheel trued up before you leave the bike shop. Later, rims will eventually become untrue due to road impact and spoke stretch. Chapter 9 has more information on wheel alignment.

Check Hub Bearing Adjustment

Once you are sure the wheel is true, check for hub bearing adjustments. Spin the wheel a bit, just enough so it rotates slowly. Watch as the wheel comes to a stop. If it stops suddenly rather than slowing down gradually, wheel bearings are too tight and should be readjusted to avoid undue wear and tear on the hub bearings and races. See Chapter 9 for further instructions on wheel bearing and wheel alignment. Now check each wheel for loose wheel bearing adjustment. Grasp each wheel in turn, at the top of the tire, and move it with your fingertips sharply and quickly from side to side. You will feel looseness if wheel bearings are too loose. Loose wheel bearings can cause wheel shimmy, especially at high speed, as when going downhill. Have wheel bearings adjusted to eliminate this sideplay and the potential hazard of wheel shimmy. Please refer to Chapter 3 for more information on wheel shimmy hazards, causes and remedies.

Headset Adjustment

The headset consists of the ball bearings, races and cones around the fork. A loose headset can cause front wheel shimmy and an accident. A loose headset will also wear out bearings faster due to road impact, and become even looser. A *tight* headset also wears out faster.

Here's how to check headset adjustment: First, straddle the top tube, with both feet on the ground. Holding the *front* brake lever tightly closed, grasp the handlebar firmly with your other hand. Shove the bike sharply back and forth four or five times (Fig. 2-21). If the headset is loose, you'll feel the looseness and also may hear a clicking sound as the fork moves back and forth. Now dismount. Check for bearing tightness this way: Hold the front wheel off the ground. Turn the handlebars so the wheel is about halfway as far left as it can move. Let go of the handlebars.

Fig. 2-21. Check headset bearing adjustment by squeezing down the front brake lever and rocking the bike back and forth, as shown. If you feel looseness or hear clicks, headset bearings are dangerously loose.

The wheel should move the rest of the way by itself. If not, with the front wheel still off the ground, lean the bike to the left. If the wheel still does not move by itself, the headset is probably too tight. Repeat this test to the right. Have the dealer readjust the headset as necessary.

Check Shifting

With the bike in a stand so the wheels are off the floor, have the dealer run through all gear combinations. If the bike has index shifting on the *rear derailleur,* you will hear and/or feel the shift lever make a slight click as it's moved through all the rear gears. As the chain travels from the smallest rear cog to the biggest one, make sure the chain moves smoothly and precisely onto all cogs, especially low-gear cog. Shift down rapidly to the smallest rear cog. *The chain must not overshift so it rubs on the spokes or on the spoke protector as you shift up. If the chain jams between the big rear cog and the spokes, it could lock up the rear wheel and cause an accident. It must not overshift to the right as you shift down to the small cog, where it could jam between the small cog and the chainstay and cause an accident.* Have the rear derailleur travel readjusted as necessary. Later, as the derailleur cable stretches, you can make this readjustment yourself (see Chapter 6).

Check the *front derailleur* the same way. Shift the chain to the smallest front chainwheel. Make sure the chain does not overshift to the left and come down onto the bottom bracket, where it could jam between it and the chainwheel. Shift the chain to the big chainwheel. Make sure the chain does not overshift to the right where it could fall off the chainwheel, down onto the crank, and cause an accident.

Check cable stretch or tautness: Shift the chain to the smallest rear cog. As you eyeball where the front derailleur cable goes, you will see that the cable lies alongside the down tube, parallel to it. Pull the rear derailleur cable upward with a finger, about halfway down the down tube. There should be no or very little slack. Shift the chain to the small front chainwheel, and check cable slack the same way. Loose or slack cables on a new bike spell trouble, because cables will stretch soon enough as it is, and if they start out loose you're going to have trouble shifting quite soon.

If shift levers are separate from the brake levers, check their clamp bolt tightness on the handlbars by trying to twist them. If loose, have them tightened.

Check Handlebars and Stem

Stand in front of the bicycle and grip the front wheel tightly between your legs. Twist the handlebars from side to side. If the handlebars move but the wheel does not turn, the stem expander bolt (Fig. 2-22) is loose and should be tightened. This is an important safety check, because a loose stem expander bolt may let you turn the handlebars but not the front wheel. Imagine sitting in a car and deciding you want to turn left. You turn the steering wheel, but the car does not respond. It keeps going straight ahead. That's the scenario a loose bike stem binder bolt could create. This situation is more likely to occur when going slow over rough terrain, where it takes muscle to steer or keep going straight. A loose stem is an invitation to disaster on any surface.

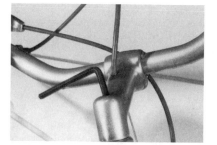

Fig. 2-22. Hold the front wheel between your legs while you twist the handlebars from side to side to check stem tightness. If the handlebars move but the wheel does not, have stem bolt tightened with an Allen wrench, as shown.

Check the handlebar binder bolt, where it's attached to the stem (unless the stem and handlebar are one piece). Twist the handlebars in a circular motion. You should not be able to move the handlebars. If they are loose, have the stem handlebar binder bolt tightened. Loosely clamped handlebars can have the same effect on braking as loose brake levers—i.e., twisting or moving when you pull hard on brake levers, and reducing or interfering with braking power.

Check Saddle Tightness

Twist the saddle in a rotating motion. It should not move. If it does, it could also move as you negotiate rough terrain. Have the shop show you how to adjust the saddle quick-release binder bolt (Fig. 2-23) and read Chapter 3 for more information. If the saddle has a conventional binder bolt, have the shop tighten it to the correct torque tightness.

Check Bottom Bracket

Grasp a crank or pedal and move it sharply to and away from the bike. If you feel any looseness, the bottom bracket bearings need adjustment. Shift the chain to the small chainwheel, slip the chain off the chainwheel and let it lie on the bottom bracket shell. Push a pedal so you spin the chainwheels slowly. Watch the chainwheels as they come to a stop. If they stop suddenly, bottom bracket bearings are too tight and will wear out faster. Have them readjusted. Chapter 7 has more information.

Check Chainwheel Binder Bolts

Make sure the shop has checked chainwheel binder bolt tightness. These are the bolts that hold the chainwheels together. The shop can check these bolts by turning them clockwise with the correct size Allen wrench

Fig. 2-23. *Make sure you know how to tighten the saddle quick-release binder bolt before you leave the shop with your new bicycle. Remember that wheels with this type of quick release are also tightened the same way. Read Chapter 3 for more data on tightening quick-release bolts.*

(Fig. 2-24), usually 4 mm. If the bolts turn easily, or can be moved more than a half turn before they are tight, they are too loose. Be sure to have them tightened. Loose chainwheel binder bolts can let the chainwheels spread apart. Then the chain can fall between chainwheels, lock the cranks and cause loss of balance and an accident. I have had expensive brand new bikes come to me right out of the shop, or the shipping carton, with loose chainwheel binder bolts. Chapter 6 has more information on chainwheel binder bolt tightness.

Check Pedals

Hold the crank arm with one hand while you rotate each pedal. If you feel roughness in pedal bearings, they are too tight and need readjustment. Move each pedal up or down. If they feel loose, bearing adjustment is loose and needs readjustment.

WHAT TO BUY BEFORE YOU LEAVE THE SHOP

Here are recommended accessories and spare items I suggest you buy while you're still in the shop. The mechanic can mount some of them; others you have to carry in a pannier.

1. *Spare tube.* A flat is inevitable. It's quicker and easier just to install a spare tube and patch the punctured one later, so buy at least one correct-size spare tube.

2. *Pump* that can be mounted under the down tube or on the seat tube. Make sure the pump has the correct *head* for your valve stem. A

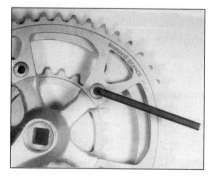

Fig. 2-24. Push chainwheels in and out to check binder bolt tightness. Loose chainwheels let chain slip down between them and cause an accident. Chainwheels are tightened with an Allen wrench, above.

Presta pump won't fit on a Schraeder valve, nor will a Schraeder pump work on a skinnier Presta value. The shop mechanic will advise you as to which pump you need. If you're not sure, see Chapter 8.

3. *Patch kit.* You will also need a patch kit and two tire levers, in case you run out of spare tubes and have to patch one on the road. Chapter 8 has tire repair instructions.

4. *Tools.* You will need a compact tool kit (Fig. 2-25) containing at least a multi-tip Allen wrench, a small screwdriver, a small adjustable wrench or 8, 9, 10 and 12 mm light wrenches, a spoke wrench and, above all, a chain rivet remover tool. If you break a chain on the road it's well nigh impossible to put it back together again without the chain tool (Fig. 2-26). See Chapter 6 for chain repair data.

5. *One or two water bottles and bottle cages to hold them.* If the bike does not come with water bottle cage(s), get at least one. If the frame has no brazed-on fittings for water bottle cage(s), install at least one clamp-on bottle cage. Two bottles and cages are advisable for long trips.

6. *Front and rear carriers (racks) and panniers (bags),* if you plan on taking long road or off-road trips. The low-rider front carrier (Fig. 2-

Fig. 2-25. *Show this picture to the bike shop to make sure you get these basic road repair tools and spare parts. Carry them on every trip.*

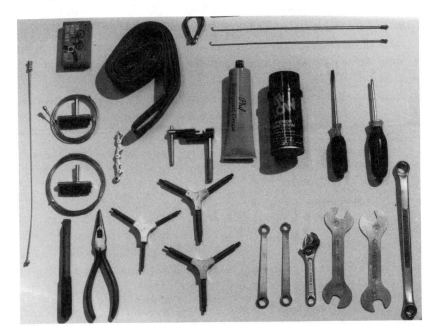

Fig. 2-26. *Your carry-along tool kit should contain a chain breaker. If the chain breaks, you will have to walk to the nearest bike shop. Chapter 6 tells how to use the chain breaker.*

Fig. 2-27. *Don't stint on panniers. This set of touring panniers, by Madden, should hold all you need for an extensive camping tour. Load is well balanced over the rear wheel. Front panniers are low to the ground for better steering control and balance.*

27) best distributes the weight of panniers on the bike frame. Use clamp-on carriers if the bike does not have bolt-on fittings. If you're taking a road or trail trip, you'll need a set of good panniers (Fig. 2-27). See Chapter 4 for pannier selections.

7. *A helmet, of course.* Your noggin is worth a lot more than the $45 or so you shell out for a helmet. Make sure the helmet is Snell approved or carries the label on the inside shell that says it meets or exceeds ANSI Z-90.4 (or later version) specifications for best impact resistance. See Chapter 3 for more helmet data.

8. *Raingear* to keep you dry on those inevitable rainy days on a tour or commute. The kind that "breathes" so body moisture can escape, yet keeps water from coming in, is best, though the most expensive (Fig. 2-28). Other excellent riding gear includes padded shorts or longer pants (Fig. 2-29) for crotch protection, summer gloves (Fig. 2-30) and gloves for colder weather (Fig. 2-31). The padding helps prevent numb hands on a long ride. The glove minimizes road rash should you fall. Chapter 3 has more information on these safety items.

9. *Computer* to tell you have far you've gone, how fast you're going, trip and total mileage, and a cadence indicator to tell you if you are spinning the pedals fast enough for good exercise. You can buy a com-

Fig. 2-28. *If you plan to tour, prepare for wet weather with raingear such as worn by the rider at left.* Photo courtesy Recreational Equipment, Inc.

Fig. 2-29. *For comfort in cold weather, roomy zippered jacket takes little room in a pannier. Pants are lined and have pleats at the knee that prevent binding when pedaling. Both garments are made by Vigorelli.*

Fig. 2-30. *Always wear gloves on a bike. If you fall they help prevent road rash. Padding eases pressure on sensitive nerve endings in the palm of your hand. Gloves are made by Kinco.*

Fig. 2-31. *These long-fingered Kinco gloves are specially made for cycling in cold weather. They are flexible, padded and insulated to retain heat.*

puter that will give your heartbeat rate, but for me that's too fancy. Just counting my pulse rate for 15 seconds and multiplying that by 4 gives me the pulse rate in beats per minute.

10. *Lights* are a must, even required in most states when you ride after dark. I prefer battery-powered lights (Fig. 2-32 and Fig. 2-33), because then I have a bright light even when I stop. A generator light, powered by rubbing on the rear tire, only gives light when the bike is moving (the wheel is turning). See Chapter 3 for light selection details.

11. *Reflective vest* is also a great safety item for both day and night riding (Fig. 2-34). I never ride without one. *Anything* that helps a motorist see you can save your life. If the bike store does not stock these vests, look in the Yellow Pages under "Safety Equipment and Clothing" and buy the vest used by roadworkers.

12. *A good lock* (Fig. 2-35) can keep your bike from being stolen. But be sure to lock the bike to something that itself won't be cut through. A parking meter post is okay if you are sure the bike can't be lifted over

Fig. 2-32. *Never bike in the dark without a light. This sealed beam unit from Rhode Gear throws a rectangular beam ahead so you can spot road hazards. A halogen taillight tells drivers you're on the road. Power is from a 6-volt sealed, rechargeable motorcycle battery in a carrying case.*

Fig. 2-33. *Here's lots of see-and-be-seen visibility in a small, lightweight, compact unit. Quartz halogen bulb in front and rear reflectors emit lots of lumens. Lights are powered by a rechargeable nickel-cadmium battery. Made by Brite-Lite.*

Fig. 2-35. *These locks are virtually impregnable to cutting or picking. If you leave your bike unattended, someone else will take "care" of it unless you lock the bike to an immovable object.*

Fig. 2-34. *Wear a reflective vest like the one worn by this cyclist for good daytime visibility.*

the meter head, lock and all. Lock your bike to a roof or trunk carrier if you travel and park outside a restaurant. Never leave your bike on the car, though, on an overnight stop at a motel. In a campground lock your bike to a picnic table, a small tree or any other immovable sturdy object. I remember one moonless night in a campground in northern California. Prowlers had crept through the camp and stole everything not locked down, including small rowboats, canoes, fishing gear, cookstoves and the like, and some bikes. I thought I heard a noise that night, but since my bike was securely chained to a picnic table I decided to ignore it. Next day my bike was still there.

13. *A bike bell* is a charming and pleasant way to tinkle your presence to pedestrians, to cyclists you are passing and to equestrians in the saddle on the trail.

SOME BASICS ABOUT FRAMES

Today's ATBs are available with frames of steel, aluminum, titanium and composite plastics such as carbon fiber. Here's a brief review of each material, beginning with steel frames and what to look for and what to avoid in such a frame.

Steel Frames

Steel has been used for bicycle frames since at least the mid-1800s. The really cheap bikes use low-carbon steel tubing that's far weaker than the higher-quality steels used in more expensive bikes. This basic weakness is, in part, compensated for by using thicker tubing, which accounts for the heavy, unresponsive "dead" feeling of these bikes.

Expensive bikes ($500 and up) use excellent tubing. Table 2-2 compares the strength of various steels in use today. You can see that the strongest tubing is double-butted chrome-moly steel (Fig. 2-36), which has an after-brazing strength of 75 kg/mm². Decals of popular frame tubing materials are shown in Figure 2-37 and will be glued to the bike frame so you see what you're buying. Plain carbon steel has a yield strength of 60K to 150K pounds per square inch (psi) and a fatigue limit of 25K to 75K psi. The better ATBs have forks that look something like the one in Figure 2-38. A cutaway section of this fork is shown in Figure 2-39.

Table 2-2 COMPARISON OF TENSILE STRENGTHS

(Note: Strengths are in kg/mm². If you wish to convert, 907 kg = 1 ton;
1 inch = 25.4 mm.)

Steel	Before Brazing	After Brazing	% Strength Retained During Brazing
Chrome-moly double-butted	82	75	91
Chrome-moly straight-gauge	79	72	91
Manganese double-butted	72	70	97
Manganese straight-gauge	67	65	97
High-tensile double-butted	60	50	83
High-tensile straight-gauge	52	43	83

Aluminum Frames

Aluminum frames use thicker tubing to achieve close to the same strength as steel tubing. I have found aluminum frame bikes give me the same

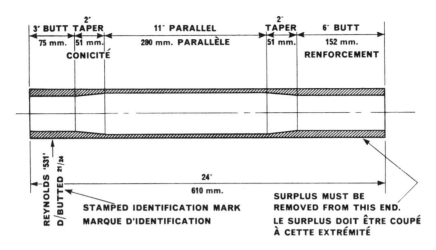

Fig. 2-36. *The strongest steel tubing for bike frames is "double-butted" where they join.*

Only the Top Tube, Seat Tube and Down Tube of a frame with this transfer are made from REYNOLDS 531 Tubing—plain gauge.

All the tubing in a bicycle with this transfer is REYNOLDS 531 — Frame Tubes, Chain & Seat Stays & Fork Blades, but it is all plain gauge tubing.

The Top Tube, Seat Tube and Down Tube of a frame which bears this transfer are REYNOLDS 531 BUTTED tubing.

This transfer signifies that the bicycle is an aristocrat, a thoroughbred — made throughout of REYNOLDS 531 tubing BUTTED for lightness with strength.

Fig. 2-37. *Look for labels like these that tell of strong, high-quality steel tubing.*

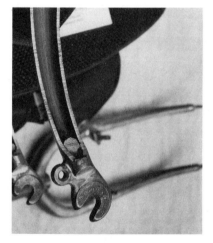

Fig. 2-38. *ATB forks take a real beating on the road or trail. They should look something like the strong fork shown here, with heavy reinforced brake bosses, strong welded joints at the steering tube and heavy-duty dropouts where the wheel axle fits. Threaded eyelets should be brazed just behind the dropouts to hold braces and a front carrier.*

Fig. 2-39. *Cutaway section of the fork in Figure 2-38.*

responsiveness and snap as good steel frames and shave two or three pounds off the bike weight. Weight savings, plus rust resistance, are the major attractions of aluminum bikes. However, aluminum frames can't be cold set (realigned) if they get bent, in which case you would need a new frame. This is a minor inconvenience, given the lightness and response of these frames. Some aluminum bike manufacturers, such as Cannondale, have a very generous frame replacement policy, should you bend a frame in normal usage. Well designed aluminum frame bicycles, such as made by Klein, are at least as strong as the best steel frames, and certainly a lot lighter. The strength of these excellent bicycles is due to the use of the strongest aluminum alloys, the wider diameter and thicker tubing made from these alloys, and, importantly, the geometry and design of these frames.

Titanium Frames

Back in 1970, an English firm sent me a titanium frame to test. First time I rode it I looked down at the bottom bracket and found it flexing about an inch to an inch and a half with every power pedal stroke. Scared the hell out of me. Shipped it back. Today the new titanium alloy frames are much stiffer and offer many advantages over frames of other materials.

Titanium combines the lightness of aluminum with the strength of steel, but at a cost ranging into the thousands. Modern titanium alloys cost five to ten times as much as steel, but are easy to weld in ambient air. However, titanium is not as stiff as comparable-diameter steel tubing, hence heavier tubing must be used, which sacrifices some of the 60 percent weight advantage of steel. Titanium has much greater fatigue resistance than steel and is even more corrosion resistant than stainless steel. The newer titanium alloys show great promise for bicycle frames, and as production goes up, price should come down from millionaire heights. Titanium 7i-74A has a yield strength of 91K psi and a fatigue strength of 45K psi.

Composites

Composites of wound carbon fiber and other plastic materials are also on the market, at a stiff price, exceeding even that of titanium. However, composites can be much stronger and stiffer than steel, highly corrosion resistant, and as light as, or lighter than in some cases, aluminum and titanium.

A CUSTOM FRAME

If you have long legs but a short torso, or long arms and short legs, or any other combination of body measurements that no stock, off-the-shelf bike can satisfy, you need a *custom* handmade bike. If you want a bike tailored to fit just you, a custom bike will do it. But you will pay upward of $2,000 for this Rolls-Royce treatment. If you do want a hand-built, custom-made ATB, there's a list of excellent, highly qualified frame builders in the Appendix. If you write or phone them, they'll send you details on how to measure your body. You can choose just the components you want, such as brakes, derailleurs, wheels, hubs, tires.

Custom frame builders complain that customers send them their own frame designs, with specific frame angles spelled out. The trouble is that unless you're a biomechanic, you should depend on the frame builder to create a frame with the correct angles for you. Frame angles differ according to frame size, so just send the builder your height, weight, arm reach from shoulder to fingertips, inseam measurement, torso length from hipbone to shoulder and any other measurement he asks for, and let him tailor the frame to these dimensions.

ANNUAL MODEL CHANGES ARE CRAZY

I have reviewed the specifications of most of the ATBs now on the market, and have selected a few models in each price range. These selections by no means imply that the bikes I do not mention are no good. These selections are simply to give you an idea as to what's on the market. I might also add that it takes upward of a year to get a book from the computer to the bookstore, and by the time this process is completed a new bike season with new models will be upon us. The annual dizziness of name and model changes, so imitative of the auto industry, is something I will never understand. Bikes simply don't change much from year to year. Back in the early 1970s when the bike boom took off, I used to go to bike shows in New York, Milan, Paris, London and Cologne. Bicycle exhibits were tucked away in the corner of the toy exhibits or motorcycle exhibits. Today there are huge annual bike shows in Atlantic City, Reno and Long Beach, California, attended by thousands of retail bike dealers. And every year new models with new names are exhibited by manufacturers. Sure there are new components that seem better than the old ones, such as index shifting and stronger, more reliable brakes. But, for the most part, the bikes you see in the store one year will be little changed from the line on sale the following year, except for the cosmetics of paint colors and names. If the dealer doesn't sell a bike during its model year, you can be sure it will be available for as long as it takes to get it purchased. Don't worry about the model year. If a bike is a good buy in one year, it will continue to be a good buy.

WHAT TO LOOK FOR IN A FRAME

Not all bikes are alike. Well, the really cheap ones, the kind I can't recommend, are all pretty much alike, awful, with poor brakes, cheap components and heavy, heavy frames. Any sturdy teenager can tear such a bike in half in short order with jumps over curbs, for example. But bikes that cost over $200, say, up to $500, are *not* all alike. Some have poorly designed frames or are carelessly assembled. Here is a quick review of what to look for in the frame of a new ATB:

Frame joints of cheap bikes are usually resistance welded on an automatic production line. Joints may be poorly mitered, or not mitered at all, and can come apart (Fig. 2-40).

Better bikes have frame tubing joined in a number of ways, all strong if done correctly. *TIG (thermal inert gas) welded frames* (Fig. 2-41) may look cumbersome but done with care are sturdy. TIG welded techniques

Fig. 2-40. Inexpensive bikes have weak low-carbon steel frames, often inaccurately mitered for close tolerance fit where tubes join. The result can be tubing that comes apart as the ATB bounces over rough trails.

Fig. 2-41. High-quality frame is TIG welded. It may look a bit crude but it's as strong as any other method of tube joining. TIG welding is a lot less labor intensive than hand brazing, so the bike can be up to 30 percent less expensive than sleeker-looking brazed frames.

are faster, require a lot less time and labor, and so these frames are usually less expensive than hand-brazed frames. Inspect the TIG welds carefully before you buy. Look for undercutting, where the heat of welding cuts away some of the metal near the joint, creating a weak spot at that point. If the tubing next to the weld looks smaller than the tubing farther away, the tube has most likely been undercut and will be weaker by the amount of metal that has been vaporized away. You don't want a frame that may buckle under stress and cause an accident. On the other hand, a quality TIG welded frame can save you around 30 percent of the cost of the bike.

A *lugged and brazed frame* is beautiful and strong, if done right. The tubing is mitered (as all tubing should be) for a smooth and accurate fit (Fig. 2-42). The tubing is joined in a lug, which makes a strong joint. However, lugged frames may use weak low-carbon steel and a cheap lug, which to the untrained eye look like an expensive lugged frame. The better lugged frames are brazed with silver solder or brass wire, at as low a temperature as possible to maintain original tubing strength.

Unlugged frames, where the joints are carefully built up with a fillet welding material (Fig. 2-43), can be just as strong as lugged frames. Here the brass fillet is spread out over a wide area to provide strength. The fillet is hand filed smooth before spray painting. The smoothly flowing lines of these joints make the frame a thing of beauty as well as a joy forever.

Fig. 2-42. Excellent example of a high quality seat post collar lug. This frame is hand-brazed, strong and beautiful.

Fig. 2-43. Note the carefully spread-out brazing material, hand applied and finished, that makes this frame as strong as TIG welded or lugged framesets. This frame looks good even before sanding and painting.

Better bikes have a *beefed-up seat collar* for strength at the stress point where the seat post is held (Fig. 2-44). Without such reinforcement the seat collar can crack or break off. However, even the strongest seat collar can break if you have the seat post (and saddle) above the danger point. As I noted earlier in this chapter, you *must* have *at least* 2½ inches of the seat post inside the seat tube. Most seat posts have a line scribed around it (Fig. 2-45), which should not show above the seat collar.

Look at the *chain stays*. Fat ATB tires require more room between chain stays than do skinny ties of road bikes. ATB manufacturers use a variety of methods to create this room. Crimped or radically bent chain stays provide this room but are not as strong as other methods, such as gradually curved chain stays (Fig. 2-46). Klein uses squared chain stays which are rigid and very strong (Fig. 2-47).

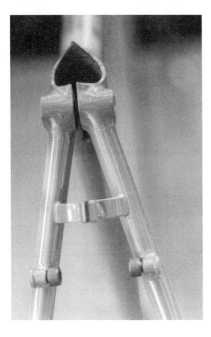

Fig. 2-44. *Top of the seat tube is a high-stress area, so better bikes have reinforced collars like this one.*

Fig. 2-45. *Seat posts usually have a scribed limit line, as shown here, to warn that at least 2½ inches of the post must be inside the seat tube. See Figures 2-14 and 2-15.*

Fig. 2-46. Gradually tapered chain stays are stronger than crimped or sharply bent stays. The bend is to allow clearance for the chain wheel.

Fig. 2-47. Klein aluminum frame chain stays are rectangular for strength.

ALL-TERRAIN BICYCLE SELECTIONS

I have selected specific ATB models in various price categories. Since componentry changes each year or oftener, I have given only the basic components. However, rest assured that component quality is equal to the overall quality of the bike, in its price range. Please remember that prices are subject to change at any time. My selections are based on bicycle design and the quality of components, together with price. Remember, model names may change, but the specifications will be the same, or close to it, as will be the price. The manufacturers I have selected make top-quality ATBs in each price category. These are all excellent bikes. The address of each manufacturer is listed in the Appendix.

$250 TO $399

Make	Miyata	GT	Marin	Schwinn	Schwinn	Trek	Raleigh	Peugeot
Model	SportRunner	Serengheti	Muirwoods	Impact	Mesa Runner	Antelope 820	Point	U.S. Express
Braze-ons*	1, 3, 4	1, 3, 4	1, 3, 4	1, 3, 4	1, 3, 4	1, 3, 4	1, 3, 4	1, 3, 4
Crankset	Biopace	Oval	Biopace	Oval	Round	Oval	Oval	Round
Frame	Cr-moly	Cr-moly	Cr-moly	Cr-moly	Hi-Tensile	Cr-moly	Cr-moly	Hi-Tensile
Frame sizes (inches)	16, 16.5, 18.5, 20.5, 22.5	16, 18, 20, 22	15.5, 17.5, 19	18, 21, 23	18, 21, 23, 25	15, 16, 18, 20, 22	16.5, 18, 20, 22	16, 18, 20, 22
Hubs**	2	2	2	2	1	2	1	2
Speeds	18	18	18	15	10	18	18	18
Toe clips	No	No	No	No	No	No	No	No
Index shifter	Yes	Yes	Yes	Yes	Yes	Yes	Yes	No
Weight (lb***)	30	NA	NA	31	33	NA	30	NA
Price****	$325	$315	$319	$399	$299	$389	$285	$275

*1, Rear carrier. 2, Front carrier. 3, Water bottle carrier(s). 4, Cable guides.
**1, Bolt-on both wheels. 2, Quick release both wheels.
***1, Quick release front wheel only, nut on rear wheel. 3, Quick release both wheels.
****Smallest frame size. Larger frames weigh a bit more.
*****Subject to change without notice.

$400 TO $599

Make	Miyata	GT	Montague	Raleigh	Cannondale	Specialized	Trek	Nishiki
Model	Valley Runner	Pachanga C	Bi-Frame M-1000	Killer Instinct	SM-400	Rockhopper	Singletrack-950	Ariel
Braze-ons*	1, 3, 4	1, 3, 4	3, 4, custom lock	3	3, 4	3, 4	1, 3, 4	3, 4
Crankset	Biopace	Biopace	Oval	Round/ Oval	Oval	Biopace	Biopace	Biopace
Frame	Cr-moly	Cr-moly double-butted	Cr-moly double-butted	6061 T8 aluminum				
Frame sizes (inches)	16.5, 18.5, 20.5, 22.5	16, 18, 20, 22	18.5, 20.5	16.5, 18, 20	16, 18, 20, 22	17, 19.5, 21.5	16.5, 18, 20, 22	17, 19, 21, 23
Hubs**	3	3	2	3	3	3	3	3
Speeds	18	21	18	18	18	21	21	21
Toe clips	No	Yes	No	No	No	Yes	Yes	Yes
Index shifter	Yes	Yes	Yes	Yes	Yes	Yes	Yes	Yes
Weight (lb***)	28	NA	29.066	28	28.2	29.9	NA	NA
Price****	$550	$590	$460	$500	$625	$532	$549	$595

*1, Rear carrier. 2, Front carrier. 3, Water bottle carrier(s). 4, Cable guides.

**1, Bolt-on both wheels. 2, Quick release front wheel only, nut on rear wheel. 3, Quick release both wheels.

***Smallest frame size. Larger frames weigh a bit more.

****Subject to change without notice.

Make Model	GT Avalanche	Marin Eldridge Grade	Schwinn High Sierra	Raleigh The Chill	Cannondale SM-600	Specialized Stumpjumper	Fat Chance Wicked Fat Chance	Trek Aluminum-8000	Fisher AL-1
Braze-ons*	Internal cable routing	1, 3, 4	1, 2, 3, 4	3 (internal cable routing)	3, 4	3, 4	3, 4	3	3, 4
Crankset	Biopace	Biopace	Round	Biopace	Biopace	Biopace	Oval	Biopace	Biopace
Frame triple-butted	GT Triple Triangle Tange Prestige and MTB tubing	Cr-moly double-butted	Cr-moly	6061 T8 aluminum	Aluminum, heat treated	Cr-moly triple-butted	Triple-butted 4130 Cr-moly	6061 T6 aluminum	Fisher 7005 H53 aluminum alloy
Frame sizes (inches)	16, 18, 20, 22	16, 18, 20, 22	18, 19, 20, 21, 23	16.5, 18, 20, 22	16, 18, 20, 22	17, 19.5, 21.5, 22.5	14, 16.5, 18, 19.5, 21, 23	16.5, 18, 20, 22	15, 17, 19, 21
Hubs**	3	3	3	3	3	3	3, 4	3	3
Speeds	21	21	18	21	21	21	21	21	21
Toe clips	Yes	No	Yes	Yes	No	Yes	Yes	Yes	Yes
Index shifter	Yes	Yes	Yes	Yes	Yes	Yes	Yes	Yes	Yes
Weight (lb)***	NA	NA	30	28	27.7	27.9	NA	NA	NA
Price****	$680	$599	$624.95	$650	$750	$759	$695	$849	$850

*1, Rear carrier. 2, Front carrier. 3, Water bottle carrier(s). 4, Cable guides.
**1, Bolt-on both wheels. 2, Quick release front wheel only, nut on rear wheel. 3, Quick release both wheels.
***Smallest frame size. Larger frames weigh a bit more.
****Subject to change without notice.

OVER $1,000

Make / Model	Miyata Sky Runner	Klein Pinnacle XCD	Kestrel MX-Z	Schwinn Aluminum Pro	Mongoose IBO C Signature	Mountain Goat DeLuxe	Mountain Goat Trench Goat	Merlin Titanium
Braze-ons*	3, 4	Cables go through tubing	1, 3 (cable routed through frame)	3, 4	3, 4 (internal cable routing)	1, 3	1, 3	3, 4
Crankset	Biopace	Biopace	Biopace	Oval	Biopace	Biopace	Biopace	Biopace
Frame	Aluminum Spectra (Uniframe)	Klein special alumi-num alloy tubing	Carbon fiber and forged aluminum Dropouts	Butted Aluminum	Titanium	Cr-moly double-butted, elliptical	Cr-moly double-butted, 4130	Titanium
Frame sizes (inches)	16.5, 18.5, 18, 20, 20.5, 22.5	18, 20, 22	18, 20	17, 18, 19, 20	16, 18, 20, 22	17, 18, 19, 20, 21, 22	17, 18, 19, 20, 21, 22	15, 17, 19, 21, 22.5
Hubs**	3	3	3	3	3	3	3	3
Speeds	21	21	21	18	21	21	21	18
Toe clips	Yes	Yes	Yes	Yes	Yes	No	No	Yes
Index shifter	Yes	No	Yes	Yes	Yes	Yes	Yes	Yes
Weight (lb)***	25	25.6	18	27.8	NA	NA	NA	NA
Price****	$1,500	$1,575	1,899	$2,900	$1,200	$2,259	$1,375	$2,700

*1, Rear carrier. 2, Front carrier. 3, Water bottle carrier(s). 4, Cable guides.
**1, Bolt-on both wheels. 2, Quick release front wheel only, nut on rear wheel. 3, Quick release both wheels.
***Smallest frame size. Larger frames weigh a bit more.
****Subject to change without notice.

OVER $1,000 (cont.)

	Specialized	Fat Chance	Trek	Klein	Fisher
Make					
Model				Top Gun XT II	CR-7
*Braze-ons**	3, 4	3, 4	3,4	Cables run through main tubes	3, 4
Crankset	Biopace	Oval	Biopace	Biopace	Biopace
Frame	Tange Prestige Cr-moly	Heat treated Aluminum	Double-butted Aluminum	Klein spec. aluminum alloy	Fisher 7005 aluminum
Frame sizes (inches)	17.5, 19.5, 20.5, 21.5, 22.5	14, 16.5, 18, 19.5, 21	16.5, 18, 20, 22	18, 20, 22	15, 17, 19, 21
*Hubs***	3	3	3	3	3
Speeds	21	21	21	21	21
Toe clips	Yes	Yes	Yes	Yes	Yes
*Weight (lb)****	26.5	NA	NA	24.5	NA
*Price*****	$1,192	$1,950	$1,229	$1,795	$1,500

*1, Rear carrier. 2, Front carrier. 3, Water bottle carrier(s). 4, Cable guides.

**1, Bolt-on both wheels. 2, Quick release front wheel only, nut on rear wheel. 3, Quick release both wheels.

***Smallest frame size. Larger frames weigh a bit more.

****Subject to change without notice.

ABOUT TANDEMS

It takes two to tango and two to ride a tandem. As in the tango, the stoker (rear rider) and the captain must be in perfect harmony, both physically and emotionally. Since both sets of pedals are joined, what either rider does can affect the other and the well-being of both. If the captain is a strong rider and likes to go all out, all the time, so must the stoker, and vice versa. If one rider looks at passing scenery and absentmindedly stops pedaling, the other rider's pedals jam. Both must know how to take off from a standing start, how to negotiate corners, how to brake. Whether a tandem is for the two of you, only you both can determine. However, I remember a cartoon in a British cycling magazine that went like this. Frame one: a friend asks a woman what happened to the tandem when she and her husband divorced. Frame two: the woman reaches into a shed, pulls out and displays her half (rear) of the tandem.

Sizing could be a problem on any tandem. ATB tandems are no exception. If the stoker is 5 feet tall and the captain a 6-footer, only a custom tandem will fit. Most stock ATB tandems come in dual sizes: a shorter-size rear section for the stoker and a larger-size front section for the captain. The theory is that the stoker will be a woman, shorter, and the captain a man, taller. I hope the liberated female cyclist takes exception to this arrangement, so that stock tandems will come with the shorter size up front. Women make excellent captains. Men make excellent stokers. Stock ATB tandems now come in sizes 16-inch rear, 18-inch front, and 18-inch rear and 20-inch front. The smaller size is for the stoker.

Burley Designs tandem costs $1,200. The Fisher MountainBike tandem costs $1,500. The Wilderness Ibis model tandem sells for $1,700. All of these tandems are excellent buys at these prices. For more information please write to the manufacturer, listed in the Appendix. There's more on riding all-terrain tandems in Chapter 3.

A WORD ABOUT WARRANTIES

Most manufacturers offer a warranty. It's in the owner's manual, usually on the inside back cover. Some manufacturers offer a 12-month warranty on the complete bicycle except for tires, tubes and cables. A better warranty by some manufacturers offers a lifetime warranty on the frame and fork and 12 months on the rest of the bike. Some manufacturers do not offer any warranty. Before you buy, read the warranty. Don't buy a bike without one. Save the *dated* bill of sale as proof of purchase date. All warranties I have read require you to pay for the labor in replacing anything broken that's covered by the warranty. For example, if you have a lifetime warranty on the frame and it breaks because of a defect in manufacturing, you will get a new frame free. *But* you may have to pay the cost of removing the old parts from your old frame and installing them on the new frame. Bike shop owners in the Portland, OR, area charge around $25 for this service. However, the cost could be greater because replacement frames and forks usually come without headset or bottom bracket set. If you have ridden the broken bicycle for many miles you probably need these new parts in any case.

SELECTING A USED ATB

You may find a used ATB for sale in newspaper classified ads, in bike magazines, from someone in your local bike club and, more rarely, in bike stores. If you find one that fits your body and your budget, here's how to check it out.

1. Go through all the inspections mentioned earlier when checking a new bike in the bike shop.

Fig. 2-48. Check for buckled tubing by looking for wrinkled paint where tubes join. This bike has been damaged by frontal impact causing the down tube to buckle, arrow.

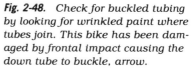

2. Inspect for tubing damage where main tubes join. Look for cracked or wrinkled paint, which indicates bent, buckled or cracked tubing underneath (Fig. 2-48). Don't buy a bike that shows such damage. The frame will be expensive to straighten, if that's possible. If it's an aluminum frame, it will have to be replaced; it can't be cold straightened. A bent frame won't track true, with both wheels in line. An out-of-line frame can cause front wheel shimmy and an accident.

So much for selecting an ATB. Now let's go on to how to ride one safely on the road and on the trail, the subject of our next chapter.

3

How to Ride Safely and Efficiently

In this chapter we'll cover safety on the trail and on the road, first aid for body and bike, wilderness survival tips and more. Let's start with on-the-road riding, because that's what most ATBs are used for, even though they are well designed for the rough stuff off-road. Let me begin with a word of apology to my female readers. Throughout this book I would appreciate your taking it as read that when I say he or him or his, I also mean she or her or hers. In the interest of brevity, I shall use the male pronoun throughout. But I am thinking of you right along. First, a word about head protection.

ALL ABOUT HELMETS AND WHY YOU SHOULD ALWAYS WEAR ONE

Never get on a bike without a helmet on your head. You can fall and strike your noggin even on a remote mountain trail. Cyclists have slipped and fallen standing still, just waiting for a stop light to change to green, suffering a head injury a helmet could have prevented. The point is, you never know when you might need a helmet, at any time, any place you ride. A good helmet protects your brain box by absorbing the G forces of a crash that would otherwise be transmitted directly to your skull. A G is a unit of force of gravity on a body at rest. The helmet protects the brain in minor impacts, collisions that could otherwise cause major brain damage. By a minor impact I mean a fall off the bike at moderate speed where your head is not the first thing that hits the ground, or hits it at a low impact. Without a helmet, even what may seem like a mild impact can cause permanent brain damage, even death.

Your brain floats in fluid inside your skull, protected against mild impacts. If the impact is severe enough, over 300 G, the brain can bounce against the inside of the skull. Such a bounce can bruise the brain and cause it to swell (subdural hemorrhage). If it swells, you may faint and die without immediate medical intervention. Make sure someone keeps an eye on you for at least 48 hours if you have had a hard fall with or without a helmet. Surveillance can bring immediate surgical treatment that relieves pressure inside the skull that can damage the brain, even cause death. A fall to the side can exert a twisting motion to the skull, in which the skull moves but the brain, on its stem, doesn't. These torsional forces can sever parts of the brain, again leading to permanent brain damage or death. I have put this scenario in nonmedical terms for clarity. I hope you get the message. To quote the label in a typical bike helmet: *"WARNING:* No helmet can protect the wearer against all foreseeable impacts."

You can't use the excuse that a helmet overheats your head on a hot day. Tests sponsored by the U.S. Cycling Federation, the governing body of bicycle racing in this country, conclusively demonstrated that helmets do not cause overheating. The tests involved two groups of competitive cyclists, trained athletes. In one test the riders wore a helmet; in the other, they were helmetless. The results "showed no statistical difference between the two groups of cyclists for external or internal body heat, heart rate, heat production or perceived discomfort."

There are two kinds of helmets on the market. One is a hard shell with a polystyrene liner about one-inch thick at the brow and ear areas and about a half inch thick at the top (Fig. 3-1 and Fig. 3-2). The other kind is an expanded polystyrene (EP) without the hard shell (Fig. 3-3 and Fig. 3-4). These helmets are 100 percent expanded polystyrene (EP). The EP is about an inch and a half thick at front and rear and about an inch thick everywhere else. A soft-shell helmet will deform more on impact than a hard-shell helmet, evidence that it absorbs the shock of impact.

If you fall and your helmet impacts the ground, return the helmet to the seller. Some manufacturers offer a replacement helmet at a reduced charge if you turn in the old banged-up one. The point I am trying to make is that once a helmet suffers an impact it is permanently deformed. The dent may not even be visible to the naked eye. When a helmet absorbs the shock of an impact, it loses the ability to absorb further

Fig. 3-1. Hard-shell helmet with polystyrene liner.

Fig. 3-2. Inside view of two hard-shell helmets.

Fig. 3-3. Expanded polystyrene (EP) helmet. This type does not have a hard shell.

Fig. 3-4. Inside of EP helmet.

shocks because it has already been deformed. Think of a spring that, once hard-compressed, loses its recoil. That spring will not spring back. Nor will a helmet spring back into the protection you paid for when it was new and undamaged. Again, *scrap the helmet you fell on!* A good new helmet costs from $45 to $65. Surely your head is worth more!

There are two helmet standards in use today, the Snell (Fig. 3-5) and the ANSI Z 90.4 (Fig. 3-6). A good helmet will display the ANSI label. A better helmet will display labels that say it has passed both ANSI and Snell tests. The Snell test is more rigorous than the ANSI Z 90.4. The Snell test requires that the helmet, with a simulated head form of 13 lb inside it, be dropped from 6½ feet onto a flat plate and onto a hemispherical anvil from a height of 3 feet 11 inches, each drop once on the four sides of the helmet. The average of all four drops shall not transmit over 300 G to the simulated head, and no single impact can measure over 330 G. The ANSI Z 90.4 test is similar except that the drops are from 3 feet 3 inches. The Snell test is both more stringent and more realistic, because the average cyclist of 5 feet 7 inches tall, on a bicycle, will have his head well above the 3 feet 3 inches of the ANSI test. The human head can withstand about 300 G without injury, although a 300 G impact can cause a headache. Over 300 G results in brain damage. A good example of a helmet that meets both Snell and ANSI tests is the LT 1100 series EP helmet (Fig. 3-7).

Snell claims that helmets meeting their test standards will protect the rider in some 85 percent of accidents. Thus helmets do have their limits. No helmet in the world can protect you against a head-first, spinal-column-crushing impact into an immovable object, such as a concrete road. That type of injury, a compression fracture of the spine, can turn you into an instant paraplegic, quadriplegic or corpse. Just ask your nearest emergency room M.D. for an even more graphic description. I have seen a hard-shell helmet worn by a rider who was killed by the impact. The exterior of the hard shell bore no evidence of the severe

Fig. 3-5. This Snell certified label denotes an excellent helmet.

Fig. 3-6. Some helmets have met both ANSI Z 90.4 specifications and Snell certification and will have both labels inside.

Fig. 3-7. *This EP helmet has both Snell and ANSI labels which signify that it meets or exceeds both specifications for impact resistance.*

impact. The interior liner had a very slight dent in it. It's possible, of course, that this was one of those accidents of such severe impact that no helmet would have protected this rider. One objective of this chapter is to help you ride so safely that such a violent collision can always be avoided.

How a helmet fits you is very important. If it's too loose, you lose some protection, because your head can bounce around inside it on impact. It should be quite snug. Helmets generally come in extra small (for kids), small, medium and extra large sizes.

Children should also wear helmets (Fig. 3-8), whether they are towed along in a trailer, carried on the bike, or ride their own bike. Also make sure any helmet you buy has a secure buckle that snaps together, like the one in Figure 3-9. These helmet straps are also adjustable to fit your head. Make sure the straps are adjusted so they are tight, hold the helmet firmly on your head, keep it from tilting back or to one side where it

Fig. 3-8. *Your child should always wear a helmet, such as this Bell model.*

Fig. 3-9. *Make sure the helmet you buy has straps that can be adjusted to fit the contours of your head, and a buckle like this one that secures the helmet to you.*

could fall off or move if you fall and hit the ground. Table 3-1 shows the relationship between hat size and helmet size. Use this table to obtain an accurate fit. Use the small Velcro pads that come with the helmet to tailor it more comfortably to the contours of your particular skull.

Never use solvents, harsh soaps or abrasive cleansing agents on your helmet. These types of cleaner can damage your helmet. Some solvents, such as gasoline and diesel fuel, can eat right through the helmet and destroy it. Some damage may not even be visible to the naked eye. Use only mild soap and water to clean your helmet.

Table 3-1 HELMET SIZING DATA

Adult Hat Size	Helmet Size
6⅜ to 6¾	X/S
6⅞ to 7⅜	S/M
7½ to 7⅞	M/L
Children's Hat Size	Helmet Size
5½ to 6	S
6⅛ to 6½	L

OFF-ROAD RIDING TECHNIQUES AND SAFETY TIPS

Off-road riding is different from cycling on the pavement. On the trail you're faced with all kinds of obstacles that may require a controlled hop to clear them. You may have to negotiate a steep, bumpy, downhill ride on slippery grass or sand. You may turn a corner and suddenly find yourself airborne as the trail takes a sudden, steep dip. Each of these situations requires skill to handle, skill that comes from experience and partly, I hope, from the words that follow.

First, Select the Tire to Suit the Terrain

You have your pick of literally dozens of tire treads to suit any type of road surface you are likely to encounter. Select a tread pattern that is most likely to give you good steerability and rear wheel traction on the surfaces you will be going over. There is no one tire suitable for every trail condition you will encounter. Unless you have been over the trail before, you won't even know what the surface condition will be. You can get a pretty good idea, though, by scanning the general area where you will be cycling. Is it sandy, muddy, grassy, rocky? All of the above? Will you cycle over pavement to get to the trail? Here's a quick review of the tire treads currently available, and the surfaces for which they are designed. But first, *a word about your rims.* Not every fat tire will fit every fat tire rim. Fat tire rim widths come in two sizes, 26 × 1.5 inches and 26 × 1.95 inches (Fig. 3-10). Fat tire sizes that will fit the 1.5-inch rim width include (all diameters are 26 inches, so I give only the tire width) 1.25, 1.4, 1.5, 1.62 and 1.75 inches. Fat tire sizes that will fit the wider 1.95-inch rim include tire widths of 1.9, 1.95, 2.125 and 2.2 inches. Do not install any of the larger width tires on the narrower rims, and vice versa. If you do, you're asking for a blowout because the tire may pop out of the misfit rim.

There are many tire treads on the market that come close to the ones I show. If you can't find the specific tread design shown here, a tread that comes close to it should work as well. Not shown is a studded tire by IRC which works well on snow but only moderately well on ice.

For paved roads use a tread on both wheels that looks like Figure 3-11, or a smoother tire like the Swallow (Fig. 3-12). These smoother tires will give you a low rolling resistance for easier pedaling. You can inflate them to 60–80 pounds per square inch (psi).

For country paved roads with a gravel shoulder use a *front tire* that has some knobs, such as the Specialized Streetstomper (Fig. 3-13), for

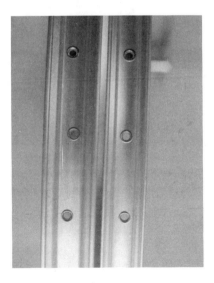

Fig. 3-10. *For safety, match your fat tire width to the rim width. The rim at right is 1.5 inches wide, is safe to use with tires up to 1.75 inches wide. The rim at left is 1.95 inches wide, for use with 1.9-inch- to 2.2-inch-wide tires.*

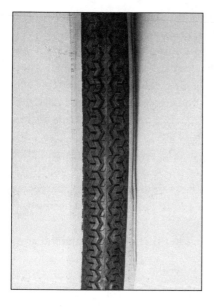

Fig. 3-11. Use this Specialized Crossroads tire with a less aggressive tread pattern for cycling on paved roads. Another excellent tire (not shown) for smooth roads is the Michelin Hi-Lite Express. Both tires give lower rolling resistance than the more aggressive knobbies.

Fig. 3-12. This Swallow model tire also offers smooth cycling on paved roads.

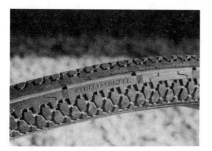

Fig. 3-13. For combination road and off-road cycling, this Specialized Streetstomper has a center ridge for street use and mild knobbies for off road use.

steering control should you have to veer off the road to avoid being struck by a car or truck. Another excellent tire for steering control on mildly rough terrain is the Mountain Trek (Fig. 3-14). Both these tires have mildly aggressive knobs that won't jar your eyeteeth on paved surfaces, but will grip loose terrain such as gravel. Then, if you do go off the road onto the gravel shoulder, the knobs on these tires will help you climb back onto the pavement as they grip the lip of the paved road where it intersects with the gravel. Use the smooth-tread tire (Fig. 3-11 or 3-12) on the rear wheel where you do not need steering traction.

There is no one tire suitable for *all* off-road riding. Some tires do better in mud than others. Some tires lack side knobs for steering traction on a fast downhill run on a dirt trail. *For mud and dirt:* a tire such as the Farmer John (Fig. 3-15) or Farmer John's Cousin (Fig. 3-16) has side knobs that help you steer around sharp corners, so either would be ideal as a front tire and both give you good traction on mud. The tread is designed to throw off mud that would otherwise cake and clog on the treads and turn the tire into a slick.

Fig. 3-14. *Another excellent combination road/off-road tire is this Mountain Trek. Center ridge makes for easy riding; side knobs grip the road if you go off into gravel or other slippery surface.*

Fig. 3-15. *Tioga's Farmer John is designed for good traction on mud and dirt.*

Fig. 3-16. *Farmer John's Cousin has side knobs that grip the terrain when you corner fast.*

There are totally bald, slick ATB tires on the market. Personally I think they are dangerous. The manufacturers advertise them as offering excellent road adhesion on smooth pavement. That may be true, if the pavement is smooth as glass and dry. But if you have to leave the smooth road to enter a driveway or veer off onto the shoulder, the adhesion becomes minimal. You can inflate slicks to 100 psi for a rock-hard tire with low rolling resistance.

If you're slogging through mud or loose sand, a more aggressive tread, such as the IRC Racer (Fig. 3-17) or the Mistubishi Competition III (Fig. 3-18), has knobby "teeth" that chew into mud and sand and is ideal as a rear tire. I would not use it on the front because it doesn't have small knobs on the sides for cornering control. If you have to ride on the road to get to your trail, use a combination tire with a smooth center tread that will give you a jar-free ride on pavement, such as the Specialized Crossroads II (Fig. 3-19). This tire has side knobs for cornering and larger knobs for ground grip on loose surfaces.

The science of which ATB tire to use on which type of terrain surface is an inexact one. New tire tread designs are introduced almost weekly, it seems. Part of the problem of staying upright on slippery surfaces goes beyond tires and into how you ride. If you corner at steep angles at high speed, you need a tire with as aggressive side knobs as possible, regardless of the rest of the tire pattern. I think trial and error is going to

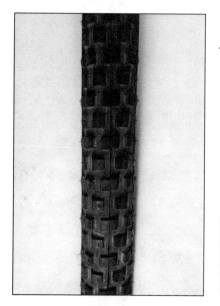

Fig. 3-17.   For mud or loose sand, the IRC Racer has an aggressive tread for good traction on mud and sand.

Fig. 3-18.   The Mitsubishi Competition III has "teeth" that chew into soft terrain, so it is ideal as a rear tire.

Fig. 3-19. The Specialized Crossroads has a smooth center ridge and
aggressive side knobs for combination terrain.

be the ultimate decider as to which tire tread to use where. One more
point. If you have to ride on knife-sharp gravel, a wide-open tire tread
pattern, such as the tire in Figure 3-18, is puncture prone. The wide-
open spaces between the tread knobs are easily ripped by gravel. I know,
because I got two flats within 10 minutes at a gravel-strewn trailhead.
Most aggravating.

As I mentioned earlier, IRC's Blizzard tire has 56 stainless steel studs
which, combined with an aggressive open-pattern tread, can go a long
way in helping you stay upright over snow, mud, even ice if you're
careful about cornering. The studs make this a fairly heavy tire of around
two pounds, but the winter traction is worth it. You are not going to
break any records cycling through mud, snow or over ice.

For good steering control you could use a fatter tire, say 2.25 inches,
on the front and a narrower 1.75-inch tire on the rear for faster cornering
as you slide around curves. If you start your trip on the pavement,
inflating both tires to 60 psi will cut rolling resistance to make pedaling
more efficient. Then, when you hit the dirt trail, reduce tire pressures
to around 35 or 40 psi for most effective ground grip. Use wider 2.25-
inch tires if you are a heavy person and/or have the bike loaded with
camping gear, or if you are going to ride on a mix of hard-packed dirt
and rocky terrain. Narrow 1.75-inch tires are less suited to paved roads.

A new ATB tire is available that is completely flat-resistant (Fig. 3-
20 and Fig. 3-21). It's the Poly-Air tire, without a tube. It has an inner
filling of multicellular polyurethane (MCP) which traps, according to its
Canadian manufacturer, "hundreds of thousands of microscopic air
bubbles" in the MCP matrix. The tread pattern, at this writing, is suitable
only for paved roads or very hard-packed soil (God forbid it should rain).
The version on the market is a tire that fits only the narrower ATB rims
(Fig. 3-10). After riding about 50 miles on a pair of these tires I can
report that they offer a surprisingly comfortable ride. I expected a bone

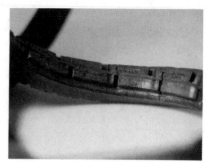

Fig. 3-20. Poly-Air makes a unique puncture-proof tire that's almost as shock-absorbent as an air-filled tire. If you race or commute over flat-producing city streets and can't afford the time to fix a flat, this is the tire for you.

Fig. 3-21. The underside of the Poly-Air multicellular flat-proof tire. Takes a bit of muscle to mount, but once on the rim it stays put.

shaker, which never materialized even over rougher pavement. This would be the tire of my choice for commuting to work, where a flat would delay my arrival, dirty my lily-white hands and be a general pain in the morning rush, wherever that is. True, these tires are heavier than pneumatic tires. On the other hand, you won't need to carry a spare tube (or a tube inside the tire, for that matter), one or two tire levers, a patch kit or an air pump. Subtract these items and the Poly-Air comes out about even or a little ahead on the weight scale.

For a hefty $12.90 you can double or, according to the manufacturer, triple puncture resistance with a polyurethane PolyTex *tube* (Fig. 3-22). The money would be well spent if you commute or plan on a long trail trip in the wilderness. You can carry only so many spare tubes and patches, so the PolyTex tube would be a good investment.

Tire casings, even on ATB tires, can be split open if they encounter razor-sharp edges (Fig. 3-23). Ignore that this is a slick tire. It could

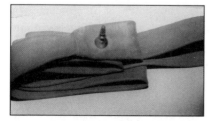

Fig. 3-22. This polyurethane PolyTex tube is extra tough and extremely difficult to puncture.

Fig. 3-23. *Even ATB tires can be slit if you hit a sharp rock. Carry duct tape to patch a tire slit until you can replace the tire.*

happen to any ATB tire. Even one with a "steel-like" Kevlar sidewall carcass. You can make an emergency repair of such slits with simple old duct tape, the gray tape used to seal the joints of heating/cooling sheet-metal ducts. Please see Chapter 8 for a short course on tire repair.

It's a good idea, before embarking on a long trip, to remove the tires and the rim strip and inspect the spoke heads (Fig. 3-24). This should be done if you have loosened a spoke to true up a wheel (see Chapter 9 for wheel truing). If you loosen a spoke, the spoke head could protrude upward, through the nipple. Then repeated road shock could force the tube and rim strip down onto the spoke. Eventually, if not sooner, the spoke will poke a hole right into the tube to flatten your day.

SAFE RIDING TECHNIQUES

This section will give you survival tips on city streets and on city and country bike lanes and trails, freeway riding and off-road cross-country cycling.

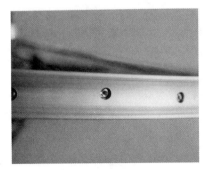

Fig. 3-24. *It's a good idea to check the rim, with rim strip removed, to make sure spoke heads aren't protruding up where they could puncture the rim. Cut off or file down any spokes that might cause a flat.*

City and Country Designated Bike Trails

Suburban areas, such as those around Chicago and other major cities, have bike trails that go through city, county or state parks. If you ride on these trails, here are a few safety tips to keep in mind:

1. Always ride on the far right side of the trail, to give clearance space to cyclists approaching from ahead or coming up behind you.

2. Be especially alert and careful about blind corners. Remember that it's easy to pedal at a rate of 10 mph, which means you are moving at 14.7 feet per second (fps). Say you are going 10 mph. You come to a blind curve. You can't see the rider coming toward you on a collision course because he is just around the curve. That rider is also moving at 10 mph. That's a combined speed of 20 mph, equal to 29 feet per second. If the rider coming at you is 29 feet around the blind curve and you are also 29 feet on your side of the blind curve, you have just *two seconds* to avoid running into each other. Table 3-2 translates speed into time. Not much time. Head-on collisions between bicycles, with lots of injury and pain, are not uncommon on such bike trails. Stay on your side of the trail, slow down as you approach a blind turn, and alert cyclists behind you as to the nature of that curve so they too can take precautions.

Table 3-2

Miles Per Hour	Feet Per Second	Seconds Per City Block*
5	7.3	38.36
10	14.6	19.18
15	21.9	12.79
20	29.2	9.59
25	36.5	7.67
30	43.8	6.39
35	51.1	5.48
40	58.4	4.80
45	65.7	4.26
50	73.0	3.84
55	80.3	3.49
60	87.6	3.20
65	94.9	2.95
70	102.2	2.74
75	109.5	2.56

*A standard city block is 280 feet long.

Be ready to take evasive action. If there are bushes to the right, steer into them to avoid a collision. Bushes are softer than pavement.

3. If the trail starts downhill, watch the grade. It can suddenly escalate from a mild 2 percent to a spine-tingling 6 percent grade inside of 20 feet. I have found that trails in city, county or state parks are often poorly marked. On some trails, for example, the cyclist may round a corner and unexpectedly find himself going down a steep hill. At the bottom of the hill he may discover that the trail turns sharply to the left or to the right, where it narrows, for some inexplicable reason, from 10 feet to 8 feet wide. This is an actual setting of a serious bike accident that occurred a few years ago on a trail in a Chicago suburb. Trail designers should erect signs warning the cyclist of all trail hazards. Signs should be placed at least 50 feet from the hazard, to give the cyclist plenty of warning. Such hazards include steep hills, bumps on the trail, narrowing of the trail, sharp hidden corners and turns, upcoming crosswalks with pedestrian traffic and upcoming highways with vehicular traffic.

Some trails parallel roads. These trails also have their safety problems, such as children who weave around on small bikes or skateboards, pedestrians and, in Europe, mopeds and small motorcycles. Don't rely on your audible signal to cyclists, skaters or pedestrians ahead that you are about to pass them. I find, sometimes, that they just ignore my call. If I yell out, "Passing on the left," I have had cyclists obligingly move to the left, into my path. The effective solution is to call out in such a way as to cause the people up ahead to look back for a moment, establish eye contact and to understand where you want to pass.

4. If the trail is gravel, and you see a cement sidewalk in the distance, be aware that gravel may have been kicked up onto the cement. Gravel on cement can cause you to skid, lose control and fall, especially if you have to turn as you cross the sidewalk.

5. Study the trail map, note where the trail intersects streets so you are prepared to stop or slow. Look left and right before crossing the street. Do not depend on a driver to slow because there is a bike-crossing caution sign facing auto traffic. Highway right-of-way rules apply at these crossings.

Designated Bike Routes

A designated bike route is part of a city street or rural road. There may be signs alerting motorists that there are bikes on the road with them. In the city, bike routes may be just a yellow line on the pavement, usually ignored by motorists who drive or even park right on them. In the country, a bike route may also be just a yellow line. Or it may be a curb or berm, or a series of small oval cement bumps which separate auto from bike traffic. The cement berm is best, of course. But whether or not there is anything or nothing which keeps traffic away from you, here are a few designated bike route travel tips for you.

Big trucks push a bubble of air in front of them. At high speed, this bubble can shove you to the right. Big trucks also create a partial vacuum behind them. This vacuum can pull you to the left. Be prepared to lean a bit to the left as the truck approaches from behind, and then a bit to the right as it passes, so this push-pull (Bernoulli effect in physics) won't cause you to lose balance and fall or steer into something undesirable, such as glass you were trying to avoid or into another cyclist (always ride single file).

Cycling on the shoulder of interstate highways and freeways is legal in much of the Far West, because there are few, if any, alternative routes, especially over mountain passes. The exception is near big cities, where cyclists are routed off the freeway and onto safer roads around or through the metro area. Avoid these highways if there is any alternative route you can take. Freeway shoulders are 10 to 12 feet wide. Stay as far to the right on the shoulder as possible so you will be as far away from traffic as you can be.

Be especially cautious as you approach on and off interstate highway ramps! As you arrive at an off ramp, where traffic on your left may exit and cross in front of you, you *must* stop. Do *not* depend on a rearview mirror to check how far away or how fast traffic is coming up from behind you. Traffic is *always* going faster than you think it is. Take a look at Table 3-2. You can see that from a block away a vehicle traveling 75 miles per hour takes only 2.5 seconds to reach you. You may never make it if you decided to beat the car across the intersecting off-ramp. Wait, you're worth it.

As you approach an off or exit ramp (Fig. 3-25), stop and look back. *Only* when you are positive that traffic coming in the right lane is not going to exit, should you proceed across the ramp. If you see an oncoming vehicle with its right turn signal blinking, of course you know enough to stop and let it turn off before you cross the ramp. But the cars that exit the freeway *without showing* a turn signal really worry me. I have looked back hundreds of times at five miles of straight road on a clear day to see a car three or four blocks away. By the time I counted off 10 seconds, that car would be next to me. Even at a quarter of a mile away, a car going 70 miles per hour will reach you in 13 seconds. Practice counting the seconds it takes for a car to reach you that you think is far enough

Fig. 3-25. Interstate freeways are legal to cyclists in many western states where there are no other roads. Watch out behind as you cross an off ramp to make sure a car is not about to exit in front of you.

Fig. 3-26. On ramps to interstate freeways are also hazardous. Stop, look, and when there is no car coming down the ramp, cross at a right angle as shown, as fast as possible.

away that you can cross the exit ramp safely before that car exits. It won't take long until you can estimate, with a comfortable margin of safety, how long you need to get across that ramp.

On ramps (Fig. 3-26) are a little safer for cyclists than exit ramps. As Figure 3-26 shows, what you do is stop at the point where the on ramp merges with the highway. When traffic coming down the on ramp is clear (i.e., when you see no cars on the ramp), simply take a straight cut to the right, across the ramp, and turn left down the ramp's shoulder. You can then safely enter the highway shoulder, at the base of the on ramp.

One final note about interstate highways. If you plan to use them, check with the state department of transportation to make sure you can do so legally. Then, check again with the state highway patrol. I was stopped by a Washington State highway patrol officer recently and told I had to get off Interstate Highway 205, because "it was illegal for me to be cycling on the shoulder of that road." I did not argue. The next day I called the Washington State Department of Transportation, which assured me that it was legal. At my request they sent me correspondence between the DOT and the state police headquarters, together with a bicycle map of the entire state interstate road system, showing where bicycling was legal and where it was not on these highways. Then I wrote a letter to the chief of the Washington State highway patrol, and sent copies to the governor, my state senator, the officer that stopped me and his boss, the lieutenant of his barracks, together with copies of the correspondence from the DOT to his department, plus my own background in bicycling. In about a week I had letters from all these people, plus a visit from the lieutenant, who was very nice, as was the chief. The lieutenant said he asked his officers if they knew that it was okay for cyclists to ride on the shoulder of some 90 percent of the state's interstate highways. Half of them said it was their understanding that it is illegal to bicycle on the shoulder of any interstate highway. This documented the stories I had been getting from local bike shops and bicyclists. Seems the police had been routinely stopping and ordering cyclists off the freeways. I am sure many long-distance cyclists had their plans cut short by such police action, because side roads are not always available. And such side roads, I have found, as are available at many off ramps are narrow, have high-speed traffic, with no shoulders, and so are far more hazardous than the interstate highway. As I noted, however, the Washington State patrol people were most cooperative once they understood the situation.

Country Roads

Roads in the country generally have narrower shoulders than interstate highways, so you have to stay on the pavement. You can, of course, go off onto the shoulder to escape an oncoming car from the rear, which may be necessary when a car or truck is coming from behind and another one is coming toward you. They generally meet right where you are, and on a narrow road there may be no room for you. Use a mirror to keep track of traffic from behind. I like the mirror that fits into the end of the handlebar (Fig. 3-27) made by Third Eye. This type of mirror gives less wobble than the kind on a stalk. I use a mirror on each end of the handlebar when I am on a freeway, so I can see traffic coming down an on ramp as well as traffic on the highway. Remove these mirrors for trail riding; they can tangle in brush on a narrow trail. You can, if you prefer, use a tiny mirror that clamps onto your helmet or glasses (Fig. 3-28), also made by Third Eye. Remember that a mirror gives you monocular vision, so it is not reliable as an indicator of the speed of an oncoming car, or as a judge of how far away it is from you. Use a mirror

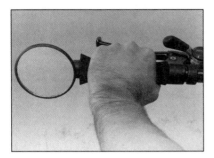

Fig. 3-27. Use a rearview mirror to keep an eye on traffic coming from behind. I prefer the kind shown here, which has no stalk, so there is no mirror wobble to distort the image.

Fig. 3-28. On the trail, where a mirror could scrape on brush, use a small helmet- or eyeglass-mounted mirror. Remember, a mirror cannot be trusted to tell you how fast a car is coming or how far away it is. A mirror only lets you know that a vehicle is coming up. Twist around quickly, use both eyes to gauge speed and distance of traffic behind you.

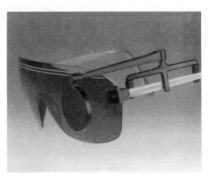

only to let you know a vehicle is there. Turn your head quickly, use both eyes to judge its speed and distance from you.

Watch out for wide-body trucks that carry extended rearview mirrors on the right side. These mirrors on pickup trucks (Fig. 3-29), towing boats and on house trailers (Fig. 3-30) have injured and killed cyclists. People that drive these vehicles often do not have the skills of a professional truck driver. Keep away from them by going over onto the shoulder, especially when traffic is coming both ways and may meet where you are, as is so often the case.

Fig. 3-29. *Beware of extended right rearview mirrors that can protrude into your lane. Avoid them by moving as far to the right as possible if you see one coming up.*

Fig. 3-30. *Drivers towing campers or driving huge motor homes are notoriously inaccurate steerers. They have extended right rearview mirrors (arrow), which have hurt and even killed cyclists. Most states have no special test or skill requirements before they can be driven. Yet these often huge, cumbersome vehicles are driven only a few months a year, by untrained drivers. State highway patrol officers are concerned about this state of affairs, and certainly we cyclists should be equally concerned.*

WHEEL SHIMMY

If you've ever felt wheel shimmy on a car you know how violent it can be. On a car you can simply slow down until the shimmy stops and you can drive to a service station for a wheel balance job. On a bike, however, wheel shimmy can be a life-threatening experience. Every split second after bike shimmy starts the front wheel side-to-side movement gets faster and wilder, and before you can even think about what to do (not much except to try to control speed by braking) the bike can dump itself *and* you on the pavement. It happened to me going down an Austrian Alpine two-lane mountain pass with a fenceless 2,000 foot drop-off on the right, a loaded logging truck coming at me from the left and some 40 American tourists speeding along behind me. I fell, was lucky enough to ride out the slide on top of the bike, with just a little skin left on the pavement and two or three bikers on top of me. Exercise-induced endorphins in my blood served as an anesthetic at the time. The pain came later. We were all fortunate. Others I know of have been seriously injured or killed because of loss of control caused by front wheel shimmy.

Wheel shimmy can be due to one or to a combination of these factors:

1. *Loose headset bearings.* See Chapter 7.
2. *Bent fork blade or chainstay.* Use an old axle or piece of wood between dropouts when shipping your bike, especially by plane.
3. *Out-of-line frame.* Wet down pavement. Ride your bike straight, and watch to see if wheels track evenly. Or check the bike frame with a Park frame alignment tool (Fig. 3-31). If you suspect the frame, the bike shop can make this check. If you have this tool, put the adjuster end against the flat side of the rear wheel dropout. Put the other end against the head tube. Screw the adjuster knob in or out (Fig. 3-32) until the tool lies flat against the head tube and the seat tube (Fig. 3-33). Now put the tool on the opposite side, without changing the adjustment. Check

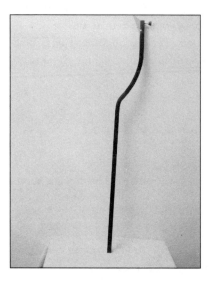

Fig. 3-31. *An out-of-line frame is an accident waiting to happen. If the bike tends to steer inaccurately or wobbles, a bent frame tube may be the culprit. A quick check with a Park frame alignment tool, shown here, can detect a bent frame.*

Fig. 3-32. Put the adjuster end of the Park tool on a rear wheel dropout, as shown.

Fig. 3-33. Turn the adjuster knob until the tool touches the seat tube. Repeat on the other side of the bike. If the tool does not touch the seat tube on the other side, a frame tube is bent. Note that the far end of this tool touches the steering tube.

that the clearance between the seat tube and the tool is the same as it was on the other side of the bike. If not, the frame is out of alignment. If it's an aluminum frame, it can't be cold straightened and should be scrapped. Check with the bike shop for the manufacturer's replacement policy. You should be able to get a new frame at low cost, but the shop will probably charge for replacing parts from the old frame to the new one. If it's steel, the shop may be able to straighten it. Personally I'd replace *any* bent frame with a new one. Perfect alignment is difficult without the jigs and fixtures used to hold frame tubes in alignment when the frame was made.

   4. *Badly balanced load.* Carry your tent, sleeping bag, clothes and other necessities as low as possible. The higher off the ground, the greater the potential for wobble and erratic steering. Use low rider carriers over the front wheels.

   5. *Loose wheel bearings,* especially on the front wheel.

   6. *Misaligned wheel,* especially the front wheel. The misalignment may be caused by

   a. Bent rim (e.g., from contact with a curb)
   b. Bent axle
   c. Inaccurately bored hub which puts the axle off center (rare, but it has happened)

d. Spoke stretch. Spokes loosen, permit the rim to gradually become untrue laterally and concentrically

The theory of wheel shimmy, simply put, is that a weight from one or more of the sources in 1 to 6 above is off center to the frame of the bike or to the wheel. Whatever the source, it is as though someone hung a weight at one point on the front wheel rim. The wheel wants to follow that weight. The weight is neutral near the ground. As the "weight" moves with the wheel it throws the wheel off balance. It's as though an invisible hand began to shake the wheel violently. The shaking is most violent at higher speeds, say over 15 mph. The faster the bike is moving, the more violent the shimmy. If you're moving at under 10 mph you may, if you're lucky, be able to slow down and stop before you dump. Otherwise the shimmy is often so sudden, so unexpected and so violent, that the bike simply falls over. Riders (myself included) who have experienced this shimmy, and who have been hurt by the dump, almost always recall nothing more than the shimmy and a sensation of being forced off the bike as it fell to one side or the other. Most car drivers have experienced front wheel wobble due to an unbalanced front tire(s). The steering wheel shakes, sometimes violently. The car has four wheels and won't turn over, so you can brake and slow down until the shimmy stops. A bike has two wheels, is lighter, has far less mass and weight than a car. Bike shimmy is sudden. You have a split second or less when you can slow to where the shimmy stops. A dump is almost 99 percent certain once shimmy starts.

Table 3-3 summarizes my recommended bike maintenance frequency by bike component.

Table 3-3 PERIODIC MAINTENANCE SCHEDULE

PART	SERVICE	FREQUENCY*	CHAPTER
Axle nuts	Check tightness	Monthly	7 and 9
Bottom bracket	Disassemble, lubricate, adjust	Yearly	7
Brake cables	Check for worn, frayed strands and replace as needed	Six months	5
Brake levers	Check tightness of mounting bolts	Six months	5
Brake pivot nut	Check tightness	Two months	5

(cont.)

PART	SERVICE	FREQUENCY*	CHAPTER
Brake shoes	Check wear, adjustment, nut tightness	Four months	5
Carriers	All mounting bolts and nuts	Four months	3
Chain	Clean, lubricate	Two months	6
Chainwheels	Clean. Check bolt tightness	Two months	6
Cranks	Check spindle nut tightness	Four months	6
Derailleurs	Check shifting. Adjust	Every ride	6
Derailleur cables	Check for frayed strands and replace as needed	Four months	6
Fenders	Check mounting nuts	Four months	3
Freewheel	Clean, lubricate. Check cog wear	Four months	6
Headset bearings	Clean, lubricate, adjust	Four months	7
Hubs	Clean, lubricate, adjust	Six months	7
Pedals	Clean, lubricate	Six months	7
Seat post	Check tightness of binder bolt	Four months	3
Shift levers	Check mounting bolt tightness	Six months	6
Spokes	Check tightness	Four months	9
Stem bolt	Check tightness	Four months	6
Tires	Check pressure, wear, cuts, gouges	Weekly	8
Wheels	Check alignment, retrue as needed	Four months	9

*Frequency of maintenance varies depending on use of bicycle. These frequencies are based on average use. If you go through water or over abrasives such as sand, or if you off-road race, your bike will need more frequent maintenance, even before every race.

RADIOS

Do not listen to a radio while you ride! Many states have outlawed radios on bicycles, for good reason. They mask the noise of vehicles, so you may not hear one bearing down on you. If you play one loud enough the noise can even drown out the siren of an emergency vehicle coming through an intersection. If you ride off-road, a radio muffles the beauty of birdsongs, the sound of wind rustling through the trees, the warning hiss of a rattler ahead on the trail, the tinkle of cowbells. Conversation with partners will be impossible. If you do carry a radio, use it only when you're off the bike, for music at night in the tent, to pick up weather forecasts, for news.

SAFE BRAKING TECHNIQUES

Use your brakes sparingly as you make a turn. Your bike rides at a greater angle to the ground when you are turning than when you are riding straight. On a turn, greater side forces exert themselves at the point where the tire makes contact with the ground. If the ground is at all slippery (gravel, wet leaves, etc.) when you brake, the bike could fall to one side. Be especially wary of braking around sharp corners at high speed. Slow down before you arrive at the turn if you're not sure how slippery the surface will be or what is around the other side of the curve.

Anticipate braking needs further in advance in wet weather. Water acts as a lubricant and cuts braking effectiveness. For example, some brakes can bring you to a stop at 15 mph within 10 feet. In wet weather, those same brakes take 20 feet to do the job. That's with aluminum rims. If you have chrome-plated steel rims the story is much worse, braking goes from 10 feet at 15 mph in dry weather to as high as 60 feet in wet weather before you can stop.

Control speed on a downhill run, on any surface, by getting your weight as far back over the rear wheel as possible (Fig. 3-34). Weight over the rear wheel improves tire-to-road adhesion and helps prevent an "endo," where the rear wheel flips up and over. The front brake provides 80 to 90 percent of the combined braking power of both brakes. As you apply both brakes, forward momentum of the bike tends to lift the rear wheel up. Try it with a book. Put a book on the table. Push it with one hand, hold it back with the other. The rear of the book, the end you're pushing, rises up off the table. Same thing happens on a bike. The front wheel grabs, the rear wheel loses traction and may even lift off the ground. Practice emergency stops by applying the rear brake first, then, instantly, the front brake. Don't rely on the rear brake alone.

A fully loaded bicycle is much harder to handle! Steering on a fully loaded bike is sluggish. You won't be able to make quick, sharp turns. Your balance will be off and the bike will seem to have a will of its own. Practice riding your fully loaded bike before taking off down the road. You'll find that after 25 miles or so handling the bike becomes more

Fig. 3-34. *Brakes work better when weight is over the rear wheel on speedy downhill runs.*

comfortable—getting on and off, starting and stopping, turning and braking will begin to feel natural. *Be aware that braking power is also drastically reduced as you load up the bike!* Remember to use greater pressure as you pull the brake levers to control speed, and be especially careful as you travel downhill. Control your speed!

Be aware that braking is adversely affected when you're *towing a loaded bike trailer* (Fig. 3-35). Take sharp turns slowly so you don't turn over the trailer or cause the trailer to hit a curb or other obstruction that the bicycle will clear but the trailer won't.

Fig. 3-35. *If you tow a trailer, remember braking takes longer. You also need to make wider swings around corners to clear curbs, and when doing so be more aware of traffic coming from behind. Go slow around corners. High-speed cornering can dump the trailer. Ask any truck driver.*

Fig. 3-37. *This isn't a fat tire, but believe me, even fat tires can fall down into and get caught in storm drains. If you can't avoid these hazards, cross them with your wheels at a right angle to the bars, not parallel to them. This applies also to bridge expansion joints, railroad and streetcar tracks.*

Fig. 3-36. *Use a rear-mounted carrier if you take your child along. The extra weight over the rear wheel improves braking.*

If you carry a child on the bike, use a rear-mounted child carrier (Fig. 3-36). You get better load distribution for safer, more accurate steering and better braking because the child's weight is over the rear wheel. The child carrier should have guards that keep the youngster's feet from tangling in the spokes, hurting the child and causing you to lose control of the bike.

Watch out for storm sewer gratings (Fig. 3-37), *bridge expansion joints and railroad tracks!* The bars in some sewer gratings are spaced far enough apart so that even fat tires can drop down in them. The bike will come to a sudden stop, the rear wheel will lift up, and you might be pitched forward over the handlebars onto your head.

WATCH FOR ROAD DAMAGE

You can't avoid every bump. Learn how to take them with maximum comfort to you and minimum harm to your tires. If you watch the road, you know when a bump is coming up that you can't avoid. As you approach the bump, have both pedals flat, so cranks are parallel to the ground. Lift your body slightly up off the saddle, so your legs and arms can absorb the road shock.

Watch out for potholes, particularly those more than two inches deep. Shallower potholes you should be able to ride over, particularly if you see them before you hit them. Steer around deeper potholes, after first checking to see if traffic permits such a detour. Be aware that if you ride right after a rainfall, deep potholes and chuckholes can be water-filled and so appear to be shallow. The most innocent-looking puddle of water on the road can mask a six-inch chuckhole that can dump you right off the bike.

HOW TO RIDE SAFELY ON CITY STREETS

In the city you share the road with passenger cars, trucks, taxis, motor-cycles, buses, other bicycles and even pedestrians. Sloane's first rule of survival when cycling on city streets is to *give the right-of-way to anyone who wants it, any time he wants it!* On a bike is no place to be macho, to argue with a behemoth of a car or truck, or even another bicyclist or a pedestrian, about who should go first, who is in the right. Better to be safe. You can always get mad later, when you're back home, safe and sound.

A review of actual typical bike accidents, and how they could have been avoided, will, I hope, demonstrate how you can avoid becoming such a statistic in the annals of accident reporting.

The data that follow come from "A Two-Year Bicycle Accident Survey," July 1981 through June 1983, made in Palo Alto, CA, by Diana Lewiston. I use this study because I believe it to be typical of all such studies. For example:

Time of day: Of all bicycle accidents reported to police, 89 percent occur between 7 A.M. and 7 P.M. Accidents peak between 7 and 9 A.M.; 11 A.M and 1 P.M.; 3 and 7 P.M.

Traffic: This may seem strange at first. But think about it. The Palo Alto study reported that there were fewer bicycle accidents on streets with high traffic counts than on streets with lower traffic counts. One can only conclude that cyclists on busy streets were the more skilled and experienced, and/or that the alertness of cyclists on less busy streets was dulled by the lower volume of cars on the road. *Lesson 1:* Be alert 100 percent of the time, no matter where you ride.

Injuries: About 84 percent of all reported accidents resulted in injury. Legs were the most frequently injured. More seriously hurt cyclists suffered multiple injuries.

Intersections: Most accidents occur at intersections. Of 200 such ac-cidents in Palo Alto, 35.5 percent were at *right-turning intersections,* where both motorist and cyclist were going straight. Most of these accidents were where the cyclist was traveling at a right angle to the motorist (Fig. 3-38). The cyclist was almost always riding *into* or *against* the flow of traffic, usually on a sidewalk. If the traffic, for example, was going north, the cyclist was riding south, in terms of the sidewalk or street on which the cyclist was riding. Most of these accidents were at a crosswalk. Most involved a cyclist 17 or under. At such intersections 11 percent of the accidents occurred at business intersections (shopping malls, etc.); 42.5 percent of the intersections had stop signs, 27.5 percent had right-on-turn signal lights. *Lesson 2:* Never ride against the flow of traffic, even if you're on the sidewalk. *Be doubly careful as you approach driveways, especially at shopping centers.* Watch out for pedestrians, especially for small children.

Right-turning intersections where the car and cyclist were traveling parallel up to the intersection, where the driver then turned to the right, in front of the cyclist (Fig. 3-39) accounted for 28 percent of the accidents in this study. In one case the cyclist was on the street, in another case, the cyclist was on the sidewalk, and in some cases both cyclist and motorist had a green stoplight. Here are the things that went wrong for these cyclists: The cyclist on the street was located in the motorist's blind spot, or the driver assumed that the cyclist would stop at the intersection and so he could safely turn right. The cyclist might have also assumed

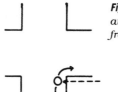

Fig. 3-38. *Most bike accidents occur at intersections. Here a car has cut in front of a cyclist.*

Fig. 3-39. *Right-turning vehicles account for some 28 percent of bike/car collisions, according to one study.*

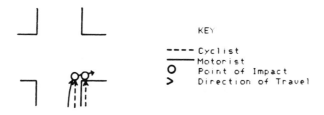

KEY

---- Cyclist
———— Motorist
O   Point of Impact
>   Direction of Travel

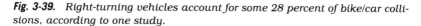

that the motorist knew he wanted to cross the intersection and would wait for him to do so. The cyclist on the sidewalk evidently made the same assumptions. *Lesson 3:* Never make any assumptions about anything, even if you have made eye contact and so believe the motorist sees you. He does not know what you have in mind, either. *Lesson 4:* Don't ride on the sidewalk, even if it is a designated bike lane. If you feel the road is too dangerous, find a safer road.

Lesson 5: As you approach an intersection, with or without a stoplight or stop sign present, and you intend to proceed straight on through the intersection, move, as soon as possible and certainly before you come to the intersection, into a position on the road that puts you behind the left rear tire of the vehicle in front (Fig. 3-40). Stay about six to eight feet behind the car. In this position both the driver behind and the driver ahead can see you. Neither can turn into you if they want to turn right, because you are not where they can do so. Oncoming cars, or cars to the left or right, can see you. In Figure 3-40, bicycle A is located behind vehicle B, and can be seen in that vehicle's rearview mirror. Bicycle C is in the best position, in the left side of the vehicle lane, to make either a left or a right turn, after, of course, waiting until oncoming vehicle B has cleared the intersection. If bike C was in the right side of the vehicle lane, vehicle D could pass to the left of the bicycle and collide with it in an attempt to make a right-hand turn. Believe me, it's not at all uncommon for a motorist to blithely ignore the presence of a bicycle and make a right turn as though the bike was not on the road at all. If you should find yourself at the curb lane, at an intersection, with a vehicle

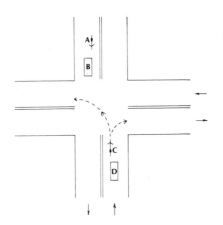

Fig. 3-40. *Here the cyclist is in a good position for a left turn but in an unsafe position for a right turn.*

on your left, make sure that vehicle proceeds straight, or completes a turn to the right, before you go straight through the intersection. Never ride parallel to a vehicle, especially on the right (blind side) as you approach and go through an intersection. *Be wary of any cars to your left if it's legal to turn right on a red signal light.* Let the light turn green, let all traffic behind and ahead clear or make sure they are not going to turn, before you go through the intersection. Next time, don't get caught between a vehicle and the curb.

Bicycle and vehicle parallel, going in the same direction (Fig. 3-41): Here the cyclists assumed, obviously incorrectly, that the motorist had seen them and would let them turn left. You can see the point of impact, at O, where the car A ran into the bicycle. *Lesson 6:* Don't try to speed ahead of a vehicle and try to turn left in front of it. Instead, let the vehicle pass, make sure all's clear, *then* make your left turn. *Lesson 7:* Bicyclist was in the curb lane, to the right of the vehicle and in its blind spot. The cyclist increased speed and swooped in front of car B. The cyclist should have been in the left tire lane of the car behind it, well before entering the intersection. If traffic did not permit the cyclist to get into that lane, the cyclist should have stopped at the intersection, let traffic clear, and only then made the left turn. Instead, the cyclist, because he was in front of a vehicle, believed that the driver of that vehicle would assume that the bike was not going to turn left and that the cyclist would maintain speed straight ahead. Also, a left-hand turn signal by the cyclist is no assurance that the driver will see it, recognize what the cyclist means by it, or slow down enough for the cyclist to turn left safely.

Fig. 3-41. *This bike accident was due to the cyclist's attempts to speed up and make a left turn in front of a vehicle, and an assumption that the driver sees him.*

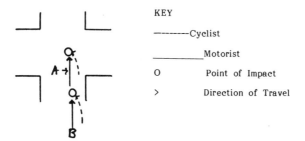

KEY

-------- Cyclist

_____ Motorist

O   Point of Impact

>   Direction of Travel

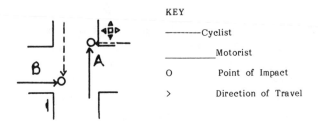

Fig. 3-42. *Here a cyclist on the sidewalk, A, does not give the motorist time to clear the intersection, having assumed that the driver would slow down or stop at the yellow. The cyclist at B was hit because he assumed that he could make it through a red light. He didn't. The cyclist assumed the car was going slow enough to give him time to "skin" through the red. Assumptions can be dangerous things.*

Failure to Yield or Obey a Stoplight Signal

Ignoring a red stoplight signal is a very common violation of both traffic regulations and common sense by bicyclists (Fig. 3-42). A cyclist (B) pedals up to an intersection, looks in all directions and thinks that he has time to go through the red light. He thinks traffic is far enough away for him to get through before a car can come close enough to endanger him. In Figure 3-42, another cyclist is on the sidewalk. The motorist has proceeded when the stoplight was yellow. The cyclist assumed that the motorist would stop. The vehicle hit the bicycle at the crosswalk. *Lesson 8: Always obey stoplight signals and stop sign warnings.* Even if the stoplight has turned green in favor of the bicycle, it's always safer to wait until all traffic has stopped at the red light before attempting to cross the intersection at a right angle to traffic. In another accident case, bicycle B had the green light, but it turned yellow when the bike was almost across the intersection. The motorist did not yield, started at the yellow, and hit the bike. *Lesson 9:* This accident was an error of judgment on the part of the driver. However, had the cyclist been perhaps more alert or more skilled, it may have been possible to have steered to the right, around the vehicle that pulled in front of the bike. This is a very iffy situation, and sometimes there really is an accident that the cyclist can't avoid. Many accidents are caused by motorists' own poor judgment, lack of understanding of the limitations of a bicycle and the knowledge that inside that steel cocoon *he* won't be the one that's hurt in a collision with a bicycle.

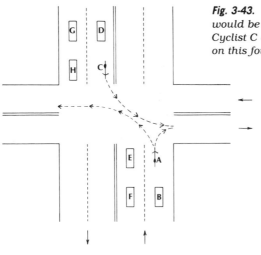

Fig. 3-43. *A right turn for cyclist A would be safe, but not a left turn. Cyclist C can safely make a left turn on this four-lane highway.*

Four-Lane Right and Left Turns

In Figure 3-43, bicycle A is in the wrong position to make a left-hand turn, but in the right position for a right-hand turn. Car B, behind the bike, may assume that the cyclist will either go straight or turn right. If the cyclist turns to the left, car B could have decided to switch to the left lane to get around the bicycle, in which case the car would impact the bike in the center of this intersection. *Lesson 10:* Bike C has the right idea. Here the cyclist has positioned himself in front of car D, in the left side of that lane. The only way car D could proceed would be to swing to the right lane to go around the bike. Or car D would have to wait until the bike had made its left turn. Of course, bike C would also have had to wait until oncoming traffic had cleared. If bike A is in a mandatory right-turn lane and has a right-turn arrow, oncoming traffic has a red signal and is blocked from proceeding. In fact, the position of bike A is the safest one to be in, in a mandatory right-turn, stoplight-protected situation. If bike A tries to turn left, it will be in imminent danger of being hit by car E or F, the drivers of which could assume that the cyclist would not risk a turn in front of them.

Compounded Errors of Judgment

As Figure 3-44 shows, the motorist did not yield to the bicyclists, and the cyclists did not let the vehicle pass, even though they may have had

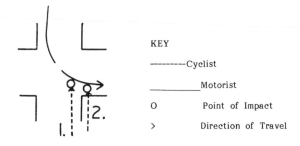

Fig. 3-44. *Here the motorist did not yield to either cyclist. Again, an unsafe assumption on the cyclist's part that the car driver would yield.*

the right of way. Who has the right of way, as I said earlier, is not important anyway. It's who does *not* get hit that's important. In my opinion, both cyclists should have seen that the vehicle was already more than halfway through its left-hand turn, and should have let the car pass before crossing the intersection.

The Benefits and Hazards of Parked Cars

I prefer to ride my bike on streets where parked cars are permitted. That's because those streets usually have an extra half lane, so people can open their car doors to get in and out of the car without interfering with passing vehicles. This special lane gives you room without having to bike in the vehicle traffic lane. It also is a lot safer to ride on this type of street than on a street where parked cars are not allowed, because on those streets, cars force you to ride right next to the curb. There's dangerously little room for cars to pass you on the left, and to the right, there's that curb.

There are, however, three hazards associated with parked cars. As you see in Figure 3-45, the driver of parked car A has, without warning, suddenly opened the driver's side door into the path of a bicycle. *Lesson 11:* As you come up to a parked car, look through the rear window and/ or the left side-view mirror to see if anyone is in the driver's seat. If so, assume the door is about to open. Slow to a crawl. Look back over your left shoulder, check to make sure that there is no traffic behind you, so you can swing out in the vehicle lane if you have to get away from a parked car opened door. In addition, as you come up to a parked car, keep your fingers on both brake levers to save precious seconds if you do have to stop suddenly.

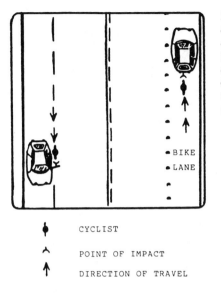

Fig. 3-45. *Cyclist at left has run into a suddenly opened car door. Cyclist at right has to go out into the traffic lane from his safe bike lane because a car has parked in the bike lane. City bike lane signs do become invisible to drivers and it's well to recognize this fact.*

CYCLIST

POINT OF IMPACT

DIRECTION OF TRAVEL

The second hazard, shown in Figure 3-45, is a car that's parked in a clearly marked bike lane. You should be able to see car B in plenty of time to go around it, carefully. First check traffic from behind to make sure there's room for you to do so. Remember, just because there is a yellow line, along with a road sign that says "Bike Lane" or similar warning (Fig. 3-46), it does *not* mean motorists will pay one bit of attention. I well remember when, after months of lobbying, we cyclists finally persuaded Chicago's city council to designate bike lanes on ap-

Fig. 3-46. *Various signs used to designate a bike route (left), a bike lane (center), and a bike crossing (right).*

A guide sign used for marking officially designated Bikeways.

The "diamond lane" gives preference to certain vehicles such as bicycles.

Used to warn motorists of a midblock bike path crossing.

propriate streets. For a few weeks motorists (with the notable exceptions of cab and bus drivers) steered clear of the bicyclist's part of the road. Then the signs became invisible, and all was as before.

The third hazard of parked cars is not often recognized as such. Here's what can happen (as it did to me). You can be riding on a nice wide suburban street, pedaling away near the curb. Suddenly, without warning, a motorist swoops in front of you, pulls to the curb and parks. You don't have a chance; you can't stop, except by running into the car's rear bumper. When that happened to me, I broke a nice new expensive Schwinn Paramount touring bike in half, I hit so hard. The front wheel stayed true, and held tight in the fork, which was more than I did, I suffered a badly sprained wrist. As I crawled out from under the rear of the car I saw a woman standing over me. I'll never forget her words. She said: "*What* are you doing under my Cadillac?" I think I'd have felt better if she had just said "car."

Use Sign Language

Signal your intentions, as shown in Figure 3-47. A motorist may not believe you, and you can't depend that he will see or understand what you're trying to tell him, but it's safer if you try. An arm straight out to the left means you intend to make a left turn. A left hand pointing up means a right turn. An arm straight down means you are coming to a stop. If the arm is down and sort of waving, it means you are slowing down. Again, don't depend on arm signals to deter a vehicle from running into you. Use them, yes, but give the right of way at all times, even if it's yours. This may seem a bit chicken to macho bike messengers who ride in major urban areas. Remember, you don't have to emulate them if they lay *their* life on the line. Play it safe!

TRAIL RIDING TECHNIQUES

On the trail you are likely to be far from a bike shop. If you have mechanical problems, or if you get a flat, you had darned well better know how to fix it, if it is fixable with the minimum tool set you can pack along. Avoid the hassles of trip delays, the stress of having to walk back, by thoroughly reviewing the following chapters on bike maintenance. Make sure your bike is in tip-top condition and that you can repair almost anything that breaks except the frame, *before* you hit the trail.

Fig. 3-47. Use these hand signals in traffic. Left hand straight out for a left turn, left hand up for a right turn and left hand pointing toward ground for a stop or slowdown.

Trail Courtesy and Consideration

Biking on the hiking trails in many state and most federal parks is, unfortunately, not allowed. The excuse is that the fat tires of ATBs will chew up the trails, that somehow they will harm the pristine beauty of untrammeled nature. I can, in a way, understand this reasoning, while I emphatically disagree with it.

Park management are civil servants. They don't want to rock any boats. They quite often are not themselves cyclists. One look at the fat knobs of an ATB tire can send them into a frenzy of no-no's. I think they view ATBs as I view trail motorcycles, dune buggies and so-called all-terrain motorized vehicles. With a mixture of horror and disgust. This view is understandable if ATBs chewed up the trail. But they don't. ATB tires wreak no more damage on the delicate ecosystem of remote mountain trails than do the fat soles of hiking boots. If you want to see trail damage, just bike behind a bunch of equestrians. Horses' hooves can make a trail all but uncyclable, especially on a clay trail or on a dirt trail after a rainstorm. I'm not even going to mention horse dumps (or cow dung for that matter), just don't run into it, very slippery and smelly. Cyclists, don't do that. Never!

Follow these rules for trail courtesy. I hope that when park officials note that we all follow them, they will change their mind about letting us bike on the narrow, truly off-road wilderness trails. Right now ATB cycling is limited, for the most part, to paved park roads and most fire roads and fire lanes. You will find state-by-state information on riding your ATB in parklands, as well as in foreign country parks, later in Chapter 4. Many of these courtesy recommendations come from the National Off-Road Bicycle Association (NORBA).

1. *Yield to hikers, equestrians, other cyclists.* Negative encounters work against us all, so be nice. Remember, you can scare a hiker or "spook" a horse if you come up behind them on silent, cat's-paw tires. Establish eye contact with those you meet. Smile a lot.

2. *Ask a rider if his/her horse is skittish, before you pass.* If the answer is yes, it may be advisable to dismount and, by mutual agreement, walk

the bike past the horse. Be careful about domestic animals such as cows, if you come upon them. Try not to alarm them as you go by.

3. *Stay on trails.* Never cut switchbacks (Fig. 3-48). Switchbacks are the gently curving trails that zigzag up a mountainside to reduce the effective grade so the climb is easier for trail users. It's tempting, I know, on a downhill run, to cut across switchbacks. Don't do it. If you leave the trail you trample delicate flora and fauna, and the sensibilities of those who care about the world in which we live. Be a good person and never leave the trail. If you go thrashing through the woods, you'll trash our chances for keeping the goodwill of those who let us in there.

4. *Be aware of the soil condition.* Don't ride on clay or muddy soil, because you'll leave fat tire tracks that tell park management and those who follow that you don't give a damn about the environment.

5. *Don't litter.* Leave nothing behind, not even soiled paper towels. Strive to leave the trail so clean no one can tell you were even on it. If it rains, never ditch your tent. "Ditching" means digging a trench around your tent to funnel rainwater away from it. Instead, use a good tent with a waterproof bottom.

6. *Observe fire rules.* Make sure you check with the ranger so you know what kind of fire you can make, if any. Sometimes dry conditions

Fig. 3-48. *A zigzag switchback eases the way up steep hills. Don't cut across these switchbacks on the way down. Stay on the trail.*

do not permit *any* kind of fire. At other times, wood fires are not permitted, yet you could use a camp stove. The rule is, always check fire rules beforehand. If the woods are too dry, you won't be permitted to ride on the trail at all. No one will be permitted on a trail when conditions are so dry a dangerous forest fire could spring up.

7. *Keep speed under control,* not only for your own safety, but so you don't dig ruts in the trail or throw a stream of dirt behind you (Fig. 3-49). Slow down as you come to a blind turn. You never know what's on the other side.

8. *Don't ride on private property* without permission from the owner. Remember, a "No Trespassing" sign may simply mean okay *if you ask.*

Safety Tips for Off-Road Riders

Bicycling on a remote mountain trail sure is a lot different from street or road riding. On the trail there are unique and different animals, easy ways to get lost, possibly bad water to drink, contour maps that are hard to interpret without a course in orienteering, to name a few of the problems. All this sounds bad, if not downright evil, I know. But, heck, I spent the first couple of chapters of this book rhapsodizing about the glories and splendors of mountain riding, the glorious vistas of breathtaking scenery and all that. Now that I've got you hooked (I hope) it's time to get realistic. I'm selfish, I want you to buy future editions of this book, which you can't do if you don't come back. Here are a few of the ways to assure your safe return:

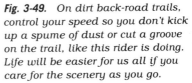

Fig. 3-49. On dirt back-road trails, control your speed so you don't kick up a spume of dust or cut a groove on the trail, like this rider is doing. Life will be easier for us all if you care for the scenery as you go.

1. *File a travel plan.* Let a park ranger and friends know your itinerary and when to expect your return. If you're not back on time, then a search party can start looking for you.

2. *Learn orienteering.* There are many excellent books on finding your way in the wilderness, where no road signs point to Manhasset, Poughkeepsie or Seattle. You should know how to use a contour map and compass to pinpoint your exact location at all times (pitch black midnight excepted). You will need a good compass, and if you can afford it, I recommend spending around $150 for an altimeter. Please see the Appendix for a list of books on orienteering. Contour and topographic maps also help you plot a course that will avoid disgustingly steep 15-percent grades. A hill that steep means you climb (spell that probably walk) 15 feet up in every 100 feet forward. In fact, a new map service now offers computer-generated maps "that give the illusion of three-dimensional landscapes, complete with peaks and valleys, providing riders with a visual idea of the terrain along bicycle routes," says *The New York Times*. The maps include the more scenic areas of the Pacific Northwest. For information write Terragrahics, P.O. Box 1025, Eugene, OR 97440.

3. *Carry a signaling mirror* (Fig. 3-50) so you can signal across a mountain valley or even a low-flying airplane for help.

4. *Learn the basics of first aid.* See the Appendix for a list of books on this subject. Take along a good first aid kit. Re health, also carry a

Fig. 3-50. *These items can be very handy when cycle camping on remote trails. At left, a signaling mirror. Center, map mileage reader. Right, an orienteering compass.*

lightweight water filtration kit so you can purify water from mountain streams and lakes.

5. *Avoid wild animals*. I know this seems obvious. But the Bambi syndrome has caused many injuries in the wild. That charming old elk, Santa Claus' sweet little deer, Smoky the Bear, cute raccoon, cuddly chipmunk, are all *wild* animals that can kick, bite, or claw if you extend a kindly hand in their direction. My advice is to admire wild animals from as great a distance as possible. Small mammals such as chipmunks, squirrels and raccoons, if friendly, are likely to be rabid and bite.

I asked large-animal curators at major zoos what to do if one meets a bear. The general response was "I hope you don't, but if you do, try curling up in a ball and playing dead. If you're lucky, the bear will go away after a few sniffs." Avoid bears with cubs. Black and brown bears can climb trees, but if you have a smooth track downhill you may be able to outrun them on your bike. However, these bears are usually not interested in you, so long as you do not antagonize them. A grizzly bear can run at 30 mph but can't climb a tree. Grizzlies are found in Yellowstone National Park, in Alaska and other Northwest mountain areas. You may find grizzlies in berry bush areas, so if you go berry gathering, particularly huckleberries, keep a sharp eye out for these nasty critters. They kill people every year in the Yellowstone area. Members of the cat family, such as pumas and mountain lions, will generally avoid you.

One question about wilderness trail cycling relates to weapons, specifically, should you carry a gun? I hate to say "don't do it" if the weapon could have saved your life. On the other hand, it's usually illegal to carry a weapon in national parks and most state parks, even with a concealed-weapons permit. Yet I know experienced ATBers who always carry a large-bore handgun strapped to a leg when in the wild, especially if their family is along, for protection against two-footed as well as four-footed animals.

About Dogs

When you're on foot, a dog may be a best friend, wriggling tail and all. When you're on a bike, the gentlest little Scotty can turn into a snarling beast. I don't know why this is. Territoriality, perhaps. My own belief is that the dog finally finds a human at a disadvantage. And it cheats. Some dogs wait until you're laboring slowly up a steep hill. They'll cut diagonally across a yard or field to get at you. Most of all, they attack from behind. If you hear the pat-pat of paws and heavy breathing coming up from behind, it's a dog after your body.

Beware of all German shepherds and Dobermans. St. Bernards can be especially vicious. Beware, too, of the owner who yells at you from his yard that *his* dog won't bite and refuses to restrain the animal. If you are bitten, try to find the owner, because he/she can be sued successfully. A case in point is a Portland, OR, man who was killed by an 85-pound bull mastiff which ran out into the street and knocked him off his bike. The jury unanimously awarded the man's family $1.5 million in damages (I'll be glad to furnish details to your attorney).

If you're attacked, here's what you can do:

1. *Pedal away if you can.* I have outrun dogs on the flat. They don't have much stamina for a long run. Takes about a mile to get away.

2. *If you're trapped* with a dog at your wheel, stop and try the friendly approach. If the dog wags his tail, lowers his head, all may be well, until you get back on the bike. Pointing a finger at the friendly dog, while urging him to go home in a loud, firm, stentorian voice, may see him slink away. If the dog bristles, holds its ears flat to its head, paws the ground, urinates and growls, the dog is ready to attack as soon as you mount the bike. If the dog does come at you, you could spray it with Halt or Mace. You can buy Halt in an animal pet shop, Mace in a sporting goods or gun store. Halt is a pepper derivative in a pressurized inert gas. Mace is tear gas. Avoid using the spray directly ahead of you if you're moving. I did and can report that Mace feels like holes burning through your skin.

Chemical sprays may not stop a big, mean animal. A nonchemical defense may be your best bet. It's a Dog Chaser, an electronic gadget that emits a high-frequency sound only the dog can hear. The sound is extremely painful to the sensitive ear of the dog. The closer the dog to the Dog Chaser, the more painful the sound. I loaned one to my postman and he fell in love with it. I tried one on a friend's Doberman, who turned tail and skulked sullenly away. The Dog Chaser won't work on your pet, who will just look up at you with mournful eyes that say, "Why did you do this to me?" The Dog Chaser costs around $60, is made by E.I. Inc., 8780 S.W. 131st Street, Miami, FL 33156.

Some cyclists use their bike pump or length of cable on the animal's nose. Personally I'd avoid that approach, not because of concern for the dog, but because man-to-dog combat may not work. You could lose. Besides, you could ruin your bike pump. Nonbiking dog lovers will hate these words, I know. Just remember, their compassion is coupled with ignorance. I like dogs, too. I have a friendly cocker spaniel and a feisty little Yorky. Both would chase all cyclists down the street if I let them.

Emergency Signals

If you are in the wild and someone in your party is hurt and needs help, use these signals that can be seen from a distance or from an aircraft.

1. *You need a doctor for serious injury:* Lay out just one tree limb, or pieces of colored fabric or anything that will attract attention, in the shape of a capital "I." Make the signal at least 10 feet long. As the aircraft swoops down to investigate, lie on ground, with your arms stretched out behind your head, if possible.

2. *You need food and water:* Lay out two signals in the shape of an "F." (Later ask yourself how come you ran out of vittles.)

3. *If you are lost* and want directions, lay out a "K." The pilot may be able to drop a map or written instructions, and with luck will miss your head, which got you lost in the first place.

4. *If you have forgotten all these signals,* make an "SOS."

5. *If there's a place for the aircraft to land,* put out a triangle.

6. *If the pilot understands* your message, he/she will signal a "yes" by dipping the plane's nose up and down. If your signals are not understood, the pilot will fishtail (move the rudder right and left).

7. *If you don't need help* but a would-be rescuer might think you do, put out two capital "LL's" and wave your right arm.

How to Use a Quick Release

Quick-release mechanisms are used on ATB seat posts to lock the saddle in place, to lock one or both wheels in the bike frame, and to lock the fork in fork-mount bicycle car-top carriers. Your safety depends on proper, safe and correct use of the quick-release mechanism. If the quick release is not safely tightened, the wheel could pop out of the fork, for example, and cause an accident. Once you understand how to use a quick release, always check its tightness before you ride the bike. This check should become a habit. If you have left the bike someplace, the quick release could have been tampered with. If the bike fell over in the garage, the quick release could be loosened. If you don't check it before you get on the bike, the bike could be in a dangerous condition. Looking at the quick-release lever isn't good enough. Just because the lever is pointing in the closed position, as described below, doesn't mean it's safely tight, for two reasons. First, the quick-release skewer (Fig. 3-51) eventually stretches, which can cause the quick release to loosen. Second, someone may have tampered with the quick-release adjuster nut (see below) and changed the original tightness adjustment.

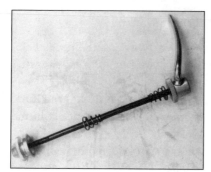

Fig. 3-51. A quick-release hub mechanism. At left, the adjuster nut. At right, the clamp lever.

Before I give you details on use of the quick release, it's vital you understand that this *is NOT a nut and bolt device.* It is a cam-action mechanism. The cam (Fig. 3-52) is eccentric and offset, and attached to the lever. The cam turns when the lever turns and tightens or loosens the quick-release mechanism, depending on which way the lever is turned. *Never try to tighten the adjuster nut alone, either with your fingers or with a tool!* The adjuster nut (arrows, Fig. 3-53), will *never* hold the wheel securely in place all by itself. On the other hand, pull tests made by Schwinn in their lab show that it takes 500 foot-pounds of pressure to pull a properly tightened quick-release mechanism wheel out of the bike frame. For example, in some 20 years of cycling, I have

Fig. 3-52. Enlarged view of a quick-release cam. The quick-release lever is attached to the cam. As the lever turns to the tightening position, the cam turns and tightens the wheel in the dropout. The dropout is where the wheel (hub) axle fits into the bike frame.

Fig. 3-53. Quick-release adjuster nut (arrows) on Campagnolo hub quick releases.

had two accidents involving the front wheel. In one, the front wheel caught in a bridge grating. The bike stopped instantly, the frame broke in half, but the *wheel stayed in the fork.* In another accident, a driver stopped suddenly in front of me. My front wheel hit the car's rear bumper at about 15 mph. The frame was totaled, yet the front wheel did not budge out of the fork dropouts.

Here is how to safely tighten the quick release:

1. Turn the quick-release lever so it is pointing toward the front of the bike (Fig. 3-54).

2. Hold the quick-release lever, in the open position, with one hand while you tighten the adjuster nut clockwise with the other hand (Fig. 3-55) as far as possible.

3. As you turn the quick-release lever toward the rear of the bike, you should feel resistance to turning when the lever is about at the 12 o'clock position, at a right angle to the frame of the bike (Fig. 3-56).

4. From the 12 o'clock position it should take *considerable* muscle to turn the lever all the way to the closed position, where the lever is pointing toward the rear of the bike (Fig. 3-57).

5. Check tightness of the quick release this way:

    a. Turn the lever to the open position (Fig. 3-54). Hold the brake shoes against the rim (Fig. 3-58) while you pull the crossover

Fig. 3-54. The quick-release unit is loose when the lever is turned toward the front of the bike and the word OPEN is visible.

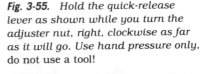

Fig. 3-55. Hold the quick-release lever as shown while you turn the adjuster nut, right, clockwise as far as it will go. Use hand pressure only, do not use a tool!

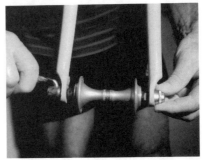

Fig. 3-56. When correctly adjusted, you should feel considerable resistance to turning the lever beginning at the 12 o'clock position, as shown here.

Fig. 3-57. In the closed position you should see the word CLOSED, and the quick-release lever should point to the rear of the bike, as above.

Fig. 3-58. To remove a wheel, hold brake shoes against the rim, then pull out the crossover cable as shown in Figure 3-59.

cable leaded end out of the brake arm (Fig. 3-59). Remove the front wheel.

b. Inspect the dropouts. They should have indents on all four sides of the dropouts that look like those in Figure 3-60. The sharp sawtooth edges of the quick release (Fig. 3-61) (or the axle bolts) and the hub locknuts (Fig. 3-62) should have made

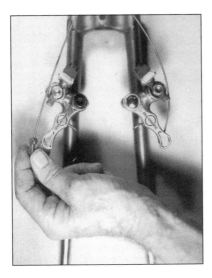

Fig. 3-60. Wheel dropouts should show indent marks like these when quick-release unit is safely tightened.

Fig. 3-59. Remove leaded tab end of crossover cable to spread brakes apart for wheel removal.

Fig. 3-61. Indent marks on dropouts (see Fig. 3-60) are made by these sawtooth edges of quick-release unit.

Fig. 3-62. Indent marks on inside of dropouts should be made by these sawtooth edges of hub locknut.

these indentations. If the wheel has been removed more than once, you should see multiple overlapping indentations. If you do not see these indentations, readjust the quick release as above.

c. Replace the wheel. Replace the crossover brake cable in the brake arm. Make sure the wheel is evenly centered between the fork blades, then turn the quick release to the closed position.

A Note About Wheel Retention Devices

The Consumer Products Safety Commission requires a wheel retention device on bolted-on front wheels but not on quick-release-held front wheels. Since quick-release hubs are more prone to accidental release than bolted-on ones, it makes absolutely no sense to me to require retention devices only on bolted-on hubs. Recognizing this problem, responsible manufacturers now have front wheel retention devices on quick-release hubs as well as on their bolted-on hubs. Schwinn has far and away the best front wheel retention device on the market (arrows in Fig. 3-63). To use this device, simply press the tab end (arrow) toward the wheel, and push the retention lever downward. When the wheel is replaced, just pull the retention lever upward until it clicks into place over the stud on the inside of the fork blade.

Yet another type of wheel retention device is actually molded into the dropout (Fig. 3-64). As you can see in Figure 3-65, if the quick release should open or is too loose, it will still be held by the outer lip of each dropout. You can't remove a wheel from this type of dropout unless you loosen the quick-release adjuster nut so the quick release will clear the dropout lip as you remove the wheel. I like this idea, because

Fig. 3-63. *The safest wheel retention device is made by Schwinn. To release, push the lever (arrows) downward, turn lever. Replace by turning lever until it snaps into the locked position.*

Fig. 3-64. *Another wheel retention device is actually a part of the drop-out. It will hold a wheel in place if the quick release is slightly loose, but not if it's very loose.*

Fig. 3-65. *To remove a wheel with the retention device in Fig. 3-64, turn the quick release to the open position (see Fig. 3-54). Holding the lever in that position, turn the adjuster nut (Fig. 3-55) counterclockwise four or five turns or until you can pull the wheel out of the dropout. Be sure you readjust the quick release after replacing the wheel. See text.*

when you replace the wheel you *have* to readjust the quick release (see above for instructions).

A third type of wheel retention device is found on inexpensive bikes (Fig. 3-66). This gadget is simply a piece of metal with a right-angled lip (arrow, Fig. 3-66). To remove a wheel, loosen the axle bolt counterclockwise far enough so the metal tab can be pulled out of the slot in the fork blade.

GETTING IN AND OUT OF PEDALS

Many ATBs now come with toe clips. Some of the toe clips also have straps. Figure 3-67 shows both kinds. Unless you're racing, I don't recommend you use cleated shoes, which have metal clips that fit over the pedal frame. However, toe clips do help keep your feet on the pedals, especially on bumpy trail descents and hill climbing. If you're straining hard uphill and your foot slips off the pedal, you could come down hard on the top tube or lose control and dump the bike. Toe clips with straps let you pull up with one foot while you push down with the other foot.

Fig. 3-66. Inexpensive bikes have a wheel retention device that goes over the axle and has a lip that fits into a slot in the fork blade. This device works if the axle nut is loose one or two turns from the tight adjustment. If the axle bolt is backed off four or five or more turns, however, the retention device can also back off and then will not keep the wheel from coming out of the dropouts. Such a retention device is little more than lip service to a Consumer Products Safety Commission requirement mandating retention devices on a bolted-on front wheel. The CPSC does not require a retention device on quick-release front wheels, yet quick releases are just as likely to be loose if not properly tightened as are bolt-on axles.

Fig. 3-67. Many ATBs now come with toe clips. Some toe clips are strapless, such as the Campagnolo pedal, right. Note that this high-quality pedal can be fitted with a plastic platform to reduce pressure from the serrated cage teeth, if desired. The platforms come with the pedals. Other conventional pedals come with toe clips and straps, left.

This push-pull pedaling adds about 40 percent to your cycling efficiency. It also makes you work harder, but if you're in good shape you'll welcome the added efficiency.

Take these safety precautions when you use toe-clip-equipped pedals, especially with toe straps:

1. *Keep toe straps loose* so you can get your foot out quickly if you need to stay upright on a fast trail descent or for a quick stop in city traffic.

2. *Practice* getting your feet in and out of the toe clips while pedaling slowly in a safe place, such as an empty playgound.

3. *Start by putting one foot in a pedal,* pushing the pedal down with that foot, and mounting the saddle to get the bike rolling, all in one graceful motion. Practice, you can do it. Tip the other pedal up with your toe (Fig. 3-68), and quickly shove your foot into the toe clip.

4. *To get a foot out of a pedal,* tip it up (Fig. 3-69), and pull your foot upward and outward in one brisk motion. Toe straps should be loose, of course.

MORE TRAIL RIDING TECHNIQUES

The tips that follow are based on my own experience on road and trail, and on that of many other experienced off-road cyclists. I am particularly

Fig. 3-69. To remove your foot from a toe-clip pedal, tilt the pedal up as shown, when the crank arm is perpendicular to the ground. Then quickly pull your foot back, up and out in one swift motion. Practice using toe-clip pedals in a safe place, such as an empty playground, until getting feet in and out of them becomes automatic and you can do it without taking your eyes off the road.

Fig. 3-68. Keep toe straps loose in city riding or on rough trails where you need to get your foot out fast to stay upright. To get a foot in the toe clip, tip the pedal up with the toe of your shoe and quickly and forcefully shove your foot onto the pedal.

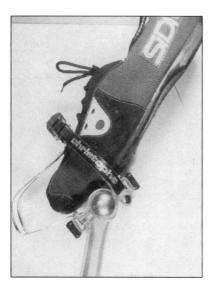

indebted to Theo Patterson, founder of the Portland (Oregon) United Mountain Pedalars, for much of this information.

The folks who started all-terrain cycling about 10 or 15 years ago had to learn the hard way how to pedal through sand, mud, shallow rivers and snow. They had to learn the new techniques of biking up steep slippery hills and getting down them safely. Hopping up and over stumps and jumping off small cliffs became almost routine.

Here is what they and thousands of other trail riders have learned.

How to Fall

Don't *practice* falling, but if you see you are losing control and have the split-second interval between this realization and the actual fall (Fig. 3-70) and Fig. 3-71), you might think about how you are going to land. For example, experienced cyclists try to do a *tuck*. That is, they try to assume a sort of fetal position (that's *fetal*, not *fatal*), with head tucked down, so they land on their shoulders, absorbing road shock in a forward roll. If you land stiff-armed, with arms straight out, to absorb road shock, which seems instinctive with most people, you're asking for a bad wrist sprain or a broken arm.

If you aren't wearing padded bike gloves you may lose a little skin off the palms of your hands as they hit the pavement. In any event, it's vital to remember that the one part of your body you don't want to hit

Fig. 3-70. *If you fall with your arms straight out you risk broken bones. Instead, try to roll or tuck, absorb landing shock on your back.*

Fig. 3-71. This rider is in a good position to tuck into a fall, in a fetal position, the safest way to land.

the pavement first is your head! A helmet protects against abrasion and offers impact resistance. But no helmet can protect against a really hard shock. If you should land head-first, on the top of your head, you could suffer a compression fracture of the spine and be an instant paraplegic or quadriplegic. It's happened, believe me.

Have an Escape Route

Always have an escape route in mind. As you ride, try to anticipate what your braking need might be. For example, a child darts out in front of you. Had you been aware of an escape route, you would have seen that even though you could not *stop* in time to avoid hitting the child, you could *turn,* either to the left into the next lane (you would know if you could because you would, or should, have been checking oncoming traffic with an occasional rearward glance or with your rearview mirror) or to the right, jumping up over a curb. You make a jump like that by pulling up on the handlebars hard, jerking them up, so the front wheel goes up three or four inches so you can go up and over the curb.

Let's say you're riding down a country lane. To your right there's a shallow ditch. To the right of the ditch there's an open field. That ditch and that open field are your escape routes if you have to turn off the road to avoid a collision. Above all, *avoid a head-on collision with anything moving,* because the combined speeds can really do you in. It's also not a good idea to run headlong into a solid, unmoving object, such as a tree or a stone wall. Dump the bike on its side, if you have to, but don't hit head-on. Or let's say you're coming to a bush-shielded intersection on your right. You know you won't be able to see any traffic coming out of that road until you are just past the bushes that are hiding your view to the right. There are now two precautions you should take. Slow down to a crawl, say two or three miles an hour. And keep your hands on the brake levers so that if a car comes at you fast you can stop before you are into the intersection far enough to be in danger.

Think, as you bike, about all the possible ways you could be in danger and how you can avoid it. For example, I routinely, traffic permitting, swing my bike over to the left side of the lane as I approach an intersection. From this position I have room to make a sharp right turn toward the curb, or into the intersection itself, if necessary, to avoid a collision with a car coming from my right. On the trail in the wild, you may suddenly be faced with a choice of jumping off a 10-foot-high clifflet you did not see in time to stop or dumping the bike in a clump of bushes. If you're not an experienced jumper (see below on taking jumps), it will probably be safer to hit the bushes or veer off onto grass if possible. Not so cheery, I know. But it's better to be on the safe side, always.

Hill Climbs

As you approach a hill, *shift to a lower gear before starting* your climb. If you delay shifting until the going is hard, you may find it difficult or impossible to shift down. You may have to either ease off pedaling pressure by turning from one side of the road to the other (not the safest of procedures) or stop, lift up the back wheel, twirl the pedals, shift down and start up again. One hazard of shifting while hill climbing is that the chain may not shift accurately, so it lies partially on one gear and partially on another. In such a case, the chain may not grab the teeth of the rear or front cogs and may slip. If the chain slips while you are exerting pedal pressure, the pedal will slip forward and you could very well lose your balance and fall off the bike or inadvertently steer to the left into another cyclist or into a vehicle. Manufacturers of the latest wide-range derailleur systems claim you can shift while climbing steep hills. For example, the Shimano UniGlide freewheel has computer-generated ridges on the cogs which they claim ease the chain movement from cog to cog under load.

If you had to stop in the middle of a steep climb and want to start up again, put the bike at an angle to the grade, lean way forward, shove off with one foot on the ground and the other foot on the pedal at the 11 o'clock position. If the trail is too steep to bike straight up, and is wide enough, try zigzagging *upward,* from one side of the trail to the other. If you have to walk, well, join the club. It's no disgrace to have to get off your bike and push it up, though my experience has been that it is always easier to pedal than to walk the bike up.

There is a new gadget called a "Rear Steer" which does make it easier to push the bike uphill. It attaches to the handlebars and clips onto the rear of the saddle and when not in use stows in its own bag under the top tube (Fig. 3-72). In use, you just grab the Rear Steer small handlebars from behind the saddle, get behind the bike and walk up. I can report that this little stroke of genius makes shoving your bike uphill a whale of a lot easier. People I rode with were most envious, and I am sure this product will enjoy the healthy sale it deserves. If your bike shop does not have one, write Rear Steer, 560 Mesa Verde Drive, Cave Junction, OR 97523, or phone 1-800-624-7889.

Another way to clomp uphill afoot is to "use your bike as an anchor to pull you up the hill," says Theo Patterson. He notes: "Set your feet, push the bike forward a few inches, apply both brakes and pull yourself up a few steps. Repeat this process until you've gotten to where you can walk or ride again. It's slow, but better than pulling up clumps of grass or breaking tree branches trying to get a grip with one hand and your dead-weight bike in the other. We're talking *steep* here. Hills this radical usually look pretty threatening on the way down."

As you strain hard up a very steep hill you may have to be off the saddle at times to maintain traction. For example, if your rear wheel spins out, shift your weight back. If you begin to lose steering control because the front wheel is flopping back and forth, move your body forward to weight that wheel. If the rear wheel spins and the front wheel flops, get your body down as low as possible, chest close to the top tube, to lower your center of gravity and to weight both wheels at once. Don't stop pedaling. Keep saying to yourself: "One more stroke, one more stroke." If the hill is both steep and long, well, you'll just need more endurance to make it.

Fig. 3-72. *Here's an invention that makes pushing your bike up a steep hill a lot easier. It's called Rear Steer. See text for details.*

All of the above refers to off-road trail riding. On a paved road you will find that in hilly, up-and-down country, like Vermont or California's Napa Valley area, all roads seem always to go up. This is because it may take a half hour to climb a hill but only a few minutes to go down the other side, where you will soon start a climb again. I found this particularly true in Vermont. Sometimes people take pity on us hard-pedaling cyclists. I remember climbing laboriously up Putney Mountain in Vermont on a hot, steamy day in August. Took a while. At the top I paused for breath in front of a wide-porched old farmhouse. On the porch a woman sat in a rocking chair, nursing her baby. She looked at me, sweating and panting. I looked at her. She said, "Would you like a beer?" Of course I said, "Yes, thank you," and chatted with her while she resumed feeding her child. Interesting lady. Turned out she had been a nun in Boston.

It's particularly aggravating to climb a steep hill section, then find that it levels out and you breathe a sigh of relief that you have come to the top. Then you round a curve and there before you is *another* steep hill. This sequence may repeat two or three times as the road winds its way up a big mountain. Bear with it, because the coast down can be fun, if you are careful. If you are sweaty at the top and the air is cool, don a light jacket or pullover to prevent chill as your body dries off. As sweat dries, it cools you by a process known as "latent heat of evaporation." The energy it takes to evaporate the moisture absorbs heat, i.e., chills you.

Staying Up Going Down

You can let gravity pull you down a steep paved road at speeds approaching 50 mph. It's a kick to pass moving cars and see the looks of astonishment from people in them as you cream by. However, folks, fun as it may be, it is a hazardous way to go. For one thing, it takes a *lot* longer to stop at high speed. If you had to slow or stop for any reason, you might very well not be able to do so in time to prevent an accident, to you! For another, applying your brakes *after* you let speed build up can heat up wheel rims and tires. We all know hot air expands. High-speed braking friction heats the air in bike tubes to where it could cause a blowout. The lesson here is to keep speed under control by using both brakes.

Off-road downhill riding takes a different technique than street riding. For one thing you may hit an obstruction that can tear the handlebars right out of your hands. If you plan on riding over rough terrain, consider installing a Pro Steer System to keep the handlebars in your grasp. The

Pro Steer (Fig. 3-73) is an adjustable hydraulic steering damper that attaches to the fork and the down tube. Cannondale has recently introduced a radical new bike with an articulated frame. It has a freeswinging rear frame with a shock absorber. I can report that this new design makes ruts, bumps and rocks virtually disappear. This bike is the most comfortable I have ever ridden.

Check out any unknown hill you approach. Is it pitted with rocks, tree stumps, roots, all of which determine how fast you can safely go? Before taking off down steep hills, flip the seat post quick-release lever and shove the saddle all the way down. If your bike is equipped with a Hite-Rite (Fig. 3-74), push the saddle down hard all the way and lock it in position with the quick release. On the flat, release the quick release and the saddle will spring back up to the normal riding position. Then tighten the quick release.

Fig. 3-73. Now you can add a hydraulic steering damper to your bike to absorb the slings and arrows of outrageous bumps. It's a Pro Steer from Odyssey/Bear Corp., 17101 S. Central Ave., Carson, CA 90746. Attaches to the fork and the down tube.

Fig. 3-74. The springlike affair attached to the seat post and to the seat tube quick release lets you shove the saddle down when you need to, yet when released it springs the saddle right back to its original riding position. It's called a Hite-Rite.

Keep your arms extended, but not locked. The rider in Figure 3-75 is displaying an unbalanced form and, in fact, dumped within a few seconds after I snapped his picture. Start off slowly rolling off the lip of the hill and begin your descent. Use your front brake to control your speed. If you rely on the rear brake you could lock up the rear wheel and skid out of control, as the rider in Figure 3-76 is doing. Note that this rider's right leg is extended outward, ready to soften the fall he is about to make. As you near the bottom of the hill, ease off the brakes and coast the rest of the way.

If you have to stop going downhill, turn to the left and put both your left foot and your bicycle down as carefully and gently as possible. That way you will protect the derailleur (right) side of the bike from damaging impact with the ground. To get started again, brace yourself against a tree while you get your feet onto the pedals and, if you have them, into the toe clips. If there is no tree handy, turn the bike across the trail (at

Fig. 3-75. This is not the safest position to ride down a steep hill. In fact, this rider dumped a few seconds after I took this photo. With his body high up, legs splayed out, the rider is in an extremely unbalanced condition. He could not absorb the shock of landing off a jump with his legs, and I am sure he suffered some groin pain.

Fig. 3-76. Here's a no-no for two reasons. First, the rider is harming the trail, as you can see. Second, he is locking up the rear wheel, which could cause that wheel to spin out and dump the bike.

a right angle to it); then mount the bike, turn the wheel toward the trail downhill and shove off.

If you are going faster than you're used to and consequently tensing up, just hang on, stay loose, stay upright and use your brakes as above to slow down. Remember, the bike's natural tendency is to stay upright. Stay relaxed so you can shift your weight around to balance your bike. If you ever rode a skateboard or skied downhill, you know what I mean by balance. Above all, don't let anyone talk you into a descent you don't feel up to. It's the riders who scar up the landscape with a wild, uncontrolled descent that make me unhappy.

ABOUT HOPS, WHEELIES AND JUMPS

A hop is when you are going five mph or faster and have to clear an obstruction on the trail (Fig. 3-77). A wheelie is a slow-speed hop up over an obstruction (Fig. 3-78). Kids pull wheelies on their BMX bikes, riding with the front wheel off the ground. Not recommended for sane adults or kids. Use a wheelie to get up over a curb, for example, or off a curb. A jump finds you briefly airborne as you fly over a hillock or down into and over a series of depressions in a trail (Fig. 3-79).

Fig. 3-78. The rider has approached this log at a slow speed and has pulled up on his handlebars to pull a wheelie to get the front wheel up and over the obstruction.

Fig. 3-77. Here the rider is executing a hop over a log.

Fig. 3-79. This is a jump *down a short hill.*

How to Hop

When you are riding on the trail you will, sooner or later, have to go over a fallen log, a projecting rock or some other impediment to your forward progress. You can, of course, simply stop, get off the bike and push the bike around the obstacle. However, a simple hop over whatever is in your way is much more fun, and faster besides. There may also be times when you have to hop to avoid a collision, as over a curb when some crazy is aiming a car at you.

Here are the four steps to a successful hop:

1. As you approach a log or whatever you want to hop over, your pedals should be flat, parallel to the ground, your butt off the saddle, legs springy, arms loose but not limp, with a firm but not "deadly" grip on the handlebars (Fig. 3-80).

2. Just before you reach the log, transfer your weight from the center of the frame (directly over the pedals) to the front wheel. Move your weight over the handlebars to compress the front tire (like squeezing down on a spring) (Fig. 3-81). The compressed front tire will help you get the front wheel up.

3. Immediately after moving forward and compressing the front tire, pull up hard on the handlebars to get the front wheel to clear the log (Fig. 3-82). Your forward momentum should carry you over the log.

4. Immediately after the front wheel goes over the obstacle, shift your weight forward to unweight the rear wheel so it "floats" over the obstacle, rather than crashing into it. The rider in Figure 3-83 has made it over the obstacle but failed to move forward to unload the rear wheel.

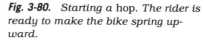

Fig. 3-80. *Starting a hop. The rider is ready to make the bike spring upward.*

Fig. 3-81. *Push your weight forward to compress the tire as you prepare to hop over an obstacle.*

Fig. 3-82. *The final step in a hop is to pull up on the handlebars to get the front wheel to clear the obstacle.*

As a result, as you can see, the rear wheel has struck the obstacle. If you do this maneuver correctly, the rear wheel may touch the obstacle but won't hit it hard and possibly dump you. Complete this jump by easing back into a normal riding position.

This four-step sequence takes but a few seconds. It's preparation, step 1; front tire compression, step 2; weight back, handlebar pull-up, step 3; and weight forward to float the rear wheel over the obstacle, step 4.

Doing a Wheelie

To do a wheelie, follow these steps:

1. Shift to a low gear.
2. Slow down to a crawl.
3. As you near whatever you want to go over (a curb or a small log, e.g.), hold your pedals at the 1 o'clock and 7 o'clock positions.
4. Immediately before your obstacle, in one combined motion, pull up *hard* on the handlebars and at the same time push forcefully down on the pedal that is at the 1 o'clock position. This combination handlebar pull-up and pedal push-down will get the front wheel up in the air and over the obstacle.
5. When the front wheel has cleared the obstacle, quickly move your weight forward to reduce rear wheel impact.

Fig. 3-83. This rider shows good form in hop, except that he did not move forward far enough to unweight the rear wheel, which as you can see struck the stump.

How to Jump

There will be times when you find yourself momentarily airborne as you come upon a depression or small steep hill in front of you on the trail (Fig. 3-84). The depression may be too steep and too short to ride down, or you may not be able to slow down soon enough to keep from taking off. If you find yourself flying through the air, probably with the greatest of unease, just keep your cool. As you land, keep your front wheel straight, so you won't veer off into the bushes. As you take off, turn the pedals parallel to the ground, get up off the saddle and absorb the landing shock with your legs and arms. You may also find yourself up in the air as you speed down a hill and immediately soar up another short, steep rise (Fig. 3-85 and Fig. 3-86). As you can see in Figure 3-86, the rider's front wheel is off the ground, as though he were pulling a wheelie or making a hop. If you see a series of short steep hills like these, keep your weight in the center of the bike, just over the saddle, with pedals parallel to the ground. Just as you clear the top of a hill, push your weight forward so you will have front wheel steering traction as you land. As soon as you establish traction, move back over the saddle for rear wheel traction and continue pedaling.

Fig. 3-84. *If you find yourself airborne over a small declivity, keep your wheel straight, balance to keep upright.*

Fig. 3-85. *Going over a series of undulating small hills takes balancing skills. Stay centered over the saddle, keep pedals parallel to the ground, and as you land, push down on the bars so the front wheel lands first for steering traction.*

Fig. 3-86. *This rider has come up a short hill at high speed so his front wheel is in the air. Note that his weight is centered on the saddle, both feet are on pedals to absorb landing shock and pedals are parallel to the ground. He is in good position at this point to lean forward and push down on the bars to get the front wheel down.*

DEALING WITH SLIPPERY AND WET TERRAIN

As you ride through sand, gravel or mud (Fig. 3-87), be in a low gear and, above all, *keep pedaling!* If you stop you may have to walk out of the slippery stuff. Get your weight back for rear wheel traction. More weight over the rear wheel provides better "bite" for the rear tire. The front wheel will also be lighter and so less likely to "wash out." Keep the front wheel straight; keep spinning in a low gear. You may not be able to pick up speed, but at least you will have forward momentum. If you stop in mud or sand, you may have to walk to more solid ground.

Fig. 3-87. *Brake carefully on gravel or rocky terrain, especially around corners. Be aware that gravel can be slippery. Think ball bearings. Be ready to balance to counteract a side slip. Keep your weight centered on the bike, grip handlebars firmly.*

Going over slippery surfaces such as ice and snow, a leaf or gravel covered trail (Fig. 3-88 and Fig. 3-89) requires a balancing act. Shift your weight around on the bike to keep upright. Brake carefully, don't let speed build up. Go around curves and corners slowly so you don't skid out. You can bike on snow (Fig. 3-90) up to a depth of about three inches. Much deeper and the snow will severely impede forward motion.

Fig. 3-88. *In slippery terrain, be in low gear and, above all, keep pedaling hard, or you will be in for a soft landing and a sticky walk to dry territory.*

Fig. 3-89. *For uphill riding on gravel- or rock-strewn trails, keep your weight a bit to the rear for rear wheel traction.*

Fig. 3-90. *You can bike on snow up to about 3 inches deep and, with care and with studded tires, on ice, but make sure the ice is at least six inches thick. Better, wait till you see people driving on the ice or ice fishing.*

You can ford shallow streams safely if you follow a few simple rules. First, get up as much speed as possible before you enter the stream. Water really holds you back. Think about cycling through molasses. Water is like that. If you can't keep going (Fig. 3-91), you will fall over.

Look before you leap. Make sure the water is no deeper than your hubs. A rider was in a race and decided to plunge off a river bank rather than take the safer but a bit longer path where the trail crossed the stream. He landed in deeper water than he could pedal out of, and wound up in the stream on his side.

ABOUT CORNERING

When cornering on the trail, put the outboard pedal, the one against the angle of lean (Fig. 3-92), at the 6 o'clock position. This keeps the pedal on the inboard side from scraping and dumping you. Your weight will also be on the inboard side which makes the tire roll flatter for more traction.

In the next chapter I will review great places to ride your ATB in this country and abroad. I'll review selected camping gear, including sleeping bags and tents, and list other necessary items you should take along.

Fig. 3-91. Get into low gear and pedal like crazy, or water resistance will dump you.

Fig. 3-92. Keep the inboard pedal up when cornering. That way the pedal won't strike the ground (as you lean into the turn) and cause an accident.

4

Riding Your ATB on the Trail and on the Road

A successful bicycle tour takes planning. In this chapter we will cover where to go, state by state, what to take, how to get there and back safely. To that end, I wrote to the tourism departments of all 50 states for information on where trail riding is permitted, guides, maps and suggestions on the best places to ride, data on campgrounds, state parks and any areas off limits to ATBs. Most states were generous with data, maps, ideas and where ATBs are and are not permitted. Following is a summary of their replies:

Alabama: State parks are located in nearly every part of Alabama. Gulf, Chewalco, Monte Sano, Oak Mountain and Cheaha, to name a few. You might try the Bureau of Tourism and Travel, 532 S. Perry St., Montgomery, AL 36130.

Alaska: This state has an enormous amount of area to explore. You might try the Kenai Peninsula, Kodiak Island (via ferry), Chugach State Park, Power Line Pass Trail, or the Bird Creek logging roads. Send for the booklet entitled "Alaska State Parks," which lists over 100 of them and tells where to write for more specific data, including maps. Bill Garry, Supt., Chugach State Park, 2601 Commercial Drive, Anchorage, AK 99501.

Arkansas: You might try either Devil's Den State Park in northwest Arkansas, Pea Ridge, Lost Valley, Buffalo River, Bear Creek Mountain or Mt. Nebo State Park for ATBs. For more information contact the Department of Parks and Tourism, One Capitol Mall, Little Rock, AR 72201.

California: The California Department of Parks and Recreation has a policy that generally restricts ATBs to the paved and unpaved roads of the state parks, unless otherwise posted. California has numerous state parks located on the beaches, in the mountains and in other scenic wilderness areas. In northern California good riding is available in these state parks: The Forest of Nisene Marks, Henry Cowell and Fall Creek Redwoods, Big Basin Redwoods, Butano, Annadel, Sugarloaf Ridge, Austin Creek, Armstrong Redwoods, Cow Mountain, Mt. Shasta and Mt. Lassen. There are many more mountains, seashore areas, scenic wilderness trails in that state that would fill up the rest of this book just to mention. Check with each park management for permission and maps. There are literally millions of acres of remote, beautiful, scenic wilderness areas available to you. Check the tour providers, professionally led tours, later in this chapter. There are many such off-road tours offered by these organizations in California. For more information, write to the California Department of Transportation, P.O. Box 1499, Sacramento, CA 95807, and the California Office of Tourism, 1030 13th St., Suite 200, Sacramento, CA 95841.

Colorado: Like California, Colorado is an ATBer's paradise. Lots and lots of trails and quiet mountain dirt roads are available in the Rockies, in the high country of Colorado. The rangers are well disposed toward ATBers. With this in mind, pick a mountain that's within a state park or wildlife area and you should have no trouble. The famous Pearl Pass is a 17-mile jaunt, with a 3,835-foot vertical climb to the summit and an 18-mile, 4,915-foot drop to Aspen, which is well worth doing. Also, the mountains around Crested Butte are famous for scenic trails. For more information contact the Colorado Department of Highways, 4201 East Arkansas Avenue, Denver, CO 80222.

Florida: No bicycles are allowed on hiking and nature trails, but they are okay on fire roads. The state says, however, that they hope to produce maps of off-road bicycle trails as part of their statewide bicycle-trails mapping effort. For off-road bicycling, try the St. Marks National Wildlife Refuge and trails paralleling rivers such as the Suwannee. There's not much in the way of mountains, as the state is mostly flat, but there are hundreds of miles of sandy beaches to ride on. Try the island of Santa Rosa. For that area and other scenic bike routes, contact Gulf Islands National Seashore, 1801 Gulf Breeze Parkway, Gulf Breeze, FL 32561. For more info write the Florida Department of Transportation, Haydon Burns Building, 650 Suwannee St., Tallahassee, FL 32301-8064.

Hawaii: I can't recommend this state for trail riding. The state is too crowded and I hear the crime rate is fairly high. Stay off Oahu, the most crowded island. For information, write Hawaii Visitors Bureau, 2270 Kalakaua Ave., Suite 801, Honolulu, HI 96815.

Idaho: There is no official position on ATBs. The state has a wait-and-see attitude. There are many great trails in the Idaho back country. Sun Valley is an ATB paradise, as is Clearwater National Forest. For a list of the dozens of ATB opportunities, I suggest you write Todd Graef, State Trails Coordinator, Idaho Department of Parks and Recreation, Statehouse Mail, 2177 Warm Springs Ave., Boise, ID 83270.

Illinois: Treats an ATB as any other bicycle. I'm not sure what that statement means. I would doubt, however, based on my experience in state parks, that you'd be hassled by an authority figure so long as you stayed on the trail and didn't wander off through the prairie, a delicate ecosystem. The state sent me a large packet of trails suitable for ATBs. In this packet are addresses of some 150 on- and off-road trails and an equestrian-trail guide. I checked with the Forest Preserve District Managers who operate these. After I explained the nature of an ATB, they either encouraged their use on equestrian trails or seemed to take a wait-and-see attitude. Some of these trails are paved; most are dirt or some rough stone that would not faze an ATB. I suggest you write for this data to Dan M. Troemper, Public Information Officer, Lands and Historic Sites, Illinois Department of Conservation, Lincoln Tower Plaza, 524 S. Second St., Springfield, IL 62701-1787.

Indiana: No response. There are many small- to medium-sized state parks in Indiana. I found them unsuitable for off-road riding, mostly because there were so few off-road trails. All of the listed rides in this state are highway trips. Write Tourism Department, Commerce Center, One North Capitol Suite 700, Indianapolis, IN 46204, for state park information.

Iowa: This tall-corn state takes a dim view of ATB trail riding. They say bikes can use all roads in state parks, but not hiking trails, because "We do not feel it is appropriate to allow bicycles on hiking trails, not due to possible environmental damage; but rather, due to user conflicts. The hikers do not appreciate being 'buzzed' by the cyclists, and the cyclists do not appreciate having to dodge hikers." Open spaces in this state are mostly farmland, so off-road riding opportunities are minimal. However, there are many miles of excellent, low-traffic country roads which offer scenic riding opportunities. For information, write Iowa Conservation Commission, Wallace State Office Building, Des Moines, IA 50319.

Kansas: I have been across the width and breadth of this state, and I can only suggest that you rule out this pancake-flat area as an exciting place to ride off-road. Roads are great, however. Write to the Kansas

Department of Economic Development, Travel Tourism Division, 503 Kansas Ave., Topeka, KS 66612, for any information on trail riding opportunities. There are state parks. I've been in some and they do not excite me. I am willing to be corrected, however. Also, no reply.

Kentucky: No reply. A fairly hilly state. However, between the coal mines, the farms, the distillers of bourbon, legal and otherwise, and horse breeders, not much room is left for trail riding. You can guess who gets priority between horse and bicycle in the Kentucky Derby, Bluegrass State. If I'm wrong, the Kentucky Division of Tourism, Capital Plaza Tower, Frankfort, KY 42302, may change your mind.

Louisiana: Chicot State Park, located in the central portion of this state, is the only state park in which trails are open to bicycles. If you are looking for other places to ride, there are plenty of rutty back roads, mostly flat, which can get you across the state, but bring food and water. For more information write the Louisiana Department of Transportation and Development, General Files Unit, P.O. Box 44245 Capitol Station, Baton Rouge, LA 70804.

Maine: No response. This state has many scenic parks to offer, and Acadia National Park, located on the state's coastline, has 16 miles of unpaved trails well suited for ATBers. Here you can enjoy the mountains and the coast simultaneously. For directions to parks and forest areas write Maine Publicity Bureau, 97 Winthrop St., Hallowell, ME 04347.

Maryland: This historic state has some ATB opportunities, such as Sugarloaf Regional Trails, maps for which can be obtained from the Maryland National Park and Planning Commission, 8787 Georgia Ave., Silver Springs, MD 20907.

Massachusetts: Now here's a state after my own heart. Gilbert A. Bliss, Director of Forests and Parks, writes and says that "Until such time as a definite policy statement is made, Mountain Bicycles are allowed on hiking trails and fire roads within the Massachusetts Forests and Parks." So pick your park and go to it. Bliss notes that a Statewide Trails Committee of trail user groups has been formed and that mountain bikes will be discussed; recommendations of this committee will influence the state's position on their use. The state has many very scenic parks, some mountainous, others along the seashore. For information, write Gilbert A. Bliss, Director of Forests and Parks, 100 Cambridge St., Boston, MA 02202.

Michigan: No response. This state has many miles of scenic dunes along Lake Michigan and has many state parks that have miles of trails which, if not challenging in terms of hills, do offer the all-terrain cyclist many opportunities to pedal into the quiet rural countryside. For specifics, write to Bill Tansil, Supervisor, Highways and Non-Motorized Planning, Michigan Dept. of Transportation, P.O. Box 30050, Lansing, MI 48909.

Minnesota: The land of sky blue waters has a large acreage of quite wild and woolly forest land suitable for ATBers, but my query about a policy remains unanswered. For information write to Nancy Mahle, Chief Bikeway Unit, Minnesota Department of Transportation, 704 Transportation Building, St. Paul, MN 55101. For maps of individual bike trails that run throughout the state, write the Minnesota Department of Natural Resources, Box 40, 500 Lafayette Road, St. Paul, MN 55146.

Mississippi: There are long-forgotten trails that run alongside the Mississippi River that Mark Twain must have seen at one time or another that would be just great for the ATBer. Or you might try the Natchez Trace, a path followed for generations by Natchez Indians and later British, Spanish and French traders. I don't know what the state's park management has to say about ATBs; they did not respond to my query. However, you might write Bill Sheffield, Bicycle Coordinator, Mississippi Highway Department 85-01, P.O. Box 1850, Jackson, MS 39205.

Missouri: Good news here! The Missouri Department of Natural Resources has approved trails for ATBs in seven state parks, and more are being planned. The state parks that have approved trails are Castlewood, Graham Cave, Knob Noster, Lake of the Ozarks, Lake Wappapello, St. Joe, and Finger Lake State Park, which sounds to be the most promising, with over 70 miles of trails open to ATBs. For maps and more information, write the Missouri Department of Natural Resources, P.O. Box 176, Jefferson City, MO 65102.

Montana: The state abounds with scenic areas that are state managed and should be open to you. Montana is one of our largest states in geographical area, yet it is sparsely settled. Check off-road riding with the Montana Travel Promotion Bureau, Dept. of Commerce, 1424 9th Ave., Helena, MT 59620.

Nebraska: Another sparsely populated state with excellent off-road touring possibilities. For information, write Nebraska Division of Travel and Tourism, P.O. Box 94759, Lincoln, NE 68509. Although the state did not reply to my query as to whether or not ATBs are permitted on state park trails, my experience has been that low-population states seldom make a fuss about judicious and careful bicycling on trails. In fact, I have a nice letter from Carl W. Wolfe, Outdoor Education Specialist, Nebraska Game and Parks Commission, in which he says the state has no prohibitions against the use of ATBs on hiking trails in their park system. He was also nice enough to report that "In checking with the U.S. Forest Service, they do not have any prohibition on the use of these bicycles on their trails." For info, write Carl at the Nebraska Game and Parks Commission, 2200 N. 33rd St., P.O. Box 30370, Lincoln, NE 68503.

Nevada: Poor paved-road riding but excellent off-road trails in state and national parks. Much of the land in this state is publicly owned and well suited for ATB riding. For maps and more information, write Department of Transportation, Map Section, Room 206, 1263 S. Stewart St., Carson City, NV 89712. For riding in state parks, write Nevada State Parks, 201 S. Fall Street, Room 119, Carson City, NV 89710.

New Hampshire: New Hampshire says: "We would not permit the use of mountain bicycles where there would be a potential conflict. . . . We have not had a request to use mountain bicycles on state park land. If the request to use this type of vehicle is presented, it would be handled on a case by case and park by park situation." My advice is to go ahead and use the trails, since ATBs are very popular in that state and they must be riding somewhere. If "conflicts" have not surfaced by now, with courtesy and consideration by all sides they should never exist. There are many opportunities for the off-road rider. Try the area around Dartmouth, the White Mountains, including Mt. Washington, and the Green Mountains. For more information, write New Hampshire Department of Public Works, Hazen Dr., P.O. Box 483, Concord, NH 03301, and William H. Carpenter, Supervisor, New Hampshire Division of Parks and Recreation, 105 Loudon Road, P.O. Box 856, Concord, NH 03301.

New Jersey: No response. Opportunities for off-road cycling are not numerous in this densely populated, highly industrialized state. A few are the Watchung Mountains and the Pine Barrens section and the shoreline. There are other mountains in the northwest. Write William H. Feldman, Pedestrian/Bicycle Advocate, New Jersey Dept. of Transportation, 1035 Parkway Ave., Trenton, NJ 08625.

New Mexico: No response. Off-road opportunities abound in this scenic state. You have a choice of desert, plains, or mountains, with plenty of trails for ATBs. State parks, so far, are quite lenient and permissive, so you should be able to ride on hiking trails and, of course, on the many fire roads and backcountry dirt roads. New Mexico Tourism and Travel Division, Bataan Memorial Building, Santa Fe, NM 87503.

New York: Stay at least 50 miles from New York City, of course. Upstaters are friendly, and the parks and trails around Lake George, the Catskills (shades of Rip van Winkle), the Finger Lakes district and the Adirondacks offer superb bicycling and scenery. For information on Finger Lakes area riding, write Finger Lakes State Park & Recreation

Commission, Rte. 3, Trumansburg, NY 14886, and the New York State Dept. of Commerce, Tourism Div., 99 Washington Ave., Albany, NY 12245.

North Carolina: No policy. Off-road riding opportunities abound in this state, notably in the Blue Ridge Mountains in the west section, the Outer Banks area in the east, and the Pisgah National Forest, to name a few. Write Mary Meletiou, North Carolina Dept. of Transportation, P.O. Box 25201, Raleigh, NC 27611, and/or Curtis B. Yates, State Bicycle Coordinator, same address.

North Dakota: Well, there are a few state parks, the Badlands in the western section, and a lot of flat prairie. The Theodore Roosevelt National Park is also in the western section and offers off-road riding. You can get more information from Norlyn Schmidt, Transportation Planner, North Dakota State Highway Dept., 600 E. Boulevard Ave., Bismarck, ND 58501.

Ohio: The state parks in this state have restricted the use of bicycles to paved roads. Hiking and equestrian trails are closed to ATBs. Don't despair, though, the Ohio Department of Natural Resources reports that the Division of Forestry has four All-Purpose Vehicle Areas where ATBs are permitted: Pike, Richland Furnace, Perry, and Maumee State Forests. They also suggest trying the many miles of gravel backcountry roads in the state forests. They recommend Shawnee, Tar Hollow, Zaleski, and Scioto Trail State Forests above the rest for this type of riding. For maps and information write Ohio Department of Natural Resources, Division of Forestry, Fountain Square, Columbus, OH 43224.

Oklahoma: No response, after several requests to state officials. Says something about what this state thinks of us cyclists. My experience with bureaucrats is that when they display a profound lack of interest in cycling they are often overweight, lazy and incompetent couch potatoes. The very thought of doing anything on a bike fills them with terror. Every time they feel like exercise, they lie down until the feeling goes away. However, if you plan to ATB in Oklahoma, stick to state parks and forests in the east and southeast section. Write Programs Coordinator, Planning and Development Division, State of Oklahoma, Tourism and Recreation Department (whew!), 50 Will Rogers Building, Oklahoma City, OK 73105.

Oregon: There's good news from this wonderful state. The authorities are by no means bureaucratic desk jockeys. What they did in formulating a policy regarding use of ATBs is an example of what other states should do. I quote from their response: "For about a year the Oregon Recreation Trails Advisory Council has been aware of a controversy developing around mountain bicycles, so they've been investigating the 'evidence' available. Following their quarterly meeting at Kah-nee-tah they took the opportunity to ride mountain bicycles which were loaned by a dealer in Bend, Oregon. The Council is aware that the Pacific Crest National Scenic Trail Advisory Council has recommended that the use of bicycles be prohibited on the Pacific Coast Trail. However, the Oregon Trails Council has not reached a consensus on the issue and has not yet recommended a specific policy for Oregon Recreation Trails. . . . There has been no indication of a problem with the use of them [ATBs] in State Parks." The letter is from Jack Remington, Co-ordinator, Recreation Trails System, Department of Transportation, Parks and Recreation Division, 525 Trade St. S.E., Salem, OR 97310. The state abounds with so many state and national parks that I can only urge you to pick a park and take off. I prefer the western section of the state; the eastern section is flatter except for outstanding mountain areas, such as the Sisters near Bend. The Umpquah National Forest in the west is an excellent example of a location for ATB riding. Get a fishing license, bring your trout rod (fishing regulations permit flies only, no live bait) and catch your dinner in the Umpquah River. Or try the Siskiyous, near Ashland; and in the summer you can bike down the mountain and attend the famous Shakespeare Festival in that city.

Pennsylvania: Well, there's good news and bad news from the Com-monwealth. First, the bad news. In his response, William C. Forrey, Director, Bureau of State Parks, says " . . . the mountain bicycles would not be allowed on our designated hiking trails." The good news is that he also states: "The use of these bicycles on fire roads is permitted on state parks and forest lands." Which leaves a lot of open off-highway terrain for ATBs. The state is loaded with parks and forests. I suggest you send for the Pennsylvania Trail Guide listing them all. The guide, kindly sent by Mr. Forrey, contains a description of each park and forest area, a map showing locations, and a roster of information sources where more data can be obtained. Kenneth Burkholder, trails coordinator, said that ATBs, as all bicycles, are required to use trails designated for bi-cycling purposes. Write for your copy to Pennsylvania Trails Coordi-nator, Pennsylvania Bureau of State Parks, P.O. Box 1467, Harrisburg, PA 17120. The guide also lists sources for national parks and trails information. Also ask for the Pennsylvania Recreational Guide, which contains a map and a list of state parks. The map also shows location of bicycle trails. Lancaster County is the Pennsylvania Dutch country and offers very scenic routes for the ATB road tourist. Write the Lancaster County Bicycle Club, Box 535, Lancaster, PA 17604, for their book of maps, at $7.00. Guided tours in the state are conducted by Four Seasons

Cycling Tours, Box 203, Williamsburg, VA 23187, and Bucks County Bicycle Tours, 211 W. Callowhill Rd., Perkasie, PA 18944.

Rhode Island: This little pancake of a state has some excellent riding possibilities along the coast and in the forest and marshes of the southeastern section. For a good state map showing rural and back roads, write Rhode Island Department of Economic Development, Tourist Promotion Division, 7 Jackson Walkway, Providence, RI 02903. Also ask for the current Visitor's Guide to Rhode Island, and for info on these bike trails: Goddard State Park; Conanicut; Greenville area of Smithfield; Tiverton, Sakonnet and Little Compton; Bellevue Avenue and Ocean Drive in Newport; and all of Block Island. The Rhode Island Bicycle Coalition has a Metropolitan Providence Bicycle Map. Write the Coalition at P.O. Box 4781, Rumford, RI 02916.

South Carolina: There are rugged mountains in the northwest, notably the Piedmont section, which offer great off-road riding in areas of scenic beauty. The coastal and central areas are mostly flat. You can get a Bicycle Guide to South Carolina from the SC Department of Parks, Recreation and Tourism, Suite 110, E. Brown Building, 1205 Pendleton St., Columbia, SC 29201. The guide is for the road biker, but it shows state parks and recreation areas.

South Dakota: No response, but data I have indicate that bikes are not permitted on trails. However, the Black Hills area does have many off-road trails and fire roads you may be able to use. I suggest you write SD Department of Tourism, 81 S. Central, Pierre, SD 57501, for maps and information. For road bikers, you will most likely not find much to look at. I've been across this state and can verify that outside of the Black Hills, the roads are boring, boring, boring.

Tennessee: Don Wick, Director of Information, Department of Tourist Development (P.O. Box 23170, Nashville, TN 37202), says: "So far as I know, there is no definitive information on off-road bike trails." However, he sent five terrific maps of choice biking roads in the state. You might ask him for a set. He also noted that bears are common in the huge wilderness areas of eastern Tennessee in the Great Smoky Mountains National Park and in the 625,000 acres of the Cherokee National Forest. He feels it might be a good idea to avoid a bear/bike encounter in those areas. East of Chattanooga are lots of state parks with trails and fire roads. In the central area you can cruise along the Tennessee River. For a road trip, try the scenic Natchez Trace Parkway. Info on the parkway is available from Natchez Trace Parkway, RR1, NT-143, Tupelo, MS 38801. The western section is fairly flat.

Texas: I had an interesting response from R. C. Hauser, Chief, Park

Operations, Texas Parks and Wildlife Department (4200 Smith School Rd., Austin, TX 78744). Mr. Hauser says: "The use of bicycles on trails and fire roads in Texas State Parks is prohibited with the exception of trails and fire roads that are specifically designated as hike and bike trails." Texas is so big it has just about every kind of ATB riding there is. I like the Padre Islands (be sure to oil the chain every day when you ride in sand or through salt water), the forest region in the east, the hill country in the west, and the back roads everywhere, once you are away from metro areas. I'd avoid the Panhandle, though, unless you like to eat wind-blown dust. For data on the hill country, write Kathryn Nichols, at the same address as for Mr. Hauser above. The Big Bend National Park is terrific for trail riding and camping. Write Big Bend National Park, TX 79834, for maps and info. Better have at least two water bottles on your frame in this desert country. I hope you have more luck than I did, though, because the authorities in this state are chintzy with their maps. Maybe they prefer horses?

Utah: This state is loaded with ATB rides ranging from easy to very, very difficult. It's advisable (always) to check map contours so you know you can handle the grade. A few of the many areas to check are Bryce and Zion National Parks, the Grand Canyon area, Yellowstone National Park (limited to paved trails, I'm afraid), and the Great Salt Lake area. For information, write John Morris, Utah D.O.T., Transportation Planning Division, 4501 South, 2700 West, Salt Lake City, UT 84114. Send for a map of the Moab area mountain bike trails, from Moab Visitor Center, 805 N. Main St., Hiway 191, Moab, UT 84532. The Bureau of Land Management, Grand Resource Area, P.O. Box M, Moab, UT 84532, also has more data on this area.

Deloy K. Peterson, of the Utah Transportation Planning Division, notes: "We do not have a state bicycle route system as none of our highways have any special provisions for bicyclists. You may ride at your own risk as part of the general traffic on any of our highways, except on portions of the interstate system where paved frontage roads or nearby alternate routes are available. Areas where you may not ride on the interstate are indicated in red on the enclosed highway map (I-84 from Tremoaton to Ogden and on I-15 from Ogden to Nehi and in the Fillmore and Beaver areas). If you intend to ride at night you must have a white light in front, a red reflector in back, and reflectors or lights visible from each side for at least 500 feet. You must not have any siren or whistle mounted on your bike for a warning device. In planning your trip through Utah there are several things you need to consider. Outside of our urbanized area between Ogden and Provo, Utah is sparsely populated. It's a long way between towns and available services and you'll need to carry everything you will want between stops. Don't forget that much of Utah is desert, with summer daytime temperatures often above 100 degrees. Along many of our routes there not only are no services, there is no shelter and no drinking water either. In these areas be sure you carry plenty of water for the long distances involved.

"Utah is also crossed from north to south with mountain ranges, and some of our highways have long, steep grades. Be prepared for long climbs—and be sure your brakes are in good shape for the downhill runs on the other side. Most of Utah is at or above 5,000 feet above sea level. Our air is 'thinner' than at lower altitudes and bikers from other areas generally find that they tire much more easily than they think they should because of the lower oxygen content. When (not 'if,' when) this happens to you, don't try to fight it by keeping up your normal pace. It won't help. Stop and rest, then pace yourself at a slower rate until you get used to the altitude. You'll feel better and, besides, Utah is too nice to rush through, anyway. Don't let all these grim-sounding things discourage you. Lots of bikers enjoy seeing Utah each year. Do remember them as you plan your trip. We want you to enjoy your visit with us, not just survive.

"Traffic on our highways shouldn't pose problems to experienced touring riders. However, if you are going to be in the urbanized area between Ogden and Provo, the peak traffic periods are between about 7:00 and 8:30 A.M., and 4:30 and 6:00 P.M. You'll probably want to avoid these times to miss having to try to find your way in a strange area and compete with the traffic.

"Our state highway map should provide basic route information to all the major points you might wish to visit. For greater detail, and more information about trails, scenic areas, elevations, etc., you might want to get the eight-map, multipurpose map set published by the Utah Travel Council. These maps show more detail and are easy to use, with each of the maps being about the size of the highway map. The set costs $8.00, and is available from the Utah Travel Council, Council Hall, Salt Lake City, Utah 84114. Our county maps are not helpful for bike trip planning; don't bother to order them."

Vermont: ATBs are limited to "forest highways and other roads where motorized vehicles are permitted," according to George E. Plumb, Recreation Division Director. He also points out that this stricture is "in conformance with the Long Trail Management System Plan (the State's most extensive trail system), as adopted by the Green Mountain Club." I've done a lot of biking in Vermont and I have noticed that roads in forest areas can be scenic and demanding in their own right, although I would prefer to use, or at least have the option of using, hiking trails as well. However, hiking trails in eastern states are quite narrow and fairly heavily used by hikers in warm weather, so in a way I can understand the restriction. I hope that through education and exposure to ATBs this attitude will be softened enough to open up appropriate hiking trails to off-road bicycling. Mr. Plumb can be reached at the Vermont Agency of Environmental Conservation, Department of Forests, Parks and Recreation, Montpelier, VT 05602.

And this for some reason reminds me, although I have said this before: there's absolutely no reason why you should restrict yourself to wilderness trails and hiking trails anyway. ATBs are great to ride on back roads, between towns, for savoring the scenery and for camping out in state parks. I can heartily recommend Route 100, up the middle of the state. One campground in particular stands out vividly. It's on the road from Route 100 to Calvin Coolidge State Park. If you want to experience a 15 percent grade, this road is it. Because the road is paved, if you have a low gear, you should be able to make it, but it will be slowly. At least your rear wheel won't skid out from under you on the pavement. The back roads from Hanover, New Hampshire, down the Connecticut River and across to Vermont and down to Brattleboro are well worth taking. Despite state-imposed restrictions on trail riding, there are actually many, many challenging and rewarding trails to ride in this beautiful state. For maps, routes and more info, write Vermont Travel Division, 134 State St., Montpelier, VT 05602 (802-828-3236); Vermont Agency of Transportation, Administration Building, 133 State St., Montpelier, VT 05602 (802-828-2568); and for a good book, ask for *Bicycling in Vermont* from the Recreation Division, Vermont Department of Forests, Parks and Recreation, Agency of Environmental Conservation, Montpelier, VT 05602.

In 1985, Mr. Plumb wrote: "It is the position of the Vermont Department of Forests, Parks and Recreation that the users of the so-called Mountain Bicycles (nonmotorized) on State hiking trails is inappropriate. These trails were developed for the specific purpose of hiking in the spring, summer, and fall seasons. In some cases, the trails also provide for snowshoeing and cross-country skiing in the winter. All other forms of trail activity (snowmobiling, ATVs, bikes, horseback riding, running races, etc.) would be in conflict with the purpose of these trails and their users. Again, this policy is in conformance with the Long Trail Management System Plan (the State's most extensive trail system), as adopted by the Green Mountain Club." Recently, Mr. Edward J. Koenemann,

Director (Vemont) State Parks and Land, wrote: "In response to your request for information on all-terrain bicycle facilities in Vermont I can speak only for state lands which are managed by the Department of Forests, Parks and Recreation. This department does not have bicycle trail maps or guidelines for on- and off-road trail riding. This information is provided through the private bicycle touring groups in Vermont. The use of all-terrain bicycles on the state lands managed by our department is limited to designated trails or roads open for other vehicular traffic. This restriction is a state statute and applies to all the lands managed by the Agency of Natural Resources. The Secretary under this statute has the authority to designate trails, however, has not done so. This restriction applies not only to all-terrain bicycles but all classes whether motorized or nonmotorized of off-road vehicles exept snowmobiles. The snowmobile regulations come under a separate statute. However, the restriction of riding only on designated trails still applies to snowmobiles. Mountain bikes are permitted on forest highways and other roads where motorized vehicles are permitted. At the present time there is no demand for development of trails for use by mountain bicyclers. If and when there is sufficient interest expressed, we will review our policies and give consideration to the development of trails which will meet this need. There are thousands of miles of lightly traveled, unpaved back roads in Vermont which are quite suitable for this activity. At this time there are only two designated trails for off-road riding. These are the D&H Railroad ROW and the old Montpelier to Wells River Railroad ROW through Groton State Forest. Most of our state parks are very small units and for the most part are fragile environments which we have some obligation to protect."

Virginia: Virginia's Parks Commissioner, Ronald D. Sutton, wrote: "As the demand for more facilities for mountain bikes grows, the Division may have to develop a separate policy for them, but until such time, they will be treated as bicycles. Therefore, you may want to include Virginia State Parks in your listing of states with no position. Bicycles are permitted on all regular park roads and on all designated bicycle trails." Seems to me this position is fairly clear. Let's hope that the Division can see that ATBs are consistent with hiking and horses and that there really is no conflict between the three means of locomotion. There are lots of good back roads in scenic mountain areas, even though we can't use hiking trails. The Blue Ridge section of the Appalachian chain, the Piedmont plains area, and the Shenandoah Valley are areas of interest. For more information, write Ronald D. Sutton, Commissioner, Department of Conservation and Economic Development, Division of Parks and Recreation, 1201 Washington Building, Capital Square, Richmond, VA 23219. For Virginia guided tours, see Pennsylvania, above.

Washington: In the summer, when it finally stops raining, this state has just about everything an off-road cyclist could want. You like the mountains? Washington gives you Mt. Rainier, Mt. Baker, Mt. Adam, the Cascades, the Olympics, and more. Do you like the seashore? She gives you Puget Sound plus hundreds of miles of ocean-hugging roads. Island hopping, starting from Seattle, taking the ferry, riding across an island, then another ferry, up to Vancouver, B.C., is a great trip. Do you like rivers? Try cycling along the Columbia River, from Vancouver to the great Bonneville Dam, and en route cross the river into Oregon to view famous Multnomah Falls, a breathtaking view if ever there was one. Do you like the narrow, twisting trails of a rain forest? Within 20 miles of Seattle there's one you could get lost in if not careful. In some forests, where biking is taboo, there are former railroad paths, wagon trails, and other primitive roads that are like a trip back to the eighteenth century. Do you like volcanoes? Bike around Mt. St. Helens.

What is the state's attitude toward ATBs on trails in state parks and forests? In answer to this query, William A. Bush, Chief, Research and Long Range Planning, Parks and Recreation Commission, 7150 Clearwater Lane, MS KY-11, Olympia, WA 98504, sent me a copy of Chapter 352-20-WAC, regarding use of motor vehicles in state parks. Nowhere in this chapter is a bicycle of any kind mentioned. I can only conclude that there is no restriction on the use of ATBs.

Jan Tveten, Director of Washington State Parks and Recreation Commission, notes: "Wheeled, operator-propelled equipment such as bicycles, tricycles, scooters and skateboards is a traditional part of the visitors' recreational use of state parks. Families cycling along park roads, and children riding tricycles and 'big wheels,' are common sights. Some state parks, such as Moran, are popular destinations for bicyclists. Bicycles are even frequently seen on pleasure boats for use as land transportation. Three years ago this agency was contacted by California State Parks concerning regulation of mountain bicycles, but this new bicycle had not yet appeared in significant numbers in our parks. This contact from California foretold of mountain bike use to come to Washington State Parks. Now, their swift appearance on the recreation scene has drawn attention to their use. Evolving use of operator-propelled equipment in parks, particularly with respect to the mountain bike, has brought staff to review how these devices fit into the overall use of state parks. The following examples typify growing concerns: At least ten bicycle accidents have been reported at Moran State Park during the past two years, most often dealing with excess downhill speed on the Mount Constitution Road. Hikers have voiced safety concerns about encountering cyclists on the trails. Use of bicycles on the Larrabee State Park trail system east of SRII, particularly in the Fragrance Lake area, has prompted hiker concerns. The Lake Washington Saddle Club has written in opposition to bicycles on the trails at Bridle Trails State Park. Sudden encounters on the trail system between horses and cyclists have endangered riders of both the horses and the bicycles. Accidents have occurred. Young operators of bicycles and skateboards often ride the wrong way on roads, impede traffic, and because of their size, are difficult for motorists to see. A special bicycle competition was proposed this past summer at Lewis and Clark State Park. The proposal brought several issues to attention of staff, including which forms of recreation are appropriate for certain park areas, commercial use of parks, and impacts of competitive riding on the natural resource and other park visitors.

"Staff then contacted persons associated with hiker and bicycle user groups to solicit their ideas about use and regulation of operator-propelled wheeled devices in parks. Although each person presented the general views of his/her constituency, the overall tone was that park facilities should remain available for multiple use recreation as long as user groups conduct their activities in relative harmony.

"With this background of information, it became clear that staff needed more information to assess the current use of nonmotorized cycles or similar devices in parks. A survey of parks was conducted this past summer: The survey results for bicycles confirmed a general problem of operator disregard for safety of pedestrians, disregard for the bicycle provisions in the motor vehicle code, and operation at night without lights. The survey substantiated the high profile emergence of the mountain bike as a form of recreation, and problems relating to these bicycles concerning competitive riding on trails, cutting trail switchbacks, riding off roads and trails, and user conflicts with hikers.

"A nonmotorized cycle or similar device is defined as any wheeled, operator-propelled equipment which transports the operator on land. Examples include, but are not limited to, unicycles, bicycles, tricycles, quadricycles, scooters, and skateboards. All wheelchairs are excluded from this definition to preclude limiting access of disabled persons.

"The use of these devices is considered appropriate on many park roads and trails, potentially over 1,300 miles. However, four exceptions to this general rule are recommended: Devices should be excluded from areas posted with prohibitory signing. This is needed to close roads or trails where conflicts exist with other park users, where public safety is an issue, or where these devices have damaged, or are likely to damage, park resources or facilities. A clear example is the concrete batteries at Fort Worden where serious personal injuries have occurred. A public meeting would be held for input before effecting a closure. Devices should be operated only on public roads in officially designated 'natural areas,' 'natural forest areas,' or 'natural area preserves.' Such classification of parks, in whole or part as outlined by Chapter 352-16 WAC, Naming of Sites and Land Classification, places constraints on recreational use: Natural areas are sites obligated to conserving a natural environment in a nearly undeveloped state for passive low-density outdoor recreation activities. These areas may be found in all types of environments. Natural forest areas are certain forest sites which are natural ecosystems designated for preservation and interpretation of natural forest processes. Natural area preserves are sites which are considered important in preserving rare or vanishing flora, fauna, geological, natural, historical or similar features of scientific or educational value and which are registered and committed as a natural area preserve through a cooperative agreement with the department of natural resources. These classifications are designated for protection and interpretation of natural resources and are intended for low-impact uses by the public. Use of mechanized devices is therefore not appropriate. This restriction would impact the public as follows:

"No public impact because of no significant present use of devices: Blind Island, Iceberg Island, Rock Island, Clark Island, Ice Caves Skull Island, Cone Island, James Island, Twin Falls Doe Island, Matia Island, Unnamed Island, Eagle Island, Patos Island, Victim Island, Freeman Island.

"No public impact because devices already restricted by WAC: Squak Mountain State Park Natural Area; Castle Rock Natural Area Preserve (Steamboat Rock); Ragged Ridge Natural Area Preserve (Mount Spokane); Little Spokane River Natural Area (Riverside).

"Public impacts possible: Bridle Trails State Park, Natural Area, entire park; Federation Forest State Park, Natural Area, entire park; Natural Forest Area, 374 of 619 acres; Fort Canby Natural Forest Area, 450 of 1881 acres; Fort Columbia Natural Forest Area, 492 of 563 acres; Ginkgo Natural Area (Ginkgo Petrified Forest State Park), trails area; Hoypus Point Natural Forest Area (Deception Pass State Park), 346 of 524 acres in Hoypus Point area; HeartLake Natural Forest Area (Deception Pass State Park), 88 of 436 acres in Heart Lake area; Leadbetter Point State Park, Natural Area, entire park; Lewis and Clark Natural

Forest Area (Lewis and Clark State Park), 293 of 534 acres; Palouse Falls Natural Area (Lyons Ferry State Park), entire Palouse Falls area; Rockport Natural Forest Area (Rockport State Park), 308 of 457 acres.

"Devices should be excluded from designated interpretive trails and exercise trails. These trails are dedicated to a single use recreation and operation of devices on these trails is in direct conflict with such use."

West Virginia: This is a state with lots of hills and mountains. It is teeming with road and off-road trails, and ATBs are welcome, according to Nancy S. Buckingham, Information Representative, WV Department of Commerce. Trails include the Greenbrier River Trail. For information on this and other WV trails, write Nancy at the WV Department of Commerce, 2101 Washington St., E. Charleston, WV 25305. She can also provide a map and listing of all the WV state parks and campgrounds. For info and maps of national parks, write Chief, Eastern Mapping Center, U.S. Geological Survey, 12201 Sunrise Valley Drive, Reston, VA 22042. Or try the commercial tour group, The Elk River Touring Center, Slatyfork, WV 26291, and Blackwater Bikes, The Mountainside Outpost, P.O. Box 190, Davis, WV 26260.

Wisconsin: This is one midwest state that's far from flat, even though it has few mountains, aside from Rib Mountain up north, worthy of the name. There's lots of scenic trail riding along the Mississippi River for hundreds of miles; there are trails in ancient Indian burial grounds, such as Kettle Moraine State Park in the east; miles of trails in picturesque Door County in the northeast, on Lake Michigan; and the cross-state trail following, in one section, an abandoned railway right-of-way from Kenosha in the east, near Lake Michigan, and ending some 350 miles to the west, at La Crosse on the Mississippi.

Bonnie Gruber, Bureau of Parks and Recreation, Box 7921, Madison, WI 53707, writes: "Enclosed is a review copy of *Biking Wisconsin's State Park Trails*. This is sold for $3.00 a copy at state parks and other Department of Natural Resources offices, or for $3.00 a copy plus $1.00 per order for postage and handling by mail or telephone (MasterCard or Visa) from the Bureau of Parks and Recreation, P.O. Box 7921, Madison WI 53707, phone (608) 266-2181. Also included is a list of our trails on former railroad grades. The trails listed as not for bicycling may be used by all-terrain bicycles, but are not surfaced for touring bikes. We also have detailed history/guide books about three trails—Military Ridge, Sugar River, and Bearskin. These are sold for $1.00 each, plus postage and handling, at those trails or the Bureau of Parks and Recreation. Off-road and wilderness trail bike riding is allowed in state parks except where posted. We do not keep a central list of what areas and trails are posted as not allowing bicycles. People interested in bicycling on other than designated bicycle trails should ask at the individual park before starting out. We are considering changing the rule so that bicycling would be prohibited except where posted. Such a change would not be effective until at least 1990. The primary reason for posting trails off-limits to bicycles is conflict with hikers. Silent bicycles coming from behind often startle hikers. The posted trails tend to be ones heavily used by hikers.

"On the bicycling trails on former railroad grades, bicyclists age 18 or older must have a daily or annual trail pass. These may be purchased at trail headquarters and other DNR offices, at some private businesses near the trails, or from trail rangers. Cyclists camping in the parks must pay campsite fees. Regular campsites are limited to a family with no more than two guests, or no more than five individuals age 7 or older. Many parks have group camp areas for larger groups; see the Visitors' Guide.

"A Special Events Recreational Use License is required for events such as races and bike-a-thons. Forms are available from park super-intendents. Sponsors of such an event must be a nonprofit organization and have liability insurance, and the event must be open to the public. An application must be reviewed by the DNR's Bureau of Legal Services before being approved or denied by the park superintendent. For more info, write or call me at (608) 267-7490."

You might also send for the booklet that lists every state park, forest, trail, and recreation area, entitled "Wisconsin State Parks, Forests, Trails and Recreation Areas, Visitors' Guide," from the Wisconsin Department of Natural Resources, Box 7921, Madison, WI 53707-7921.

Wyoming: In cycling through this state a few years ago, I had a frontier sort of feeling about the state and the people in it—outside of the big cities, that is. (I wondered what signs saying "Open Range" meant, the first time I saw one. This eastern boy thought it meant some sort of military firing range, and the cycling went gingerly. Then, over a rise, I saw the road clogged with cattle, and it came to me that the sign meant no fences. You learn something every day.) I had no response to my query about ATBs in state parks. Yellowstone is in Wyoming, and bi-cycles are okay there, but only on roads open to cars as well. This is also the state of the Grand Tetons, judge by some to be the most beautiful of all mountain areas in the United States, the Wind River Range, and the Bighorn Mountains. For specifics, write the Wyoming Travel Com-mission, Frank Norris Jr. Travel Center, Cheyenne, WY 82002. (I hope you have better luck than I did. They do need public relations help.)

BOOKS ON NATIONAL, REGIONAL AND STATE BIKE TRAILS

Here are books that preplan the route for you, point out areas of interest both scenic and historic, guide you to the best campsites and more. Books like these roll so frequently off the press that I can only suggest that if you can't find one that covers the area of your interest, check with your library, bookstore or bike shop.

Don and Lolly Skillman. *Pedalling Across America*. A diary of the joys, trials, tribulations and rewards of their journey from Ashland, OR, to Virginia Beach, VA. Rewarding reading, with lots of sage advice, for anyone contemplating a bike trip across the United States. 150 pages. Vitesse Press, Brattleboro, VT.

Erin and Bill Woods. *Bicycling the Backroads Around Puget Sound*. A guide to 54 recreational bicycling routes in the Puget Sound Basins, from Olympia to the San Juans, from Port Orchard to the Cascades. Has maps and elevation profiles. 206 pages. The Mountaineers, Seattle, WA.

Erin and Bill Woods. *Bicycling the Backroads of Northwest Washington*. Covers routes from Seattle north to lower British Columbia, the Hood Canal side of the Olympic Peninsula, Kitsap Peninsula and Whidbey Island. 206 pages. The Mountaineers, Seattle, WA.

Erin and Bill Woods. *Bicycling the Backroads Around Southwest Washington*. Gig Harbor to the Columbia River. The Mountaineers, Seattle, WA.

John S. Friedin. *25 Bicycle Tours in Vermont*. Mapped and planned tours you can take in this beautiful state. 174 pages. Backcountry Publications, Woodstock, VT.

Eric Tobey and Richard Wolkenberg. *Northeast Bicycle Tours*. 130 planned tours in New York and New England. Maps, location of bike shops, fun places to see and visit, mileage charts, campgrounds. 280 pages. The Tobey Publishing Company, Inc., New Canaan, CT.

Michael McCoy. *Mountain Bike Adventures in the Northern Rockies*. ATB trips in Yellowstone, the Sawtooths, Jackson Hole, Sun Valley, Flathead River, the Black Hills, Idaho Panhandle and the Bighorn Mountains. 40 trips in the exhilaratingly beautiful and wild mountains of the West. The Mountaineers, Seattle, WA.

Tom Kirkendall. *Mountain Bike Adventures in Washington's Cascades and Olympics*. Covers over 1,000 miles of legal ATB trail and rural road rides in scenic mountain areas. 222 pages. The Mountaineers, Seattle, WA.

Paul M. Van Aken, Jr. *The California Bicycle Tour Atlas and Service.* Bike tours with maps, elevations, campgrounds, the works, the length and breadth of California. Pacific Sports Actualities, Berkeley, CA.

California Coastal Access Guide. If you like bicycling close to the water, camping next to the ocean, want to see the whales and other aquatic wildlife, this book is an excellent guide. 238 pages. Published by the University of California Press, for the California Coastal Commission.

Michael H. Farny. *A Cyclist's Guide to New England Over the Handlebars.* From Maine to Connecticut, a thorough look at the best road bike tours in this historic, scenic part of the Eastern States. 176 pages. Little, Brown and Company, Boston.

Dave Gilbert. *The American Bicycle Atlas.* Over 100 tours covered in detail, this book offers details on where to bike in the United States. 268 pages. American Youth Hostels, Inc., E.P. Dutton, New York.

Eric Newby. *Round Ireland in Low Gear.* Eric Newby and his wife Wanda rode their ATBs around Ireland, on the flats and, hence the title, up and down the mountains. If you plan a bike trip to Ireland, read this book first. 308 pages. William Collins Sons & Co., Ltd., London, England.

Richard Crane and Nicholas Crane. *Bicycles up Kilimanjaro.* An ATB saga of a challenge with man and machine on Africa's highest mountain. Riding through snow and over ice can be fun. This book proves it. 156 pages. The Oxford Illustrated Press Limited, Sparkford, Nr. Yeovil, Somerset, England.

The National Park Foundation. *The Complete Guide to America's National Parks.* Comprehensive data on all 360 U.S. national parks, including maps, mailing addresses, phone numbers, directions, permits, fees, facilities, regulations, weather, points of interest, and more. At $10 a copy, a real bargain. Cost is tax deductible as a contribution to the nonprofit-chartered National Park Foundation, P.O. Box 57473, Washington, D.C. 20037. 1-202-785-4500.

Hasse Brunelle and Shirley Sarvis. *Cooking for Camp and Trail.* Camp fare is more than dehydrated foods, as this book will prove. The Sierra Club, San Francisco, CA.

Hasse Brunelle and Winnie Thomas. *Food for Knapsackers and Other Trail Travelers.* Take this book with you. Lots of excellent data on food, menus, preparation, nutrition, equipment and recipes. The Sierra Club, San Francisco, CA.

These are but a sampling of the dozens of such books covering almost every country on the globe. For bike touring guides to specific countries, again, see your library or bike store, and refer to *Books in Print.*

SOLO VS. GROUP RIDES

If you go alone:

a. You have complete freedom of where and when to stop.

b. You can go as fast or as slowly as you wish.

c. You can select your own routes and itinerary.

But:

d. It can be lonely out there.

e. You will have to carry your own equipment—tent, stove, cookware, etc.—the weight of which could be split with a partner.

f. If you get hurt or if your bike malfunctions, you're on your own. There will be no one at hand to render first aid or cycle on for help if it's needed.

If you go with a guided tour group:

a. You won't get lost: Routes are planned and in most cases ridden by the tour guides before you set wheel on the trail.

b. No hassles: Permits are taken care of. Food is supplied and served, in most cases. An expert mechanic will be on hand. Cooking gear and tents may be provided by some tour outfits. Insurance coverage is usually provided. The route is planned well in advance and selected for scenic beauty. Most leaders are trained in first aid.

c. You'll be with people: It's a lot more fun to share the adventure with others.

d. You ride a bike without a load; the tour provider's sag wagon carries all your gear.

e. Guided tours are great for singles!

But:

f. On the minus side, you have to go when and where the trip is routed, can't deviate from the itinerary, or lay over if you feel like it. You do lose a certain amount of freedom and independence. I like both kinds of trips, the professionally planned tour and the sturdily independent one. There's nothing that can go wrong with my bike that I can't fix, unless the frame breaks.

COMMERCIAL BICYCLE TOUR ORGANIZATIONS

There are literally hundreds of commercial tour providers scattered throughout the United States. Many are small, local outfits, tucked away in a small town or rural location—which is not to imply that these organizations do not provide a worthwhile service. They do, so far as I can determine. In fact, I believe tour providers who offer regional tours are to be preferred over some big outfit located in a major city. The local providers know the area, the terrain, the best campsites, restaurants and other facilities on a first-name basis.

On the other hand, if you want tours in foreign countries, the major tour groups offer the best value, in my opinion. They are usually well capitalized, have clout with carriers, know the language and the customs problems, can provide visas and whatever else is needed to make your tour a happy, hassle-free vacation on two wheels. A stranded traveler you don't want to be.

Select a tour provider with at least three years' experience in the areas you want to go to, who advertise in bicycle and travel publications, and who can offer names of clients you can check with.

Here are a few of the professional tour organizers and providers that have been in business for at least three years, most for a lot longer, who appear to be well financed and adequately staffed. For additional listings, see your travel agency, the classified ads in bicycle magazines and ask your local bicycle shop for their own experience and referrals.

American Youth Hostels, Inc., P.O. Box 37613, Washington, D.C. 20013-7613, phone 202-783-6161. Send for their World Tour Catalog, which lists both U.S. and international tours.

The BikeCentennial, P.O. Box 8308, Missoula, MT 59807. A top-notch touring outfit. Tours in the United States and abroad.

Sobek Expeditions, Angels Camp, CA 95222. America's premier tour provider. Tours in the United States and abroad to just about any country you can name.

Vermont Bicycle Touring, Box 711-JG, Bristol, VT 05443, phone 802-453-4811. *The* premium tour provider in New England, also conducts tours overseas. A very professional outfit, in business 17 years.

Bike America, P.O. Box 29, Northfield, MN 55057, phone 507-663-1268. Major tour outfit, tours coast-to-coast in the United States, tours in various states. Specializes in the United States.

Steve Wineke, Halfway, OR 97834, phone 503-742-5722. A small but experienced local tour provider located in the scenic Hells Canyon district of eastern Oregon.

Bicycle Adventures, P.O. Box 7875, Olympia, WA 98507, phone 206-786-0989. The premium tour group specializing in the Pacific Northwest. Very well equipped on every front. Experienced group leaders. Suggest you start with their tour of Puget Sound's San Juan Islands.

Timberline Adventures, 7975 E. Harvard, #J, Denver, CO 80231, phone 303-759-3804. Specializes in the mountain country of the Rockies, in the Pacific Northwest, and in the California wine country. Reasonable prices, group discounts.

The above is just a minuscule list of tour providers. For additional listings I suggest you subscribe to *Bicycle USA,* a monthly magazine devoted to bicycle touring, which lists a multitude of providers. This is a publication of the American Wheelmen, the oldest bicycle club in the United States. Cost, $18 for an individual subscription. Send your subscription to Bicycle USA, 6707 Whitestone Rd., Suite 209, Baltimore, MD 21207, phone 301-944-3399.

ABOUT OVERSEAS ATBING

Whether you elect a planned trip with a tour provider, go it alone or bike with one or more friends, you need to keep these points in mind:

1. **Packing Your Bike for Shipment:**   Most airlines have bike boxes at terminals in major cities. They generally charge $10 for the box. To use the box you have to remove your handlebars and drape them over the top tube. Then remove the front wheel and the pedals (screw the pedals back on the inside of the cranks so they don't rattle around inside the box). If your bike has a front carrier, you'll probably have to remove it to get the bike to fit inside the box. Put a dummy axle or a block of wood in the front wheel axle dropouts to protect your fork blades from being bent.

You can check, as baggage, two pieces of luggage, and carry a third piece of luggage aboard the airplane. The bike box can, according to the carriers I checked with, go free as one of the two permissible pieces of checked luggage. However, verify this yourself before you leave for the airport. Some airline ticket agents aren't all that familiar with the regulations. It's best to call the 800 phone number of your carrier, ask for the international agent and get verification. Armed with that, you can argue, successfully, with the agent at the airline's terminal.

There's lots of empty space in the bike box, even after you put the bike in it. Fill this space with your panniers, clothing, camping gear, whatever. Remember, the maximum allowable weight for one piece of checked luggage is 70 pounds.

Save the $10 airline charge for their bike box by bumming one from a bike store. They have to dump the box a new bike comes in anyway. This way you pack the box at home, at your leisure. You can leave this box at the overseas hotel you stay in the first night and pick it up when you leave. Or discard the box at the overseas terminal and buy another from the carrier on the return trip. Be sure to get a good night's sleep, though, to beat jet lag, before you take off on your bike cross-country. I have tried both ways. At first I would unload the bike at the terminal, assemble it, attach my panniers, and cycle to a hotel. The problem is that you are often tired on arrival, so have trouble finding your way around the foreign city even with a map, and can get in an accident as you strive to cope with reverse traffic patterns. I have had a couple of close calls in England because of arrival fatigue that cut my alertness at intersections, where I found myself looking the wrong way. So stuff the bike box in a cab, get to a hotel, and get a good night's sleep before you take off.

2. Customs Problems: If you take anything made outside the United States with you, be sure to predeclare it at the terminal customs office. Make sure the declaration slip is complete, and be sure the agent signs it. I'll never forget the time I returned from Holland to Chicago. The customs agent in Chicago found a German-made camera strap on my camera, and insisted I had purchased it overseas and wanted me to pay duty on it. I protested mightily that I had bought the strap when I bought my obviously well used 10-year-old Japanese camera. After that encounter, I predeclare *everything* foreign-made I bought in the United States—bike, camera, watch, spare tubes and tires, the works. Customs agents aren't happy about this, but they are obliged to go over these items with you. The only problem here is that the agents have to inspect predeclared items, so you will have to repack your bike bag after this inspection. However, you probably don't have to predeclare your bike if it has a U.S. name label, say, Schwinn, on it. But if you had, on an earlier trip, bought, say, a Colnago in Italy or a Rene Herse or Alex Singer in France, get the customs agent to acknowledge this so you don't have to pay duty on it twice.

The political situation in some countries at this writing would keep me from going to them now. Perhaps by the time you read this book travel there will be safer. Right now I'd stay away from China, South

Africa on humanitarian principles, Northern Ireland, Czechoslovakia, those parts of Russia and any other country currently in turmoil.

Check with the local embassy of countries you plan to visit as to what inoculations, if any, you will need. Carry written proof of shots with you. Also ask your travel agent or tour provider about needed shots.

3. **About Money:**   Get foreign currency in the United States to save time on arrival and to have cash for cabs, food, hotel, etc. *Never* cash traveler's checks at a hotel, you'll pay a premium. *Always* cash them at a local bank in the country you're in.

4. **About the Language:**   I have biked extensively in France, Germany, Italy, Sweden, Austria and Great Britain. In France don't even *try* to converse in French unless you are sure of your pronunciation. My college French did not cut the mustard, literally. In a cafe in a little town in the south of France, I asked for a ham and cheese with mustard. The waitress brought me a loaf of French bread, sliced the long way, with mustard on the slices. No ham, no cheese. When I again asked for ham and cheese, with my best accent, she took the bread with a facial expression somewhere between a snarl and a cheeky grin and came back with the ham and cheese between the slices. The French *hate* foreigners to mangle their lovely, very precise language.

Don't bother about learning simple phrases such as "How much." You probably won't understand the reply. It could help if you understand direction-finding words such as right, left, and compass words. Better yet, try to find someone who speaks English for directions. Once I stopped in a small rural village in Germany, about 20 miles from Aachen, for directions to that city. It was November, near dusk and cold. Somebody found the inevitable returnee who had lived in Milwaukee. Every town in Germany has at least one such person who speaks English. Even then, though, about 15 people wrangled for 10 minutes in the town square about the best way for me to get to Aachen. No decision. Finally I tore myself away and, map in hand, found what looked like a good road. It probably is today, but then it was in the early stages of construction, a swath of mud through which I biked, walked and stumbled to Aachen, arriving at 10:30 P.M.

5. **Health Problems:**   If you have a medical problem, such as I had in Luxembourg, better know the local name for the problem so the local doctor can help if he does not speak English. In my case, I was suffering the tail end of a bout with an inner ear balance disturbance. I thought I had it licked. But the air travel brought it back. In the morning I woke up with the bed whirling around like a 78 rpm record player, and I had to hold onto the bed to keep from being whirled off into space. When

things quieted down I called the desk. They called in a doctor who did not speak English, but who, I could tell from his unsympathetic mien, was convinced I was simply badly hung over. Finally I remembered a word that seemed vaguely French and said, "Vertige, docteur," or something like that. His face brightened, the harsh look disappeared and he became, once more, a doctor. He prescribed a motion sickness medicine which did help a lot. Interestingly, even though dizzy, I could ride my bike okay, unless I looked upward at a passing plane or a tall building. So if you have a health problem that seems under control, just be sure you know the words for it in the language of the country you visit.

WHAT TO TAKE IF YOU GO ALONE

IIere's a list of essentials if you tour alone or with another person.

Bike Equipment

1. Patch kit, extra tubes and fold-up verion of your tire. Roll of duct tape. Tire lever.
2. Pump, of course.
3. Basic tools, including chain rivet remover, hub cone and headset wrenches, Allen wrenches to fit derailleurs, carrier mounting brackets, brakes. Wrenches to fit pedals, bottom bracket spindle bolts, brake and derailleur cable clamp bolts and nuts, spoke wrench (See Figs. 2-25 and 2-26.)
4. Spare parts, including brake and derailleur cables, extra chain links, spokes and nipples.
5. Tube of bearing grease.

Let me remind you that on a trail trip, far from a bike shop, you better know basic bike repairs, or have someone with you who does. Overseas, so-called bike mechanics in third-world countries can really butcher your bike. One woman I heard of got stuck in, I think it was Pakistan, with dry hub bearings. She left the bike with the local guru mechanic. On her return she was horrified to find the "mechanic" *hammering* the axle bolts back onto the axle. I recommend you carry instructions on coping with bike mechanical problems. One such book is my own *Sloane's Handy Pocket Guide to Bicycle Repair.*

Other Gear

See the section in this chapter on what to wear on bike trips. There's a wide variety of such clothing available. Let me add to this a word of advice. Wear anything you like on an off-road trip. But on a road trip, particularly in Europe, carry a decent dress-up outfit, preferably wrinkle-proof, so you can eat in good restaurants without looking like a bum. My first trip to Europe, back in 1970, saw me traveling with 40 or so fairly well-to-do Americans who belonged to the International Bicycle Touring Society (IBTS). These people knew that Europeans usually are elegantly garbed in the better restaurants. On one Sunday afternoon, our group stopped at a fine restaurant in Austria. Most others on the tour had worn, for that October day, fine knickers, good shirt, tie and a jacket carried in the pannier. I wore my usual grimy shorts, shoes still muddy from the previous day's ride in the rain, a somewhat bedraggled jacket. I went to the bar for a drink and noticed that some people moved to the other end of the bar, as far as possible from me. They were members of my group. I will say that Europeans in general do dress better than the average American, or that at least they are more clothing conscious. I did have decent clothes, but they were back at the hotel.

CAMPING GEAR

Here's a rundown on some tents, sleeping bags, cookstoves, and camping odds and ends I have come to love on damp, rainy, misty, freezing nights in the wilderness.

Back in the 1960s, before bicycle touring became fashionable, my son, his friend and I went on a bike tour of Vermont. We packed our panniers full and hung on our bikes whatever was remotely connected with camping. You name it, we had it, and then some. After struggling up a few mountains, we decided we were carrying too much stuff. I estimated my gear weighed at least 50 pounds. The teenagers' stuff weighed much more, I saw to that. So one night we sat around the campfire and began to sift through our luggage to see what we could do without. First, we could do without a week's worth of daily clothing change. Cut that back to one change. We'd wash clothes every night, let it flap from the bike to dry as we pedaled the next day. Then, I made the biggest goof of the trip. I culled the cookstove and its fuel bottle. I shipped all this stuff back home at the first post office we came to. The next morning, stoveless, we went out collecting wood for breakfast. Ever try to build a fire with wet wood? By 10:30 we finally finished breakfast. Dinner was also a disaster, timewise. It had been raining a lot in Vermont. Things got better when we discovered dry twigs and small tree limbs deep in the woods. But we bought another stove that very afternoon, at the first general store we came to. Well, let's discuss stoves.

Stoves

The stoves that use butane or LP gas light instantly at the touch of a match. You don't have to mess with gasoline. On the minus side, you have to pack in and pack out about three butane containers for each week of the trip. Butane stoves take longer to heat than gasoline. It takes butane about 8.5 minutes to boil a quart of water. A gas stove can do it in from 3 to 4 minutes. If you cook for two, for example, one 6.5-ounce butane cylinder lasts for at least two days. You get about 2.5 to 3 hours of use out of a cylinder. I use from two to three cylinders a week on a trail ride. Butane stoves are inexpensive. They cost around $25. The cartridges for them weigh about 10 ounces and cost about $2.50 each. One stove with cartridge weighs around 22 ounces. A very compact stove that can double as a camp light is the Hank Roberts. It uses LP gas cartridges that cost $3 each and burns at full blast for around three hours. The stove itself, with camp light adapter, costs $39. It's slow though, takes 7 minutes to boil a quart of water at sea level. Gas stoves cost a lost more, but they also give you a lot more heat.

Going all the way up the price scale, the MSR multifuel X-GK stove boils a quart of water in just 3 minutes (at sea level), burns for 99.8 minutes on a 2-pint container of fuel, burns almost anything, including all auto fuels, gas, kerosene, No. 1 and 2 diesel fuel, and several kinds of solvents. This is a rather expensive stove, at $89.95, but it's the best one on the market, in my opinion, particularly when unleaded stove gas isn't available in some foreign countries. On the basis of some rather extensive bike-pack trips in this country and abroad, my experience has been that it takes about 15 minutes of stove time to prepare the average meal, but that depends on how much heat the stove puts out. I was able to get by with about 60 ounces of unleaded gas for a week with the MSR, which is not a lot to carry. How much fuel to carry is a matter of what and how much you will cook. If you bring mostly dehydrated food, you will need only to heat water and can get by with very little fuel. I suggest you practice cooking at home on the stove you will take. Cook the kind of food you will pack and check cooking times and fuel consumption. Don't take anybody's word for this. Don't guess, know for sure.

A less expensive version of this stove burns only white gas and heats just as fast.

The Coleman Peak I stove has been recently improved, and the new version, which boils a quart of water in about 4.5 minutes at sea level, uses unleaded gas. The tank holds 11.8 oz of fuel, which will last 1 hour and 15 minutes at full blast or will simmer for 2.5 hours. It costs $45.

The camper's standby, a stove I had been using for at least the past 10 years and finally gave to one of my sons, is the brass Swedish SVEA. It throws a very hot blast but is a bit tricky to light in a brisk wind. I have no figures on how long it takes to boil a quart of water at sea level, but my recollection is that it does so quickly, in around 3 minutes. It costs about $45.

Tents

The single most costly camping item you need is a good tent. The el cheapo cut-rate-store tent of heavy canvas weighs a ton, won't breathe and isn't worth the money to mail it home. In the wild you need, above all, comfort. You also need a tent that is lightweight, easy to set up and take down, packs compactly, is waterproof, not just water-resistant, has a small vestibule to keep your panniers in out of the rain at night, without crowding the tent sleeping area. How big the tent should be depends on the compatibility of your partner and how comfortable you are in tight quarters. Two-person tents are marginal for two, in my experience, but then I like a little elbow room. A three-person tent with foyer is ideal.

Tents I have used and like are the following:

My favorite tent is a Moss StarTrak with foyer (Fig. 4-1). It sleeps two with room to spare, has a floor space with vestibule of 49 sq ft, weighs 6 lb 8 oz (that's only 3 lb 4 oz each), sets up and takes down in

Fig. 4-1: *Compact, lightweight Moss tent has room for two, can be open to the stars at night.*

a jiffy, folds compactly for bike carrying, costs around $365 and is worth it. After all, ten nights in a hotel would cost you at least that much. Moss's StarGazer model (Fig. 4-2) weighs 6 lb 12 oz, has 52.1 sq ft of floor space with vestibule, costs around $399 and sleeps two with space to spare, and could sleep three. Both tents are open to the sky but come with a separate rain cover that goes over the entire tent. These are extremely well made, intelligently designed tents I can recommend without reservation. If your sporting goods store can't supply them, write Moss, Inc., Mt. Battie St., P.O. Box 309, Camden, Maine 04843, phone 207-236-8368.

Comparable tents are available from other major sporting goods firms, such as REI. If an REI store is not near you, I suggest you send for their excellent catalog, which lists everything you could possibly need for a bike camping trip. Use their toll-free number to order your catalog: 1-800-426-4840.

Other Camping Gear

For off-road trail rides into the wilderness, you really have to know orienteering, how to find your way with contour map and compass. I urge you to take courses in this subject. Your local sporting goods outfitter should know who offers them. For orienteering you will need a good compass, such as a Silva tracking model. An altimeter is a handy adjunct to a contour map, because that type of map has lines showing altitude. If you know about where you are, and have an altimeter to tell which contour line you're on, you're halfway to orienteering accurately. I use the Thommen 15,000-ft altimeter (Fig. 4-3), find it highly accurate, light, easy to read and, at around $160, a comforting instrument to have in the wild.

Fig. 4-2. Larger Moss tent has ample room for two or three. Sets up and takes down quickly, folds compactly.

Fig. 4-3. *An altimeter, with a contour map, is a navigation aid in the wilderness. This Thommen model is good to 15,000 ft altitude. Beyond that, your bike will need wings.*

Books on Orienteering, Map Reading, Use of the Compass: If you can't find a class in orienteering, next best is to read a good book about it. Here are some excellent examples:

Bjorn Kellstrom. *Be Expert with Map and Compass.* Orienteerists say this book is their "Bible." Once you read it, you'll agree. Covers map symbols and what they mean, travel by map alone, by compass alone, with both together, finding bearings, sketching maps and wilderness travel. 214 pages. Charles Scribner's Sons, Inc., New York.

Hans Bengtsson and George Atkinson. *Orienteering for Sport and Pleasure.* Emphasizes orienteering as a sport unto itself. 215 pages. The Stephen Greene Press, Brattleboro, VT.

June Fleming. *Staying Found.* A practical guide to the use of map and compass. 159 pages. Random House, New York.

Harold Gatty. *Finding Your Way on Land or Sea.* This book is subtitled "Reading Nature's Maps." Teaches you to use Mother Nature herself to find your way, without the use of maps or compass. 272 pages. Stephen Greene Press, Brattleboro, VT.

W. S. Kals. *Land Navigation Handbook.* This is the Sierra Club's guide to the map and compass. Also covers use of the altimeter as an aid to finding your way on the land. 230 pages. Sierra Books, San Francisco, CA.

Please also review Chapter 3, which covers rescue procedures in the wild.

You will also need:

1. First aid kit.
2. Set of cookware.
3. Food (see books listed on this subject in the Appendix).
4. A flashlight and camp light. Some years ago I ran across a solar-powered flashlight. I've been looking for it ever since. It's ideal for extended wilderness trips for obvious reasons.
5. Tinkle bell on the bike to alert hikers and equestrians to your presence.
6. The other stuff, such as clothing, sunglasses, raingear, soaps, etc., I leave to your imagination and ingenuity. Take a couple of two- or three-day wilderness shakedown rides. You'll soon find out what you need.

Sleeping Bags

Next to the tent, a good sleeping bag is worth every cent you pay for it. Here are a few tips:

1. Down is lighter and packs into a smaller sack, but if it gets wet you might as well pack your body into a large ice cube.
2. Synthetic-fiber-filled sleeping bags will still keep you warm even when wet. (Take along a couple of sturdy plastic garbage bags to wrap stuff you want to keep dry.)
3. Bags with a hood, which can double as a pillow, keep your head warm on cold nights. Your head is prone to suffer heat loss, and when it does you can be uncomfortable, even though the rest of you is surrounded by the sleeping bag.
4. Bags come in two styles, the square boxlike shape and the mummy bag, which tapers like a cowboy boot. The mummy bag is lighter at a given temperature rating and clings closely to your body to fend off the cold. But its shape gives my feet claustrophobia; however, my wife likes that style. I gladly put up with the extra weight of a box-shaped bag, one I can roll about in with comfort, twist and turn to my heart's content, wiggle my toes, crack my ankle bones.

Select a bag that is rated at a lower temperature than you think you will be exposed to. You can always unzip the bag if it gets too warm, but you can't compensate for a bag that does not have enough "fill" to keep you warm on a cold night. I'd opt for a bag rated at 50 degrees F for the flatlands and 20 degrees F for the hills, in the warm season.

Some bags, such as the Moonstone Minima, have snap-in liners so you can tailor them for varying temperature extremes and cost about $185. The Moonstone Minima weighs only 2.5 lb. The Caribou Quasar bag is rated 0 degrees F to −10 degrees F, and is my own favorite. It's roomy, light, around 4.2 lb with stuff sack, costs around $180. Heavier than the Minima, but I like its roomy comfort.

One more point: a foam pad of some kind under your sleeping bag protects you against cold and moisture seeping through the tent bottom and also protects against the tiny pebbles and twigs you never seem to sweep away before pitching the tent. The Therma-Rest pad can be pumped up to move you away from the cold earth.

PANNIERS TO CARRY YOUR GEAR

Panniers are the bags you strap on your carrier which hold your outing gear. There are far too many makes and models of panniers on the market today for me to cover them all. I will, however, make general recommendations and give you criteria to use in selecting them.

1. *Buy the size you need.* Pannier sizes range from around 750 to 2,900 cubic inches.

2. *Secure mounting on the carrier.* Back in 1972, I was bouncing along a cobblestone street in Brussels, in the midst of traffic, when my left pannier jumped off the carrier and fell into the street. That was the pannier that was carrying, among other items, my prized $1,200 Hasselblad camera. I think I broke all records for instant dismount and pannier retrieval before a car could run over it. Ideally, the pannier should be secured to the carrier so well as to be virtually a part of it. There should also be no pannier side sway that could cause instability of the bike. Panniers with simple hook mounts that dangle from the end of a spring may be okay for road rides. But on a rough trail or road, I prefer a positive strap fastening, such as the Needle Works (Fig. 4-4), which holds the pannier securely to the carrier.

3. *No load shifting inside the pannier.* What you're carrying inside the pannier should stay put. If it moves around as you pedal, the weight shift could reduce the stability of the bike. Well-placed interior and/or exterior compression straps (Fig. 4-5) keep the load from shifting around.

4. *Proper load distribution inside the pannier.* Heavy items should be placed in the forward part of both front and rear panniers. Keep

Fig. 4-4. *This is how a pannier should strap to your carrier. Note positive retention straps holding this Needle Works pannier on the carrier. This carrier is an early Bruce Gordon and has since been redesigned to permit access to the wheel axle nut or quick release.*

Fig. 4-5. *Exterior straps hold the load in this pannier from swaying, and contribute to stability.*

weight as far forward as possible to help keep the front wheel on the ground, especially on sandy terrain.

5. *Rectangular shape panniers give better side clearance.* A pannier that's more rectangular in shape (see Fig. 4-6) is better than a pannier that's more square in shape, with the same cubic capacity, because it will not bulge out as much as a square bag. The rectangular pannier gives you a thinner profile for clearance on narrow off-road trails. You don't want the pannier to catch on anything projecting from the side of the trail, such as tree branches.

6. *Load isolation is important.* The pannier should be compartmented (Fig. 4-7) so you can stow items for convenient retrieval. When you want something, you should be able to find it without an exasperating and time-wasting search through the load.

7. *Other pannier design features to look for.* Check for loose, unstitched fabric inside the pannier, behind zippers. If there is such fabric, I guarantee it will fray and the loose ends and threads will catch in zippers, a major cause of zipper failure and lost tempers. Fabric ends inside as well as outside the pannier should be neatly stitched, as in

Fig. 4-7. *Many pockets, as on this pair of Cannondale panniers, permit intelligent gear stowage. You'll find what you are looking for without fumbling through bigger pockets.*

Fig. 4-6. *Narrow-profile panniers offer greater clearance from branches and other trail protrusions.*

Figure 4-8. Back stiffeners should be removable and replaceable because they can become bent and warped. Tie-downs and other straps should not dangle where they can be caught in the spokes. A rain cover, one that's durable and easy to install, is a real plus for two reasons other than rain protection. The cover protects the pannier from wear and tear on the trail, and from sharp trail projections or from tears that might

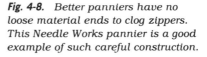

Fig. 4-8. *Better panniers have no loose material ends to clog zippers. This Needle Works pannier is a good example of such careful construction.*

occur if you dump the bike. It's a lot easier and less expensive to repair or replace a cover than the pannier itself. Second, a cover makes the pannier less attractive to thieves because it's more difficult and slower to get into. Every extra second a thief has to spend getting to the target increases the likelihood of his (or her) being caught. (A cable and lock will be yet another deterrent, especially when you camp, but be sure to lock the bike to a tree.)

8. *Handlebar bags.* A small bag fastened to the handlebars is a convenient carrier for frequently used items, such as wallet, small flashlight, dog-deterrent spray, extra maps, keys. Buy the kind that's quickly removable, yet fastens securely, such as the Cannondale (Fig. 4-9). When you stop for lunch, you can unsnap the bag and take it with you. A plastic map cover (Fig. 4-10) atop the bar bag lets you check the map without digging for it in your panniers.

Fig. 4-9. I nominate this Cannondale bar bag as the best on the market. It's roomy, has five pockets and a map carrier. It clips securely to the mounting bracket, bottom left, yet you can unclip it in seconds to take the bag with you into a store, restaurant or tent. Comes with a carrying strap.

Fig. 4-10. A map holder on a bar bag is a real convenience.

HOW TO PICK A CARRIER

Now let's take a look at the bike carriers that carry your bike panniers.

1. *The carrier should fit your bike.* Not every carrier fits every bike. Cheap ATBs don't have brazed-on fittings (Fig. 2-18), to which carriers can be bolted. Without these fittings, carriers must be clamped to the bike frame. These clamps can work loose; when they do, heavily loaded panniers can slide down and interfere with pedaling, possibly cause an accident. Buy a carrier that can be bolted to your bike frame.

2. *Carriers should be rigid, without sideway.* Look at the carrier you have in mind. If you can find one installed on a bike, push it from side to side. If it moves easily, think how it can move when heavily loaded. I like the Blackburn (Fig. 4-11) and the Bruce Gordon (Fig. 4-4) carrier. The Gordon hand-brazed, mitered, tubular steel carrier is an exceptionally well made unit that's very stable. The carrier should be sturdy. If the carrier breaks on the trail, and you're carrying a lot of camping gear, you will be faced with a major decision. You can abandon all but absolutely necessary gear, and hide the rest in the woods. If you're lucky, it will still be there when you get back, if you can find it. What's necessary depends on how far you are from civilization and the weather. In a pinch, you could do without your tent and sleeping bag if you have warm clothes. You will need your food, though you may be able to ditch the stove and cookware if you have enough food that does not require cooking to get you back. If you can get back within the day, then, of course, you can hide your gear and hope it's still there when you return. A discreet blaze

Fig. 4-11. The locking mechanism holds the Kirtland pannier securely on the carrier. The Blackburn aluminum carrier is strong and light, accepts any pannier on the market.

mark on a tree can help you locate it on the return trip. Ideally, though, you should have a carrier strong enough that it won't break. It should have cross bracing for strength and rigidity. The carrier should be able to withstand the stresses and rigors of trail riding, and have the strength to stay together should the bike fall on its side or collide with a solid object, such as a boulder or tree trunk.

3. *Other features to look for.* The carrier should be adjustable so the top can be parallel to the ground. If the frame tilts toward the rear, the pannier tends to slide in that direction, which puts load weight toward the rear instead of toward the front of the bike. When fastened to the frame it should not move when pushed from side to side.

4. *Carriers, fat tires, and fenders.* Be careful about buying a carrier that's not made specifically for an ATB. Carriers made for skinny-tire street bikes often do not have enough clearance for the fat rear tire. Check this point out before you pay for the carrier and go to all the trouble of installing it—or trying to install it.

5. *Install only a low-rider front carrier* (Fig. 4-4), which keeps the load as close to the ground as possible for greater bike-handling stability.

6. *Wheel removal.* The carrier, front or rear, should not interfere with wheel removal. The front carrier, in particular, must permit use of the quick-release lever. Some older carriers have struts located right next to the wheel axle (Fig. 4-4), which makes wheel removal a real pain. You should be able to remove the front wheel without removing the carrier. Hold the carrier you like in place, where it mounts, to check this point. The carrier must also not interfere with the brake arms or brake cables (nor should the panniers).

CARRYING YOUR BIKE ON A CAR

A good bike carrier, one that fits on the roof of your car, is a must if you plan to carry your bike anywhere. Here's what to look for in a carrier:

1. *The carrier must fit your car:* Carriers are made for specific makes and models of cars. For example, if your car has no rain gutters, you need a gutterless carrier.

2. *The carrier should be lockable to the car:* The mounting brackets should have locks. The same key should fit all four bracket locks.

3. *Mounting should be convenient:* I like the carriers that use quick-release fork holders (Fig. 4-12) and sturdy, ratcheting type straps to hold

Fig. 4-12. This Thule rooftop bike carrier clamps the fork blades in a quick-release unit. Rear wheel is held by sturdy straps. All four carrier mounting brackets are key-locked to the car roof.

Fig. 4-13. Yakima cartop bike carriers use this ratcheting type holding strap on the rear wheel which provides a very secure rear wheel hold-down. The strap base slides in a groove in the bottom of the rail.

the rear wheel onto the carrier rail (Fig. 4-13). However, be sure to remember to pick up the removed front wheel and stow it in your car. I've left wheels behind. Don't you do it!

4. *The rail should be long enough* to fit the longer wheelbase of your ATB or your tandem.

5. *Use a special carrier if you carry your bike in a pickup truck* (Fig. 4-14) to prevent damage to bike and truck.

6. *Spray your roof carrier with DayGlo orange paint* so you can find your car readily in a crowded parking lot. Trying to find your car at the

Fig. 4-14. Use a pickup truck bike holder, such as this Yakima model, to keep your good bikes from rattling around in the truck bed.

airport, in the wee dark hours of the night, after a long, tiring airplane trip, can be most discouraging. DayGlo can also help identify your car from a distance.

7. *Consider a rear- or trunk-mounted carrier* (Fig. 4-15 and Fig. 4-16) if you drive a van or can't lift your bike to the roof of your car. Select a carrier that won't rub on your car or permit the bike to do so. Be particular about this point, because some of these carriers, the cheaper ones, are ill-designed, possibly by auto body shops.

Carriers that meet the above criteria are Yakima, Thule and Rola. There are probably others.

Caution: Remove panniers, handlebar bag, pump and water bottle from your bike before installing it on a carrier. You'll cut wind resistance, noise and improve gas mileage when you do. The pump can bounce off and be lost.

Fig. 4-15. *If lifting your ATB to a roof-top carrier is a burden, use a trunk carrier that fits any car, even this station wagon.*

Fig. 4-16. *This Hitchrack, by Wild Side Designs, fits a van or a camper.*

CHECK THESE REFERENCE WORKS

In Chapter 3 I covered what to do if confronted by a wild animal, and how to avoid such confrontation in the first place. In addition, I would urge you to become familiar with the basics of first aid, such as caring for fractures and concussions, avoiding and treating heat stroke, hypothermia (exposure to cold) and hypoglycemia (low blood-sugar level, which causes a real energy droop), CPR (dealing with a heart attack), poison ivy and poison oak exposure, and snakebites, to name a few possibilities. There are many books on administering first aid in the wilds. Here are a few of the better ones:

David Patten. *The Outdoor Survival Book.* Covers use of maps of all types, camping gear, food and food preparation, camping in all kinds of weather, first aid and weather forecasting. 160 pages. David & Charles, North Pomfret, VT.

James A. Wilkerson, M.D. *Medicine for Mountaineering.* This is *the* definitive book for survival in the wild. Covers first aid for just about anything that could happen to you, from any source. Even pregnancy. Chapters by eminent physicians on their specialty. Don't leave without it! 365 pages. The Mountaineers, Seattle, WA.

W. W. Forgey, M.D. *Death by Exposure, Hypothermia.* How to avoid harm from being too cold or too hot is what this book is all about. Prevention, alleviation and cure are detailed. Discusses clothing, sunstroke and heatstroke, overexposure to cold water and many other factors relating to the effect of temperature on the human body. 175 pages. ICS Books, Inc., Merrillville, IN. See Appendix for additional books.

These books on health remind me, once again, as I said in Chapter 1, to keep in shape all year you need to exercise all year. Jumping on the bike as soon as the snow melts is a route to pain if you tear a muscle by overexertion. When you can't ride outside, your best bet is to ride inside, on a bike trainer, such as the one in Figure 4-17. This is a new model, made by Avenir. When winter goes, fold and stow this trainer away. In bad weather, mount your bike by the rear axle, with the rear tire over the fan shaft, and pedal your way to year-round fitness. Use the trainer for a half hour every day. Watch your pulse rate. Keep it at your aerobic fitness level. Calculate that level by subtracting your age from 220 and multiplying the result by .75. If you're not bathed in sweat

Fig. 4-17. An excellent way to keep in shape is to use a bike trainer, such as this Avenir model, which folds compactly out of the way when not in use.

at the end of 30 minutes, you've been goofing off. Stimulate your pedaling cadence by playing fast music. If you get bored, watch an interesting TV show and forget about the time. If it's hard to maintain your aerobic level for 30 minutes, you're out of shape. Take it easy the first couple of times on the trainer. Start out riding for 5 minutes, and add 5 minutes each day until you can sustain a fast pace for at least 30 minutes. But get your physician's okay first.

OTHER ITEMS TO TAKE

If you're going on a safari, where water is scarce, take an insulated monster water carrier. If you can't find a solar-powered flashlight, a Tekna quartz light is compact and throws a powerful beam (Fig. 4-18).

Fig. 4-18. Get powerful light with a quartz flashlight, such as this Tekna compact model.

Fig. 4-19. Carry a small kerosene camp light, such as this one. Adds a cheerful note to any campsite.

A first aid kit can be a lifesaver, as well as a convenience. Take a water-purifier kit along if you plan to drink stream water, available from any outdoor sporting goods store or REI catalog (see Appendix). This kerosene-burning camp light (Fig. 4-19) doubles as a saucepan cooker. A candle camp light gives enough light to play cards by. Keep a journal of your trip with a water-resistant notebook and wallet combination. Carry a compact rescue blanket, which offers some cold protection if, say, your down sleeping bag gets wet.

BICYCLE CLOTHING

In all areas of cycling today things change rapidly. Everything seems to be redesigned, improved, renamed or discontinued. The same condition exists in the area of clothing designed for cycling. Remember that there will continue to be innovation and change as you read or refer to this information about bicycle clothing. This section includes pattern design, fabric technology, garments for specific climatic conditions, specific off-road wear, women's clothing, safety innovations and cycling gadgetry.

It is said that clothing makes the person; but in a book about cycling, one could ask, does clothing make a cyclist? The reply could depend on the person who is cycling and whether that person is an avid or a casual cyclist. The reply could also depend on the cyclist's body build, personal preference and pocketbook. The beginning cyclist might ask about the need for specialized bicycle clothing. After all, some folks ride in whatever they happen to be wearing when they feel like cycling. They seem to move along pretty well and look comfortable enough. So, why the special clothing?

If you are a beginning or an avid cyclist who would like to know more about the dynamics of some bicycle clothing, read on. Let's begin with an explanation of clothing (active-wear) design. Some cycling active-wear on the market today seems to fit the body so closely that it appears to leave just enough room for the bones, muscles and skin. This skintight fit is aerodynamic; garments cling so closely that they add very little wind resistance. Garments are light because fabrics are lightweight (it's not much fun to carry around excess baggage on a bike). Some fabrics are stretchy; they move as the body moves. Better cycling fabrics breathe; in other words, they allow cooling air to flow over the body (breathing = ventilation). Conversely, in this ventilating process, fabric should allow perspiration to be wicked away either to outer layers of clothing or to the outside air. Some types of active-wear offer protection for the skin and insulation for the body, with minimal bulk and weight. In other words, cycling active-wear is streamlined, utilitarian and comfortable.

Streamlined utility and comfort are basic to the design of cycling jerseys and shorts (in later paragraphs, other specific types of clothing, e.g., ATB and women's clothing, will be discussed). There are variations on a few common themes of design detail for both jerseys and shorts. So, get out just a few sewing terms you might remember from basic survival home economics in high school and let's begin.

Basic Jersey Pattern Design

Usually the jersey front and back panels and the sleeves are designed in one of two ways. One jersey pattern is constructed simply by sewing a single-unit frontpiece to a single-unit backpiece at side and shoulder seams (Fig. 4-20). The second jersey pattern is a combination of narrowly cut front and back panels and four contoured side panels (two under each arm) (Fig. 4-21). As a result there are more seams. Whenever side panels appear in nonactive-wear, it means that that portion of a garment will allow more flexibility of movement while it more accurately fits proportion and shape. Therefore, in theory, a jersey with side panels should have a more defined fit and allow for unhampered movement. However, the designers of both types of jersey patterns are working with stretchable fabric, which would automatically allow for close fit and body flexion. Choice of side panel detail would be up to the individual taste or body shape and size.

Fig. 4-20. *Jersey with single-unit frontpiece joined to a single-unit backpiece at side and shoulder seams.*

Fig. 4-21. *A combination of narrowly cut front and back panels and four contoured side panels (two under each arm).*

The sleeve design detail also has two basic pattern options. One option is the set-in (cap) sleeve, which, according to advertising, has been cut to allow for the forward body and arm position of the biker. A set-in sleeve is cut in one flat piece, stitched together at the underarm seam, and the resulting sleeve is sewn into the armhole opening of the jersey (Fig. 4-20). The second sleeve pattern option is cut so that it begins at the neck edge and extends over the shoulder to the mid-bicep or wrist in one continuous piece. When the sleeve sections are sewn to the front and back of the jersey, the sleeve seams lie diagonally from neck to underarm (a raglan sleeve) (Fig. 4-22). The raglan sleeve is used most often in jackets. Both types of sleeve, if cut properly, should prevent pulling and binding across the upper back and arms.

Other design details of cycling jerseys are somewhat standard. One standard detail is the added length of the back panel (sometimes called a tail), which is designed to cover the waist-to-hip area. When the body is bent forward, this is an area where gaping easily occurs in an ordinary shirt and shorts combination. At times, the entire tail or the hem is

Fig. 4-22. *A raglan sleeve.*

elasticized as added insurance against shirt sneak-up or to prevent flapping in the breeze. Another standard feature of jerseys is a two- or three-
section pocket across the lower back. This sectioned pocket is handy for
storing things you might need while riding, e.g., a quick snack and maps
or directions. A final standard feature is a stand-up and close-fitting collar
with a front zipper that extends into the body of the jersey (some collars
taper down to the zipper). Snug fit should prevent wind resistance that
other types of collar might cause by catching or flapping in the wind.
The zipper is designed to be opened with one hand for ventilation. A
casual or an off-road cyclist might choose to wear a cotton or cotton/
polyester blend T-shirt with a crew neck. A crew neck lies flat against
the neck. One drawback to a crew neck is that it does not protect the
neck from chill on cool days. A more detailed description of fabric types,
characteristics and value to cyclists will follow in later paragraphs.

Shorts Design

As jerseys have optional design details, so do cycling shorts. There are
two basic shorts designs, which can have various modifications or additions. Shorts are designed to stretch and move with the rider in any
riding position without bunching up or binding in the crotch or at the
waist. The first type of shorts design is the skin-fitted nylon/spandex
model (Fig. 4-23). These shorts are sewn together in a series of panels,
which may vary from four panels in one pair of shorts to eight in another
pair. Without going into detail, it can probably be assumed that quality
of the contoured fit and the amount of mobility the shorts allow are in
direct proportion to the number and cut of panels in the shorts. The legs
of the shorts are also cut to about midthigh to prevent the inner thigh
from brushing constantly against the bike saddle. In time, brushing can
cause irritation and chafing of the inner thigh. Grippers have been added
to the inside of leg hems of some shorts to prevent any fabric creep while
riding. Shorts have an inner back pocket tucked inside a high-rise back
waist which protects the low back area. They also have a lower-cut front
waist to minimize bunching when the biker leans forward. For additional
adjustments at the waist, some shorts have drawstrings inside the waist-
band.

Another type of shorts design is for casual riders, for riders who are
figure conscious, or for off-road cyclists. These shorts are usually made
with a fabric that has a tougher, more resilient (yet soft to the touch)
finish. Based on the combination of fibers in the fabric, some of these
shorts do have limited stretch. These shorts are generally cut in panels

Fig. 4-23. *Skin-fitted nylon/spandex shorts.*

but the cut is fuller, the shorts roomier. The legs also appear to be shorter than the nylon/spandex shorts and some have a V-slit in the lower side-leg for added ease. Some also have elastic or a drawstring in the waist-band.

Crotch Liners

Finally, one of the most important parts of any pair of cycling shorts, as far as comfort and anatomical protection is concerned, is the crotch liner. The shape of most liners usually looks like a pliable eggshell that has been flattened and has had a broad V inserted at the narrow end. This is called a Y-cut liner. The flattened shape protects the crotch and sit-bone area. The pubis is protected by the V insert, which cups up and over the nose of the saddle. In some liners, seams are required for construction and could be a source of irritation if they are bulky or poorly placed. Cannondale Corporation (for one) now offers a molded one-piece Ultra-Suede chamois liner that has a second layer of fleece bonded to its underside to provide wicking action and extra cushion. The original and probably still most expensive liner is made of chamois, which is not as washable as the synthetic liners. Chamois is claimed to offer more resistance to saddle chafing. Most often, the chamois liner is one layer thick.

Usually, unlike chamois liners, the synthetic liners are constructed in layers. Each layer is a different type of fabric, and each fabric has a separate purpose. For example, the Descente liner has four layers: (1) the top layer (closest to the crotch) is a chamois mimic (sometimes called Ultra-Suede) to reduce the risk of chafing (it is quick drying and pliable); (2) a layer of fleece to aid in moisture absorption; (3) a layer of polyurethane padding to cushion the road bumps and to help prevent numbness; and (4) a tricot layer which, it is claimed, allows the liner to move with the body and not the outer fabric of the shorts, further reducing the chance of irritation. Another liner that sounds unique is the Spenco Biosoft gel. This liner is a sandwich of (1) Supersuede synthetic chamois; (2) terrycloth; (3) foam gel; and (4) tricot. Spenco adds the gel, which, they claim, is "fluidlike" and "cushions both vertical and lateral pressure" when the crotch, sit-bones and muscles meet the saddle.

There certainly are differences in liners. For instance, compare those already mentioned with those used most often in the casual cycling shorts. These liners are generally made of a single layer of polyester fleece.

Fabrics for Cycling Active-Wear

Construction detail for dynamic fit is only one of the necessities for cycling active-wear. Quality fabric is also a necessity. Fabric used to manufacture active-wear is a film or sheeting, woven or knitted from fibers of various types. Active-wear fabrics, at a basic level, should mimic our skin's excellent adaptive and protective qualities. For example, one of our skin's many functions is to moderate the extremes possible in body temperature. When our normal core temperature is maintained, we are able to perform at an optimum level of focus and energy. When we are active, we perspire, and perspiration gradually evaporates in order to cool our skin and body core. If perspiration did not evaporate, we'd have heavier bodies, which would slow us down. When our body is chilled, our skin tightens up and puckers up, which, along with surface hair and a subsurface layer of fat, provides insulation and prevents heat loss. Our skin serves as a protective shield for underlying muscle. It is also soft, lightweight, and flexible enough to allow muscles and bones to move freely. Finally, skin can be washed and dried without shrinking, and, when clean, does not retain odor.

Ideally, fabric should perform as well as or better than our own skin, especially while we are active. Many fiber and fabric manufacturers today are searching for ideal fabrics. It is exciting to read about research and high technology being used to develop efficient fabric for active-wear. New synthetic fabrics are being designed to meet the distinct thermostatic needs (temperature maintenance) of athletes. Modern fabrics accomplish this by wicking perspiration from the skin. Excess moisture is held in a sort of suspension in or between fibers of the cloth until it exits through evaporation, which takes very little time. Rapid evaporation prevents saturation, and fabrics remain lightweight. Another advantage of some newer fabrics is toughness and durability. They provide excellent abrasion-resistant surfaces while maintaining good looks. Some fabrics resist or repel water and wind or insulate against cold. Most synthetics wash easily and dry rapidly, without shrinkage or color fade. If washed properly, they are nonabrasive, supple, and retain their shape. Odor retention is not the problem it once was.

Some folks believe that synthetic, technologically designed fabrics are best. Others believe in, and will use only, natural fabrics such as cotton, silk and wool. One reason for using only natural-fiber fabrics is that some people have allergies to synthetic fibers. In the following paragraphs, qualities of both natural and synthetic fabrics will be reviewed. It will be easiest to describe fabrics according to the climatic conditions in which they could be used.

A note: there are many trademark names for fibers or fabrics that appear to be similar in character and function. Trademark names for some similar fabrics are included in following paragraphs, which should be helpful to you when you shop and read labels.

Lightweight Fibers/Fabrics: Moderate to Hot Weather

Fabric that is used to construct cycling active-wear for moderate to hot weather should have the latest synthetic's advantageous qualities, discussed earlier. Most of the fabrics mentioned in this category are used primarily for jerseys, shorts and some jackets.

Natural fibers such as cotton and silk can be soft and smooth to the touch and give a relaxed comfortable feeling when worn. Cotton does not require too stringent washing/drying procedures, although it takes longer to dry than synthetics. On the other hand, silk does need special handling when washed/dried. It can retain odor unless washed with gentle detergents made especially for silk and other fine washables (try REI's ReFRESH). Both cotton and silk are generally less fade-resistant than synthetic fabrics. Neither fabric has as much wicking capability as synthetics. When they become saturated with moisture, fibers swell and block ventilation, creating a soggy jersey. On a day of cool breezes a soggy jersey next to your skin can be extremely chilling. Both fabrics might be used more effectively as a second layer over one of the wick-efficient synthetics.

Synthetics

Of the synthetics specifically targeted for active-wear, nylon, polyester, and acrylic are primary. All three are tough, resilient, and can be dyed in vivid, fade-resistant colors. You will find these fibers blended, layered, sandwiched around insulating fibers or fabric, laminated to membranes, or coated with film or finish. Sunlight can weaken these fibers. Black absorbs more rays than light colors do; therefore, black or dark garments will not wear as long.

Among the synthetics (knit rather than woven fabric) are Du Pont's 100 percent Coolmax, Milliken Mill's WickTec, Descente's X-Bio (a dual-layered fabric of cotton and polyester), Toray's Fieldsensor and Asahi's Sofilia Sport. Du Pont claims to have achieved an ultrafine, soft and light fiber with dynamic wicking and insulating characteristics in its newest development, Microfine (fabric by Milliken Mills). Following are a few active-wear items in which these synthetics and others like them are used: jerseys, tanks, bras, and mesh liners and inserts. Some active-wear manufacturers using these fabrics are Blackbottom, Cannondale, Descente, Hind and Lite-Speed.

In a class by itself is spandex. Spandex is an elastic fiber. When knitted together with other fibers, the result is a stretchy fabric. Active-wear made from this fabric will fit closely but not tightly because it adapts to your shape and movement. Body oils and tanning oils and lotions, as well as perspiration, can discolor or yellow spandex. Common trademarks are Du Pont's Lycra, BASF's Vivana and Zefsport, and Hoechst-Celanese Corporation's ESP. Some uses for spandex/nylon fabrics are skin-fitted cycling shorts, bib shorts, tights, full-body tights, portions of gloves, and T-back tops and bras. Spandura is a heavier, more abrasion-resistant type of spandex that may be used in the side panels of off-road shorts.

Finally, a group of fabrics that are woven (some with a textured finish) rather than knit, are more abrasion- and snag-resistant (tough wearing), and have a light cottony feel are Du Pont's Supplex, ICI Fiber's Tactel, and Allied Signal's Trek. When Du Pont's Cordura is added to the fiber mix, the resulting fabric is extra rugged. These fabrics are used most often for casual and off-road shorts and various styles of jackets.

Wind and Rain Gear: Jackets, Ponchos, Tights

Wind and rain gear sold for cycling is either "resistant" or "repellent." To date there is no fabric that is absolutely windproof or waterproof. The term "resistant" means that the garment will shed rain or wind for a short time and then penetration will occur and you'll get wet. The term "repellent" means that the garment is the closest to waterproof that you will be able to purchase (fabric stays dry the longest). Buy only garments with labels that state that they have sealed seams, or prepare to seal them yourself with seam sealer. If they are not sealed, they will leak.

In order to make a garment resistant or repellent, manufacturers use finishes or coatings (Burlington's Ultrex, Du Pont's Zepel), membranes (MicroPore Inc.'s Microtex, Akzo's Sympatex), or fabrics specifically woven for this purpose (Allied Signal's Dryline, Toray's Entrant, W. L. Gore's Gore-Tex, Helly-Tech's Tactel). Note: Gore-Tex is a well-known example of a microporous fabric. Its pores are minute, and wind/rain cannot pass through although perspiration vapor, from inside, can. Not all of the materials mentioned above allow garments to breathe.

Venting systems are added to some jackets. Mesh fabric, zippers, and strategically placed openings are common to these systems. A mesh insert is sewn across the upper back and shoulders (the yoke). It is covered by a second separate piece of fabric (generally the same fabric that has been used in other parts of the jacket). Vapor dissipates through large holes in the mesh. The outer fabric resists/repels the wind/rain. Vents, with or without mesh, may be part of underarm seams. Sometimes underarm seams are zippered to form vents. Zipping and unzipping the vents and jacket front, in varying degrees, give you control over the amount of venting you need.

Ponchos are a one-piece rain covering. Make sure yours has elastic thumb loops to prevent fly-up. It should have a contoured hood large enough to fit over a helmet. The hood should have a drawstring or adjustable closure to ensure a close fit; otherwise it could block peripheral vision.

Looser-fit nylon shell pants and cycling tights are also part of the wind/rain gear scene. If you choose the nylon shell variety make sure that the knee area has stretch or pleated panels for flexion. Another must for these pants is an adjustable ankle band, strap or clamp, which keeps the pants leg out of the chainwheel. Side zippers make it easier to get pants on and off. Cycling tights are made of stretch fabric. The nylon/spandex tight is not necessarily rain functional. However, there are some with top-leg panels of wind/rain-resistant or fleece-bonded insulating fabrics. Blackbottom makes all-weather tights with pleats at the knees (Fig. 4-24). Lite-Speed's version has a roomy knee panel (Fig. 4-25). What you wear under any wind/rain gear will depend on weather conditions at the time of your ride.

Boots, also known as booties, to pull on over cycling shoes (in rainy or cold conditions) are available (Fig. 4-26). They either pull on or have zippered backs. Neoprene, a molded (yet stretchy) material which can be sandwiched between layers of nylon, is used as insulating material in boots. It is durable, blocks wind and (when wet) maintains body warmth. Cannondale Corporation and Performance offer cycling boots. Neoprene is also used in headbands and facemasks.

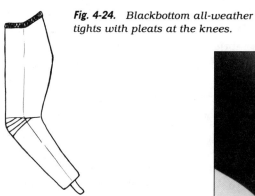

Fig. 4-24. *Blackbottom all-weather tights with pleats at the knees.*

Fig. 4-25. *Lite-Speed's tights have a roomy knee panel.*

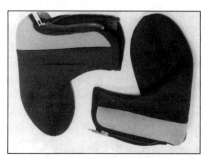

Fig. 4-26. *These booties can zip over bike shoes for cold-weather comfort.*

Weightier Fabrics: Cool to Frigid Weather

If you cycle in cold weather or in areas where temperatures can fluctuate drastically or suddenly, it is wise to be familiar with causes, effects and prevention of hypothermia.

Much touted requisites for cold-weather dress are still true. One, it is important to wear a hat because a great amount of heat is lost from a bare head. Two, layering is also an old standby and is still the best defense against variable and/or cold weather. Wearing clothing in layers makes it possible for you to adjust, not only to weather but to your body's heat and perspiration output. Gloves that are flexible, thin, wind/rain-resistant, and warm are a must. Finally, a wind/rain shell is the icing on the cake. This lightweight covering takes the brunt of wind, rain or snow. It can increase the effective warmth of a wool shirt/sweater or polar fleece jacket without adding much weight.

Following is one system for layering garments. Choose at least three layers and adjust them depending on your body's requirements and harshness of the climate. The layer closest to the body should be long underwear. Follow this layer with appropriate active-wear. A final layer is some form of outerwear which might incorporate batting as an insulator. An active outdoor person should, in each layer, choose the fabric and garment that gives the most warmth for weight, as well as maximum flexibilty and comfort.

Underwear Layer: To be most effective underwear should fit snugly. Silk underwear works only if you perspire lightly. Washable lightweight wool or wool blends are effective if you are not allergic. Even when wet, wool can keep the body warm and dry in wind and rain. (SuperWash wool is Australian merino wool, which is soft, nonabrasive, durable and washable.) Polypropylene is a synthetic with excellent wicking action. It insulates against wind. It stays warm when wet although it does not stay wet long. Follow washing instructions carefully (REI's ReFRESH). Machine drying can cause the fabric to feel abrasive. New technology has eliminated the odd odor previously associated with this fiber. Du Pont claims its Thermax (hollow-core fiber) fabric meets and exceeds all of polypropylene's characteristics. (Cannondale Corporation's Team Issue Superskin Tight, Helly-Hansen's Lifa Super and Performance's Underwear of Thermax are examples of available underwear.) Other items that fit in this underwear category and are also available in the same fabrics are socks, knit hats, earbands, glove liners and helmet liners.

Active-Wear Layer: This group includes all the styles of active-wear described earlier. However, jerseys have long sleeves, higher collars, and are made from fabrics that insulate, such as SuperWash Wool, Du Pont's Thermax, W. L. Gore's Thermodry, and Allied Signal's Hydrofil. (Active-wear available: Performance's Apex and Terminator winter jerseys.) Winter tights are also available in the above fabrics. Another option to tights is leg and arm warmers, tubular casings that slide over the arm and legs. (Baleno offers both spandex/nylon and fleece in single- or double-knee styles. ShaverSport also has leg/arm warmers.) A fabric used for jerseys that has not been mentioned is synthetic fleece (pile). Synthetic fleece is lightweight and soft. It comes in varying thicknesses known as weights. It resists water and, when water is absorbed, dries quickly. The warmth-to-weight ratio is excellent. Some stretch and resist pilling. Neck warmers, earbands, vests, jackets and jacket liners are also made of pile or fleece. (Names to look for are Du Pont's Polarlite and Polartek, Maiden Mills' Polarite and Polarplus.)

Insulating Layer: Synthetic insulation, in the form of batting, is lofty (thick in appearance but lightweight). It is constructed to trap body heat and to prevent its rapid dissipation to colder air. Trapped warm air maintains warmth. Batting is designed to imitate goose down which (when dry and of good quality) is the best insulator for its weight. Synthetics, however, absorb less water and retain much of their warming capability even when wet. Jackets, parkas and insulated pants are among the active-wear items in this group, as well as other smaller but equally important items such as balaclavas, gloves, insoles (3M's Thinsulate) for shoes, earbands, and ear coverings that slip onto helmet chin straps (Helmuffs) (Fig. 4-27). Insulation material represented in this group is also used in sleeping bags. (Trade names: Wiggy's Lamilite, Du Pont's Holofil II, Moonstone Mountaineering's Moonlite, Hoechst-Celanese's Novaloft, 3M's Thinsulate.)

Off-Road Wear

For cyclists who use their all-terrain bikes on roads or city paths, the active-wear already described is recommended. The active-wear needs of an off-road cyclist are somewhat different. The off-roader sits in a more upright position on the bike, and terrain is varied and, at times, much more difficult. An upright position places less stress on the back and sleeves of a jersey. On hot days or dry trails, underarm mesh-inserts provide rapid evaporation and cooling. Rough terrain calls for tough, padded or reinforced shorts or tights. If shorts are worn, then thick wool knee shocks or neoprene guards protect vulnerable shins and kneepads cover knees. Socks (for any type of cycling) should be chosen carefully.

Fig. 4-27. Helmuffs fasten to your helmet.

Look for flat toe seams, extra cushioning on top for protection on the upstroke, dual layers that have been designed to protect against friction (which can cause blisters), and added padding for heels. Long-sleeved shirts help protect arms from abrasive foliage. Stretchy shorts or tights are necessary for the muscular expansions/contractions and twisting/turning movements required to climb hills and to maneuver tricky terrain. Sorry, jeans are too confining—you'll exert more energy and wear out sooner because you are working against stiff fabric.

A few of the manufacturers producing off-road-specific lines (who sent either samples or literature) are PearliZumi, Cannondale Corporation, Hind, and Lite-Speed. In any case, check your local bike stores for these and other active-wear options for off-road biking that will suit your needs and taste.

To give you a bit of a head start, here's a rundown of active-wear samples or brochure descriptions. Unfortunately, some brochures were in black and white; therefore, it is difficult to comment on color effect, although, for the most part, colors are bold and/or bright.

PearliZumi's line is labeled "Gonzo Abusive." This line includes (1) loose-fitting shorts made of abrasion-resistant fabric which feature large pockets with snap closures, (2) specially padded briefs to be worn under loose-fit shorts, (3) heavier-weight spandex shorts with removable impact hip-pads, (4) knicker-length shorts with padded knees, and (5) jerseys with extra fabric lamination as an added protective layer.

Cannondale Corporation has a line called "Shred Threads." This line includes (1) an anorak made of nylon Supplex which features Polartek inserts and drawstring waist and collar, (2) shorts Cannondale calls "hip baggy sport shorts," which have poly/Lycra mesh briefs complete with crotch liner, and (3) a heavyweight long-sleeved shirt. This line sports vivid "Victory Blue," "Jungle Green" and ebony color combinations.

Hind's brochure lists the "Explorer" and "Maniac" lines. The "Explorer" group includes (1) a "rayon/polyester mini-mesh" jersey and (2) cargo-pocketed nylon shorts with built-in liner. The "Maniac" line includes (1) a jersey similar to the "Explorer" model with the exception that it has long sleeves and (2) heavyweight spandex shorts "with protective panels." Aqua, cobalt, "purple haze, sunset" colors are used in various combinations with white, black and slate to produce striking color designs.

Finally, Lite-Speed (from Eugene, OR) not only supplied brochures and informational articles (about fabrics and active-wear construction) but provided generous samples. Everything from jerseys and shorts with DayGlo zebra-swoosh detailing, to jerseys with spirited rainbow bands across chest, collar, and cuffs, to tie-dyed loose-fit Supplex shorts was included. Although Lite-Speed does not have (at this time) an off-road-specific line, they do have a quality line of both loose-fitting and spandex shorts that would serve very well for off-road wear. "Knickerskins" are spandex shorts (Fig. 4-28) that are cut below the knee and would provide protection for off-road cycling. Another unique item from this company's line is a pair of briefs called Underskins. Underskins are made of very lightweight nylon spandex. The uniqueness is found in the contour-cut crotch liner. Its fleece liner is constructed with pocketlike spaces which can be fitted with foam pads of varying thicknesses. This system of

Fig. 4-28. Lite-Speed Knickerskins are spandex shorts, cut below the knee, that provide protection for off-road cycling.

interchangeable pads (Fig. 4-29) is called Airskin Padding and can be used in Lite-Speed's Pedaler (nylon/spandex) and Traveler (Supplex nylon) shorts models (Fig. 4-30). Add as many layers of this padding as you need for protection against pubic bone pain on rough trails. Ultra-Max III fabric (similar to Coolmax) is used to construct most (if not all) of their jerseys.

Gloves for Off-Road

Gloves for any type of cycling need to pad palms against road/trail shock, have finger openings that fit snugly without binding, and have no bulky seams in the palm. If your ride could be a chilly one, you will need

Fig. 4-29. System of interchangeable pads is called AirSkin Padding and can be used in Lite-Speed's Pedaler (nylon/spandex) and Traveler (Supplex nylon) shorts models.

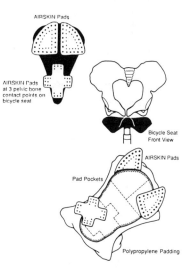

Fig. 4-30. Lite-Speed's Traveler (Supplex nylon) shorts.

gloves with some sort of insulation, e.g., wool or synthetic dot-gloves (dot-gloves have little gripper dots on the palm and fingers), glove liners, or Thinsulate lining. In addition to the above characteristics, off-road gloves need to have longer finger lengths for added protection against scrapes, an effective gripping system for control on rough trails, and, hopefully, fabric that provides excellent ventilation. Two examples of available gloves: (1) Terra Firma Mountain Gloves, in Campmore's catalog, have washable synthetic leather palms, terry/spandex backs, longer finger length, and Tuff-Grip on palm, thumb and index finger. (2) Specialized has extra sturdy gloves for trail use (Fig. 4-31.).

Women's Active-Wear

Until recently, many manufacturers have used "unisex" sizing only. However, women differ from men in their anatomical structure. The differences are longer legs than torso, smaller and higher waists, larger hips, and wider pelvis. Therefore, some companies are now extending their lines to include active-wear constructed and sized specifically for women. All of the aforementioned manufacturers, as well as other manufacturers (Bellwether, Blackbottom, and Descente) now have women's lines. Hind ("For Women Only" label) and Cannondale are two companies who also redesigned their crotch liners (butterfly-shaped) to provide more accurate cushioning. Along with better fit come new items of active-wear which directly accommodate female anatomy. One item is T-back bras (or crop top), with or without mesh liners, for added support. The T-back (Fig. 4-32) allows for support as well as freedom from mid-

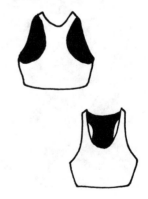

Fig. 4-32. T-back bras (or crop top), with or without mesh liners, give added support.

Fig. 4-31. Specialized has extra sturdy gloves for trail use.

shoulder straps, which can slip or bind when the body is in cycling position. It also affords the coolness of a swimsuit-style top (and you should keep sunscreen applied). Another article designed with cooling quality in mind is the sleeveless tank top which has the same construction as cycling jerseys with the exception of sleeves. Blackbottom offers a more feminine look in its jersey and culotte combo. Hopefully, women's active-wear lines will improve with age and ingenuity.

Designed for Safety

Safe riding at any time of the day (and, if you must, evening) is absolutely necessary. Safety-conscious cyclists can promote safety in their active-wear additions and choices. Reflector tape is a safety feature that can be added to active-wear. Reflective leg or arm bands and vests can be worn over other garments. Cyclists can choose more visible colors that are called DayGlo or neon. Finally, Hind is offering reflective 3M Scotch-lite (300 times brighter than white, visible at 2,000 feet) decorative panels on side-thigh and rear of their Night-Blade shorts.

Gadgets

There are numerous gadgets for cycling, e.g. suspenders, watches, cyclometers, seat pads, and helmet covers. Some, such as sunglasses, have a more vital function. If you buy glasses especially designed for cycling watch for scratch/shatter/fog resistance, good depth perception and upper and peripheral vision in the cycling position, ultraviolet ray blockers, and ventilation. Some glasses are designed to use interchangeable lenses for different light conditions. Others have elastic headbands or built in sweatbands. Most all specially designed sunglasses are spendy.

Conclusion

Sunglasses are not the only costly accessory items for cycling. To complete a functional active-wear wardrobe requires some expense. At the least, be an informed buyer, shop, consider, and choose wisely (based on your own needs and pocketbook). You need to (1) talk to other cyclists, (2) read labels, (3) ask questions and continue to ask questions until you are satisfied, (4) try on garments (bend, sit, and move in them), (5) check construction details (try zippers for ease of movement, see that layers of cloth are evenly sewn into seams, look for broken seam threads and even hems, stretch the stretchy garments and listen for thread pops, and (6) think about the safety factors you need.

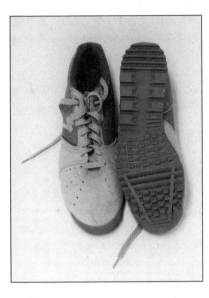

Fig. 4-33. Wear ventilated off-road shoes such as this Specialized model.

Fig. 4-34. Nike trail shoes have grip pattern in a heavy sole for foot protection.

Fig. 4-35. Use good hiking shoes in cold weather. Note the aggressive sole pattern that provides ground-gripping stability when you need to put a leg out to stay upright.

Shoes

In hot weather wear low-cut, well-ventilated shoes designed for off-road riding, such as Specialized (Fig. 4-33) or Nike (Fig. 4-34). These shoes have thick, sturdy soles that protect the tender underside of your feet from the pressure of pedaling on sawtooth-edged pedals. The shoes also have a grip pattern in case you have to put a foot out to stay upright or have to walk your bike up a slippery trail. Wear good hiking shoes (Fig. 4-35) in colder weather and on rougher terrain.

Now let's get down to the nitty gritty of bicycle maintenance, starting with brakes in the next chapter.

5

How to Give Your Brakes a Break

You're tearing down a steep hill on a country lane or a dirt fire trail in the woods, going all out. Around the next curve there's an angry rhino waiting to gore you, or a troop of Boy Scouts marching four abreast, a rattlesnake warming itself in a pool of sunshine, possibly a horse and rider on a narrow trail. This is abolutely no time for your brakes to fail or malfunction. You never know what's right there around the bend, on the road or trail. You need to be able to stop, or at least to keep your speed under control. In this chapter you'll learn how to use your brakes and how to keep them in safe operating condition so they work when you need them.

TOOLS YOU WILL NEED

You need the right tools to work on your brakes. The bicycle industry has yet to standardize the sizes of nuts and bolts used. Such lack of uniformity is, in a way, understandable since bicycles and bicycle components sold in the United States are made also in Japan, Taiwan, South Korea, France, Germany, Italy, Great Britain and other countries.

For example, some brakes need a 19-mm wrench to equalize spring tension to keep brake shoes evenly spaced from the rim. Other makes of brakes use a 2-mm Allen wrench for the same purpose. The tool list that follows may include more tools than you need for the brakes you have, but the overrun will be small and inexpensive. If your bike shop does not carry a particular tool, let me refer you to The Third Hand. This outfit carries every bike tool known to man, and some unknown ones. Their catalog is enough to make a bike mechanic swoon. To reach The Third Hand, phone them at 916-926-2600, FAX them at 916-926-2663 or write them at Box 212, Mt. Shasta, CA 96067. They are a boon to cycling folk.

Torque Wrench: Torque is the force required to produce a twisting motion around an axis, as when you turn a nut or bolt to tighten or loosen it. You need a torque wrench to ensure that the bolts and nuts on a bicycle are safely tight. Bicycle component manufacturers specify tightness in inch-pounds, so buy a torque wrench calibrated in inch-pounds. If you have to use a foot-pound torque wrench, translate the inch-pound specification into foot-pounds by dividing by 12. For example, if you need to tighten a nut to 36 inch-pounds, divide 36 by 12 to obtain the correct torque of 3 foot-pounds. Bicycle component manufacturers located outside the United States commonly use metric measurements instead of inch-pounds or foot-pounds as their torque specifications. Use Table 5-1 to change metric torques to inch-pounds or foot-pounds.

Table 5-1 CONVERSION OF METRIC MEASUREMENTS TO INCH-POUNDS OR FOOT-POUNDS

cm-kg $\div$ 1.15 = inch/pounds
cm-kg $\div$ 13.8 = foot/pounds
m/kg = foot-pounds $\times$ .1383
Foot-pounds = m-kg $\times$ 7.2329

Foot-pounds $\times$ 12 = inch-pounds
Inch-pounds divided by 12 = foot-pounds

Throughout the technical section of this book I will give torque specifications in inch-pounds for every nut and bolt on a bicycle. Take it easy if you use a foot-pound wrench, because that monster can snap off a bike bolt with just a slight overtorque.

Use a torque wrench to tighten or to check the tightness of a bolt or nut. Turn the torque wrench clockwise (tightening direction) to test the tightness of a nut or bolt. If you turn the torque wrench in the loosening direction (counterclockwise), you will find that the "breakaway" measurement is a lot less than the torque you applied when you tightened the nut (clockwise). For example, I tightened a nut to 150 inch-pounds (clockwise). Then I turned the torque wrench counterclockwise to loosen this nut. The nut turned (broke away) at 100 inch-pounds, which, of course, did not accurately reflect my original tightening torque of 150 inch-pounds.

Use a torque wrench to *check how tight* a bolt or nut is by turning the nut or bolt with the torque wrench in the tightening direction. As you apply pressure on the wrench, watch the nut or bolt carefully. Stop the instant it starts moving. The reading on the torque wrench is the tightness of the bolt or nut. Use a torque wrench to tighten a nut or bolt. Watch the indicator as you turn the wrench. Stop the instant the indicator reaches the torque setting you want.

There are three types of torque wrenches. The beam-type torque wrench (Fig. 5-1) is not as accurate as the click type (Fig. 5-2) or the dial type (Fig. 5-3). However, it is inexpensive, around $25 from Sears

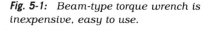
Fig. 5-1: *Beam-type torque wrench is inexpensive, easy to use.*

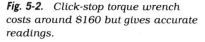
Fig. 5-2. *Click-stop torque wrench costs around $160 but gives accurate readings.*

Fig. 5-3. *Dial-type torque wrench is the most accurate, easiest to use but most expensive, around $173.*

Roebuck or an auto supply store, and is adequate for home use. The click type, made by Proto Tools, costs around $160. The more accurate dial type, also made by Proto, goes for around $173. I recommend the dial type for use by bike shops or bicycle clubs or wherever a lot of bicycle repair and maintenance is performed.

Use Table 5-2 as a general guide to safe tightness of brake parts. These torque specifications are from brake manufacturers' technical literature.

Table 5-2 TORQUE SPECIFICATIONS FOR BRAKES

Part	See Fig. No.	Tightness in Inch-Pounds
Brake shoe in brake arm	5-4, 5-5	50–80
Cable carrier binder bolt	5-6	50–75
Crossover cable binder bolt	5-7	50–75
Brake arm mounting bolt	5-8	50–75
Brake lever mounting bolt	5-9 (E)	50–65

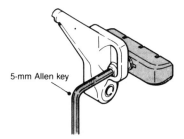

5-mm Allen key

Fig. 5-4. Brake shoe is held in brake arm by a binder bolt. Check its tightness every few months, depending on bike use.

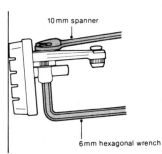

10 mm spanner

6 mm hexagonal wrench

Fig. 5-5. Another way of securing the brake shoe in the brake arm permits toe-in as shown.

Fig. 5-6. Make sure the main brake cable is tightly held by the cable carrier binder bolt (pencil). Tighten this bolt to 50–70 inch-pounds.

Fig. 5-7. *Tighten the crossover cable binder bolt in the brake arm to 50–75 inch-pounds.*

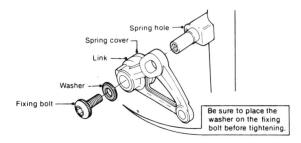

Fig. 5-8. *Brake arm fixing bolt should be tightened to 50–75 inch-pounds.*

Fig. 5-9. *Tighten the brake lever binder bolt (arrows) to 50–65 inch-pounds.*

More Tools

To work on your bike you need some way to hold it up off the floor and at a convenient height. You could hang your bike by padded hooks from the ceiling, but the bike won't hold still that way. Best solution is a bike workstand, such as the Park stand which collapses compactly when not in use (Fig. 5-10) or a Blackburn bench stand you can bolt to a workbench (Fig. 5-11). You also need:

    1. A set of Allen (hex) wrenches in 2, 2.5, 3, 4, 5 and 6 mm sizes (Fig. 5-12).

    2. Wrenches in 8, 9, 10 and 11 mm sizes (Fig. 5-13).

    3. A 19-mm thin cone-type open-end wrench if you use SunTour XCD brakes so you can adjust spring tension to keep brake shoes evenly spaced on each side of the wheel rim.

Fig. 5-10. A good workstand, such as this foldable Park unit, makes bike maintenance a lot easier than struggling with a bike that wants to move around as you work on it. The stand arm is rotatable so you can get at the bike right side up or, as shown, work on the bike when it's upside down.

Fig. 5-11. Bolt this Blackburn bike holder to your workbench to make bike maintenance a lot easier.

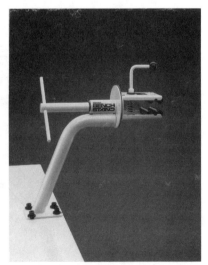

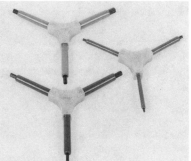

Fig. 5-13. *You need these metric wrenches from Park for brake maintenance and for other work on your bike.*

Fig. 5-12. *A set of Park metric Allen wrenches is a must for shop and on-the-road maintenance.*

4. Cable cutter. Optional, but snips off brake and derailleur cables neatly, so ends don't unravel before you can solder them closed. This tool is made by SunTour and does work very well.

5. Soldering iron and solder. Optional, but a neat and easy way to solder cut ends of cables to keep them from unraveling. This also makes it easy to remove cables for servicing components and reinstall the same cable.

6. A Park third hand (Fig. 5-14) or a NSH third hand (Fig. 5-15) to hold shoes tightly against the rim while you adjust the cable. You could use a toe strap, but the third hands shown here are far easier to use.

7. A Park fourth hand (Fig. 5-16). Holds the cable taut while you tighten the cable binder bolt.

8. No. 282 LocTite (the kind that does not harden to ironlike consistency but does keep nuts and bolts from rattling loose). Use LocTite on all bolts and nuts *except* hubs, bottom brackets, pedal bearings and headsets. Keep it away from brake shoes and rims!

BRAKING TECHNIQUE

Before we get into brake maintenance, here's a brief review of safe brake operation. First, remember that your *front* brake provides some 90 percent of the total braking power of *both* brakes combined. Let me illustrate. Place a book on the table, with one end against one hand. Think of that hand as the front brake. Now, with your other hand, push the

Fig. 5-15. *Another type of third hand is a cable clamp which holds brake shoes tightly against the wheel rim.*

Fig. 5-14. *Use this third-hand tool by Park to clamp brake shoes against the wheel rim when making brake adjustments.*

Fig. 5-16. *Hold the brake cable taut with this fourth-hand brake tool from Park, when removing cable stretch or installing a new brake cable.*

other end of the book. You will see that the brake hand stops the book, but the rear of the book rises up off the table. That is what happens when you apply the brakes. The rear wheel tends to rise in the air and lose contact with the ground. Obviously, the less contact, the less braking power. If for some reason your rear brake is not working (for all the reasons I cite below in the brake adjustment section), the front wheel may lock up. When that happens you could be pitched forward off the bike and get hurt—which is a good reason to make darned sure *both* your brakes are in good working order.

Always apply both brakes at the same time, never the front one alone. If you apply only the front brake you risk an "endo" or a pitch over the handlebars. Another reason for the poor performance of the rear brake is its much longer cable. Just the part of the cable that goes through the spaghetti tubing measures 9 inches on the front and some 30 inches on the rear brake on a typical ATB. The extra 21 inches of cable tubing means a lot more friction at the brake lever. It takes more hand pressure to apply the rear brake than the front one. The longer rear cable also stretches far more than the shorter front cable. If you're going downhill fast, keep your weight as far back as possible for maximum braking ability. If you have to make an emergency stop on the flat, shift your bottom as far back on the saddle as possible as you brake. That way you put more weight over the rear wheel for safer braking.

Brake before you corner! If you brake *as* you corner, the bike could skid out from under you. Slow down *before* you come to a sharp turn. Keep the inboard pedal upright for maximum pedal-to-ground clearance.

Practice braking on a variety of surfaces, such as sand, gravel or cement, until you become familiar with how the brakes work and how you and the bike react. Be especially careful on slippery surfaces, such as sand, snow, mud or ice. Avoid braking so hard that you lock up one or both wheels.

Wet weather cuts braking power substantially! Be aware that you will likely travel *60 feet* on the flat at 5 mph before you come to a stop in wet weather. Slow down and apply brakes sooner when it's raining.

If your bike has steel rims, remember that brakes don't grip as well as they do on aluminum, especially in wet weather.

Brake shoes harden with age. As they harden, you lose braking power. You may be able to come to a gradual, *anticipated* stop, even with hardened brake shoes. But rocklike brake shoes won't stop you in an emergency, when you need full braking power. If you have had your bike for over two years, I recommend you replace all four brake shoes, even if they *look* okay. (Please see brake shoe replacement instructions later.) When you do buy new shoes, take the old ones to the bike shop for an exact same replacement.

The Consumer Products Safety Commission requires that a rider of 150 pounds, going at 15 mph on a flat, smooth, dry surface (such as a concrete roadway) with the wind velocity less than 7 mph (direction not specified) be able to stop within 15 feet of initial brake application (both brakes). As a practical matter, the heavier you are, the longer it's going to take you to stop. Conversely, the lighter you are, the sooner you can stop, so muscular heavyweights should anticipate braking needs for a safe, controlled stop.

Check your brakes every 500 miles or every two months worth of *riding* time (not calendar time). Here's how. On a dry, hard-surfaced traffic-free street, chalk a length of 15 feet. If you have a speedometer on your bike, fine. If not, just get going at a good clip, to an estimated 15 mph, which is a lot faster than you may realize on a bike. Most of us, if we don't know, almost always think we're going faster than we are. Once up to speed, apply both brakes, carefully at first. If you overshoot and can't stop within 15 feet, make several tries. Apply the brakes harder each time. If you always overshoot, your brakes are defective. Here's how to keep them in safe operating condition.

BRAKE MAINTENANCE AND SAFETY

I would like to repeat a warning I made in Chapter 2: that is, never buy a bicycle from any store other than a store that sells *only* bicycles. A professional bicycle store has trained mechanics who check and, if necessary, readjust the brakes before you ride off on your new bike. Other outlets have back room stockboys who may be untrained bicycle mechanics. The abysmal condition of new bikes (particularly their brakes) on disply at general merchandise stores or discount outlets is testimony to the hazardous condition of many of these bicycles. The Consumer Products Safety Commission did a good job of mandating what it takes to make a safe bicycle. The trouble is these regulations seem to stop with their printed manual. Or the CPSC may pass a bike at the factory, but they seem to be understaffed when it comes to checking "assembled" bikes at the retail level. Nor do CPSC requirements include the credentials of bicycle assemblers at the retail level. Even the most expensive bike can have bad brakes if assembled by some klutz of a stockboy and purchased by an unwary customer. When it comes to bikes, caveat emptor, "let the buyer beware," should be your motto, because it's your life that's on the line.

What to Check

A loose bolt or nut on a brake can spell disaster! I received a new ATB from a manufacturer to test for this book. On my very first ride the main front brake cable slipped right out of the cable carrier (Fig. 5-6), leaving me with just the rear brake to stop with. Fortunately I was going slowly on a traffic-free road. I know, I know, I should have squeezed the brake lever hard first, to make sure the cable binder bolts were tight. That's the danger of making assumptions; you could be wrong. Assuming effective quality control can be hazardous to your health! The crossover cable end, where it's held by the binder bolt in the brake arm (Fig. 5-7), may also slip if that bolt is not tight enough. The crossover cable is the short cable that rides in the cable carrier. One end of the crossover cable has a leaded tab (Fig. 5-17) that can be pulled out of the brake arm when the brake shoes are squeezed together, to let the fat tire fit past the brake shoes when you remove and replace the wheel. The other end of the crossover cable is held in the brake arm by a binder bolt (Fig. 5-7). Check all brake nuts and bolts at least every six months to the safe torque tightness in Table 5-2.

Loose Brake Shoe Binder Bolts and Nuts: If the nut that holds the brake shoe in the brake arm (Fig. 5-4 and Fig. 5-5) works loose, *the brake shoe can dodge down under the rim* (Fig. 5-18). If that happens, no brake. Or as has happened on three road bike accident cases on which I was an expert witness in the ensuing litigation, a loose brake shoe binder bolt permitted the brake shoe to pop up so it rubbed on the tire wall. Figure 5-19 shows a bike where this happened. You can see that the brake shoe is tilted upward so there is rubber-to-rubber contact between the brake shoes and the tire sidewall. This contact brings the brake shoes even closer to the tire than it was to the rim, because the tire is fatter than the rim. (ATB fat tires are more vulnerable to such wheel lockup.) When the front wheel locks up, all the forward momentum of the rider and the bike is concentrated on the front wheel axle. This

Fig. 5-17.   *Fit the leaded end of the crossover cable in the slot on the brake arm. To remove a wheel, squeeze the brake shoes against the rim and pull the crossover cable leaded end out of the brake arm. This spreads the brake shoes apart so you can pull the fat tire wheel out of the bike.*

Fig. 5-18.   *If the brake shoe binder bolt works loose, the brake shoe can dodge down under the rim, as shown here. If this happens you will lose braking. Avoid this hazard by checking tightness of the brake shoe binder bolts every few months.*

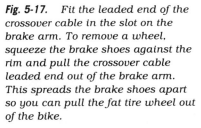

Fig. 5-19. *Another reason to make sure the brake shoes are held tightly in the brake arms. Here, as you can see (arrow) the brake shoe has moved up to where it grabbed the rubber tire sidewall. When the rider braked, the front wheel locked up and caused an accident. The accident involved a skinny-tired road bike, but can also occur on a fat-tired ATB.*

instantaneous transference of force or energy is absorbed by the fork blades as the bicycle comes to a screaming halt and propels the rider off the bike, over the handlebars, or to one side or the other. In the three accidents I noted above, the fork blades were bent backward in an identical S-shaped pattern (Fig. 5-20). Two of the bike accidents occurred in the Midwest, the other in the Northwest, thousands of miles and three or four years apart. These accidents resulted in serious injury to the rider. They happened on mild, dry days on smooth concrete.

There are two possible scenarios that contributed to these accidents. When the rider applied the brakes, one or both brake shoes popped up and grabbed the tire. Instant lockup. The brake shoe binder bolts were loose enough (possibly had become loose because of vibration) to permit the shoes to work their way upward and grab the fatter tire. Instant lockup. Yet another reason for brake shoe pop-up and rim grab is lack of toe-in. Toe-in is where the front of the brake shoe contacts the rim first, as described later in this chapter. If the *rear* of the brake shoe contacts the rim first, the shoe may dig into the rim and force it upward, where it will grab the tire and cause instant wheel lockup and an accident. A combination of no toe-in plus insufficiently tightened brake shoe binder bolts can make brake shoe tire grab quite likely. Please see the brake shoe adjustment section of this chapter for toe-in instructions.

Exposed Springs: The springs on some brakes are exposed and could pop out from behind the stub that holds them in tension (arrow, Fig. 5-21). If you have such a brake, make sure the spring is in proper position, at full tension, especially if you have worked on the brake or if you have transported your bike.

Fig. 5-20. *The is the bike in Figure 5-19. Note that the front wheel lockup that occurred when the brake shoe grabbed the tire also forced the fork blades backward.*

Fig. 5-21. *Some ATB cantilever brakes have an exposed spring. Make sure the spring is held in tension, behind the brake arm stub (arrow). Otherwise the brake shoe will drag on the wheel rim.*

Handlebar Height Adjustment: I have said this before, but I'll say it again. If you have moved the handlebars up or down on your ATB, you *must* readjust the front brake shoe rim clearance. If you *raised* the handlebars, the brake shoes move *closer* to the rim, so close you may have wheel lockup. If you *lowered* the handlebars, the brake shoes will be *farther* from the rim. If you lowered the handlebars a lot, you may have little or no front brake.

Types of Brakes

Take a look at your bike so you can identify which type of brake you have. All types of brakes have adjustments in common, but some have special requirements you should, for your own safety, know about. There are four types of brakes used on ATBs: *cantilever* (Fig. 5-22), *U-brakes* (Fig. 5-23), *cam action* (Fig. 5-24), and two makes of *hydraulic* design, the Mathauser hydraulic brake (Fig. 5-25) and the Magura hydraulic brake (Fig. 5-26). Both of these hydraulic brakes can be retrofitted, so you can remove your manual brakes and install a pair of hydraulics if you wish. Have this work done at the bike shop, for safety reasons.

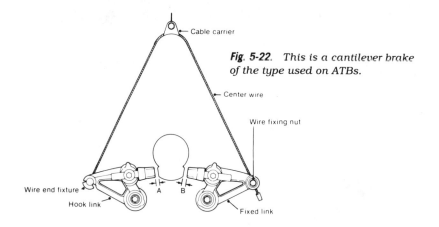

Fig. 5-22. This is a cantilever brake of the type used on ATBs.

Fig. 5-24. This cam-action brake is powerful, but is not widely used by bicycle manufacturers on models built after 1990.

Fig. 5-23. A U-brake design is used on some ATBs.

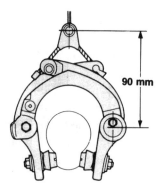

Fig. 5-25. This Mathauser hydraulic brake is powerful, offers precision braking control, eliminates the hassles of cable stretch. An excellent brake.

Fig. 5-26. The Magura hydraulic brake mounts on cantilever brake bosses.

Hydraulic brakes have been on automobiles and motorcycles for at least 56 years. It's about time bicycles had their advantages, which include zero cable stretch and more controllable, graduated and powerful braking action, without any sacrifice in weight. As of this writing these brakes are being introduced.

Cable Stretch

Brake cables stretch over time, sometimes over a very short time, such as during your very first ride. When cables stretch, brake shoes get farther away from the rim. If brake shoes get too far away, the brake lever may bottom out on the handlebars and still not stop you. In addition, as brake shoes get farther away from the rim, braking response time and stopping power are reduced. I'd like to see you go right out to the garage, now, and check your bike for brake cable stretch. Pull on each brake lever as hard as you can, and hold the levers tight. Do they bottom out on the handlebars? When you push the bike while gripping the levers closed, will one or both wheels turn? Let go of the brake levers. Look at the brake shoes. Are they more than ⅛ inch away from the wheel rim (Fig. 5-22)? If so, your brakes are unsafe. You can remove the minor cable stretch at the brake levers. Major cable stretch requires more work.

Let's start with minor cable stretch. These instructions apply to all types of cable-actuated brakes.

How to Remove Minor Cable Stretch

If brake cables have not stretched too far, you can remove this minor cable stretch with a simple adjustment at the brake lever. Both front and rear brake levers have a cable adjuster barrel (Fig. 5-27) to remove minor cable stretch. This barrel has two parts, a locknut (L in Fig. 5-27) and the barrel body (M, Fig. 5-27), which is threaded into the brake lever itself.

Here's how to remove minor cable stretch with the adjusting barrel:

1. Hold the adjuster barrel (M in Fig. 5-27) with one hand while you turn the adjuster barrel locknut (L in Fig. 5-27) a few turns counter-clockwise to loosen it.

2. Hold the barrel locknut while you turn the barrel counterclockwise until brake shoes are about ⅛ inch from the wheel rim. Tighten the barrel locknut against the brake lever body.

Fig. 5-27. Make minor brake shoe-to-rim clearance adjustments at the brake lever. Turn the knurled locknut, L, counterclockwise to loosen it. Turn the adjuster bolt, M, one way or the other to correct brake shoe clearance (see Fig. 5-22).

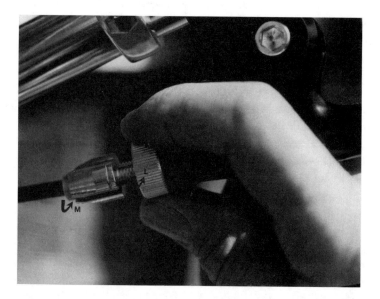

3. Readjust the above until brake shoes are ⅛ inch from the wheel rim. *Note:* This adjustment will be easier if you hold the brake shoes against the rim.

Comment: I prefer more than the ¹/₁₆-inch brake-shoe-to-rim clearance specified by brake manufacturers for two reasons:

   a. *If the brake shoes are within the specified 2-mm clearance (that's a tad over ¹/₁₆ inch) from the rim, and you grab the brake levers, you have little choice but to have the brake shoes pressed hard against the rim, or not at all. I prefer a ⅛-inch clearance so I can modulate brake pressure more accurately. Remember, with only a ¹/₁₆-inch shoe-to-rim clearance the brake lever does not have to travel far to achieve wheel lockup.*

   b. *At the ¹/₁₆-inch shoe-to-rim clearance, any misalignment in the wheel will likely cause one of the brake shoes to drag on the rim, at least until the wheel is retrued. The tendency is to turn the cable adjuster (see below) at the brake lever to move the brake shoe farther away. Do not do this! All you will do is decrease braking power and response time. Instead, true the wheel (see Chapter 9).*

4. If you cannot bring brake shoes ⅛ inch from the rim with these minor adjustments, major cable stretch has occurred and your bike is unsafe to ride until it is removed.

Removing Major Cable Stretch

1. Turn the brake barrel locknut clockwise until it is almost flush against the brake lever body.

2. Turn the brake lever adjuster barrel clockwise as far as possible. Now the adjuster barrel is in position for fine tuning of later minor cable stretch, but brake shoes will be now very far from the wheel rim, much too far for safety. Turn the locknut counterclockwise until it is tight against the brake lever body. Now you are ready to remove major cable stretch.

3. Hold the brake shoes against the rim with a third-hand tool (Fig. 5-14) or with a strap tool (Fig. 5-15).

4. Hold the main brake cable binder bolt in the crossover cable carrier (R in Fig. 5-28) with an 8- or 9-mm wrench (depending on manufacturer). Loosen the binder nut (A in Fig. 5-28) with a 9- or 10-mm wrench.

5. Remove cable slack by pulling on the main brake cable with a pair of needle-nose pliers or use a fourth-hand tool (M in Fig. 5-28).

6. While you hold cable tension on the main brake cable (H in Fig.

Fig. 5-28. Brake cables (H) stretch with use. When they do, brake shoes get too far from the wheel rim for safe braking. For major brake shoe clearance adjustments, clamp brake shoes to the rim, loosen brake cable carrier binder nut (A), use the fourth-hand tool (M) to hold cable tight. Then remove cable slack. Hold binder bolt (R) with one wrench and tighten its nut (A) with another wrench to 50 to 75 inch-pounds. For purposes of identification, the cable carrier is E and the crossover cable is L.

5-28) to remove cable stretch, tighten the cable carrier fixing bolt as shown in step 7 below.

7.   Hold the binder bolt (R in Fig. 5-28) with one wrench, while you tighten its nut, A, to 50 to 75 inch-pounds. Remove the fourth-hand and the third-hand tools if you used them. Check the tightness of the cable fixing bolt by squeezing the appropriate brake lever closed as hard as you can. If the cable slips out of the cable carrier binder bolt, repeat the steps above until the main brake cable will not slip. This tightness check is important, because if the cable slips, the brake is inoperative and you could have an accident if you need to stop and can't. Proceed to fine-tune brake-to-shoe-to-rim clearance as shown in minor stretch removal section above.

Round Cable Carriers Require Special Treatment

Some brakes use a two-piece flat-shaped cable unit (Fig. 5-29) instead of a cable carrier with a channel (Fig. 5-6). As Figure 5-29 shows, the main brake cable, A, is clamped in the carrier, B. The *end* of the main

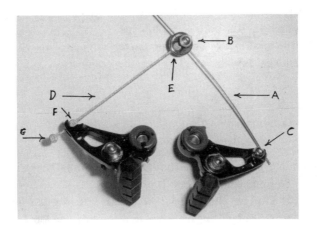

Fig. 5-29. *Round cable carrier. Main brake cable goes through the carrier to the brake stem. See text for parts description.*

brake cable is held by a binder bolt in the brake arm, C. A separate shorter cable, D, has three lead tab ends. One tab end fits into a mating hole in the carrier, E. The other lead tab fits into a slot in the brake arm, F. The remaining tab, G, is a pull tab so this shorter cable can be removed from the brake arm to spread brake shoes apart so the wheel can be removed. To spread brakes apart, squeeze brake shoes together, then pull tab end of cable out of the brake arm. For this type of cable carrier, remove major cable stretch this way:

1. Follow steps 1 to 3 above to readjust the adjuster barrel and clamp brake shoes against the wheel rim.

2. Hold the cable carrier binder bolt with an Allen wrench and turn the binder bolt nut (B in Fig. 5-29) counterclockwise two or three turns, or just enough so the main brake cable is loose in the carrier.

3. Turn the cable binder bolt on the brake arm (C in Fig. 5-29) with an Allen wrench counterclockwise two or three turns, just enough so you can pull the main brake carrier slack through it (and through the cable carrier, too). Use pliers if necessary.

4. Tighten the cable binder bolt on the brake arm to 50–75 inch-pounds.

5. Push the cable carrier up so the main brake cable and the shorter cable are the same length. This is important so both brake shoes can be pressed evenly against the wheel rim when the brake lever is squeezed.

6. Tighten the cable carrier binder bolt to 50–75 inch-pounds.

7. Check cable binder bolt tightness by squeezing the brake lever hard. Retighten binder bolts if cable slips.

8. Use the brake lever adjuster barrel as shown above to remove any remaining cable slack and to bring the brake shoes ⅛ inch from the rim.

Other Brake Shoe Adjustments

1. *Brake shoes should be about ¹⁄₃₂ inch, no more than that, from the rim top* (left in Fig. 5-30). Shoes should also be parallel to the rim (center, Fig. 5-30). To make these two adjustments:

2. Hold the brake shoe binder bolt with one wrench (an Allen or open-end wrench, depending on brake make) while you loosen the binder bolt nut with another wrench (as shown in Fig. 5-31), or use a 10-mm wrench (Fig. 5-32) (depending on make and model of brake). Move the brake shoe up or down until it is ¹⁄₃₂ inch below and parallel to the rim top.

3. *Brake shoes should toe-in* (as shown in Fig. 5-33). On some brakes this toe-in can be made by rotating an eccentric washer at the brake binder bolt. Toe-in permits the rear of the brake shoe to contact the rim last. Toe-in also helps reduce squeaking when you apply the brakes hard. Leave about ¹⁄₃₂ inch at the trailing (rear) end of the brake block.

4. *After making all the adjustments above, both brake shoes should be equidistant from the wheel rim.* Depending on the make of brake, there are several ways to equalize brake shoe distance on both sides of the rim. First, however, check the wheel to make sure brake shoe drag is not caused by an out-of-line wheel rim. Spin the wheel. Watch where the rim passes a brake shoe. If the rim comes closer to, then farther away from, the shoe, realign the rim before more adjustments. Please see Chapter 9 for wheel truing instructions.

Fig. 5-30. *Keep brake shoes aligned with wheel rim, left, and parallel to the rim, center. Toe-in the brake shoe, with the closest trailing edge of the brake shoe about ¹⁄₆₄ to ¹⁄₃₂ inch from the wheel rim.*

Align the brake shoe   Shoe and rim   Open about
with the rim surface.   should be parallel.   0.5—1.0 mm.

Fig. 5-31. Adjust brake shoe by holding the binder bolt with an Allen wrench, loosening its bolt with another wrench and moving the shoe up or down and aligned with the rim. Shoe should be about ¹⁄₃₂ inch from rim top and parallel to it.

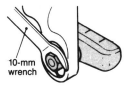

Fig. 5-32. On some brake models, a 10-mm wrench loosens the brake shoe binder bolt in the brake arm.

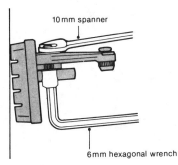

Fig. 5-33. Adjust toe-in so brake shoe rear contacts rim last. Loosen brake shoe binder bolt, turn eccentric washer just behind the binder bolt head to adjust toe-in, tighten binder bolt nut while holding binder bolt with Allen wrench, as shown.

Keep brake shoes the same distance from the rim (assuming you have made all the adjustment steps above first) by adjusting brake arm spring tension. Some brakes have an adjuster that can be turned with a 2-mm Allen wrench (Fig. 5-34). The SunTour XCD brake requires a 19-mm wrench (Fig. 5-37) to adjust spring tension. You could also use an adjustable crescent wrench to turn this spring tension nut (Fig. 5-35).

5. *Replace brake shoes* when they wear past the tread and/or become age-hardened or coated with aluminum oxide scraped off an aluminum rim. To replace a shoe, loosen the brake shoe binder bolt (Fig. 5-31). Twist the shoe up so you can pull it out of the brake arm. Replace with a new shoe. Some brake shoes have a directional arrow (Fig. 5-36). Make sure this arrow points in the direction of rim rotation. Years ago some cantilever brake shoes came with one end open. If the open end faced

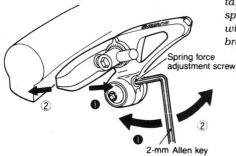

Fig. 5-34. Keep brake shoes equidistant from the wheel rim by adjusting
spring tension on brakes provided
with such a tension screw. Newer
brake models are so equipped.

Fig. 5-35. Use a 19-mm wrench, or
an adjustable crescent wrench as
shown here, to adjust spring tension
on SunTour XCD brakes. Hold the
brake arm mounting bolt with an
Allen wrench when making this adjustment.

Fig. 5-36. Follow directional arrows or embossed directions when installing
new brake shoes. The arrow should point toward the front of the bike.

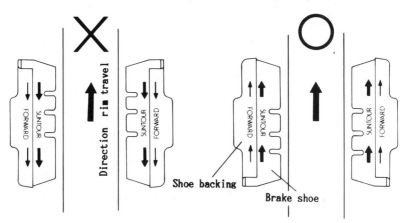

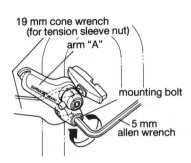

19 mm cone wrench
(for tension sleeve nut)
arm "A"

mounting bolt

5 mm
allen wrench

Fig. 5-37. Check brake main mounting bolt tightness, which should be 50 to 80 inch-pounds.

toward the front of the bike, the brake shoe block would pop right out of its holder on the first brake application. Do not install such a brake shoe on your bike! Readjust brake shoes as above after installing new ones. I recommend installing all four brake shoes rather than just one, for safer, more even braking. Tighten brake shoe binder bolts (mounting bolts) to 50 to 80 inch-pounds. When you replace brake shoes, check tightness of the brake shoe binder bolt by twisting the brake shoe firmly. If the shoe moves, retighten the binder bolt. The shoe must be held very firmly in the brake arm for safety.

6. This is a good time to check the brake mounting bolt tightness (Fig. 5-37), which should be 50–80 inch-pounds.

Brake Cable Installation

Brake cables will eventually fray, wear out and require replacement. Here's how to do it:

1. Hold brake shoes against the rim with a third-hand tool (Fig. 5-14).

2. Loosen the cable carrier binder nut (Fig. 5-6). Pull cable out of the carrier. If your bike has a round cable carrier, see instructions on these carriers above and loosen the main brake cable at the brake arm so you can remove this cable for replacement with a new one.

3. Align the brake lever adjusting barrel so the groove matches the groove in the brake lever (Fig. 5-38). Screw the adjusting barrel all the way in, toward the brake lever.

4. Lift the brake cable upward (Fig. 5-39) and pull the leaded tab end out of the brake lever. If there is a tiny cable end adapter in the brake lever shot where the cable end fits, be sure to save it and use it with the new cable.

Fig. 5-38. *Align adjustable barrel and brake lever slots, O and N, so brake cable can be removed or a new one installed. Leaded end, S, fits into a slotted cut-out in the brake lever.*

Fig. 5-39. *Remove a brake cable by pulling it up until you can pull the leaded end out of the brake lever. Don't lose the tiny little inner cable and adaptor if you need to use it on the replacement cable.*

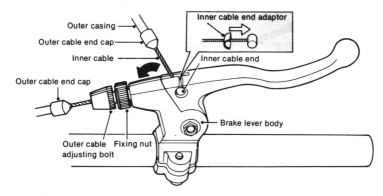

5. Pull the old cable out of its spaghetti tubing, shove a new cable in the tubing and reverse the above steps. Realign the brake shoes as shown earlier in this chapter. *Note:* Campagnolo brake levers (Fig. 5-40) have a unique feature. They accept either ATB type cables (A in Fig. 5-40) or road bike cables (B in Fig. 5-40). Since road bike cables

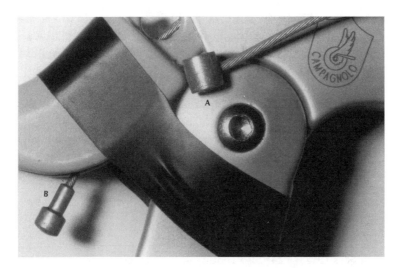

Fig. 5-40. *Campagnolo brake levers accept ATB brake cables, A, or road bike brake cables, B.*

are, at this writing, more readily available than ATB cables, this feature could be a blessing. *Also note:* Only a leaded end no bigger than 7 mm will fit into the new Shimano SLR brake levers. For a replacement that fits, take your old cable to the bike shop for an exact duplicate.

About U-Brakes

U-brakes require a few adjustments separate from those outlined above, although they also require those, such as brake-shoe-to-rim clearance, shoe alignment, toe-in.

1. If your ATB has a U-brake installed at the chainstay level and its brake shoes wear down, a brake arm may contact and rub on the chainwheel (left, Fig. 5-41). The solution here is simple. Move the toe-

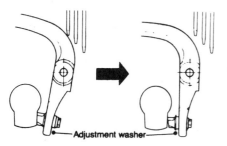

Adjustment washer

Fig. 5-41. *If a U-brake arm rubs on the small chainwheel, as shown at left, move the toe-in adjustment washer from the outside to the inside of the brake arm, as shown at right.*

in adjusting washer to the inside of the brake arm (at right in Fig. 5-41).

2. Note that there is a brake spring tension equalizer bolt which is adjusted with a 2-mm Allen wrench, to bring brake shoes equidistant from the rim (Fig. 5-42).

3. The distance between the bottom of the cable hanger (where the main brake cable spaghetti tubing is held) and the cable carrier should be at least 20 mm (¾ inch or more), as shown in Figure 5-43.

4. The distance from the center line of the cable carrier binder bolt and the center line of the brake arm binder bolt (which holds the brake arm in the bike frame) should be 90 mm (3½ inches), as shown in Figure 5-44.

Cam Brakes

Cam brakes (Fig. 5-24) also require a few special adjustments, which are as follows:

1. To remove a wheel, squeeze the brake shoes against the rim and pull the cam plate out from between the brake arms (Fig. 5-45).

Fig. 5-42. *Keep U-brake shoes equidistant from the wheel rim by turning the spring-force adjuster clockwise or counterclockwise. This drawing also shows the toe-in adjustment washer.*

Fig. 5-43. *Keep the top of the cable carrier of U-brakes 20 mm (¾ inch) or more from the main brake cable hanger. Make this adjustment at the cable carrier binder bolt or the cable slack adjuster on the brake lever. You will need to change brake-shoe-to-rim clearance when you do this adjustment.*

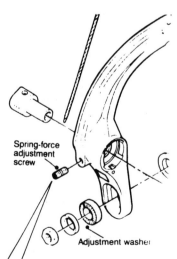

Spring-force
adjustment
screw

Adjustment washer

Installation of the center wire

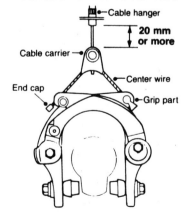

Cable hanger

20 mm
or more

Cable carrier

Center wire

End cap

Grip part

**The best setting is so that the
clearance between the cable
carrier and the pivot boss is
90 mm.**

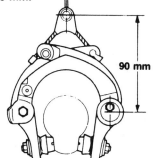

Fig. 5-44. *Keep the distance between
the center line of the brake cable carrier bolt and the center line of the
brake arm mounting bolt about 90
mm (3½ inches), when brake shoes
are held against the wheel rim by
the brake lever.*

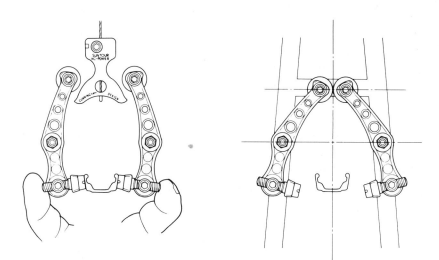

Fig. 5-45. *Remove a wheel from a bike equipped with cam-action brakes this
way: squeeze cam-action brake shoes against the rim, and pull the cam up
from between the brake arms, left, so brake shoes can spread wide enough,
right, for fat-tire clearance.*

   2. To keep brake shoes equidistant from the rim, use a 15-mm wrench
on the adjusting bushing of the brake arm (Fig. 5-46). Turn the bushing
clockwise to increase spring tension, counterclockwise to decrease spring
tension.

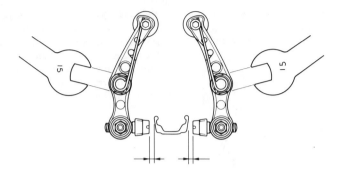

Fig. 5-46. *Keep cam-action brake shoes equidistant from the wheel rim by turing the brake arm mounting bolts with a 15 mm wrench, one way or the other, as necessary.*

A Word About Brake Levers and Brake Shoe Clearance

There are two lengths, or perhaps "styles" would be a better word, for the brake levers that come on ATBs. The "four-finger" design (Fig. 5-47) was until recently original equipment on most ATBs. Now the "two-finger" brake lever design (Fig. 5-48) has become popular. I like the "two-finger" design because you can brake with just two fingers, which means you can keep the other three fingers on the handlebars for steering control. This is an important feature if you're negotiating rough or tricky trails and you need all the steering control you can get.

Some brake levers have a "reach adjuster" (Fig. 5-49 or Fig. 5-50) that moves the lever closer to or farther away from the handlebars,

Fig. 5-48. *A "two-finger" brake lever lets you apply the brakes with two fingers while you keep other steering control with the rest of your hand.*

Fig. 5-47. *A "four-finger" brake lever.*

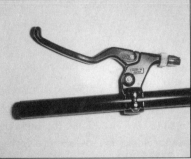

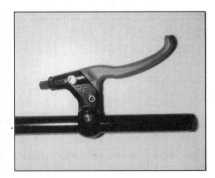

Fig. 5-49. *Most brake levers on better ATBs have a "reach adjuster" that takes a 2-mm Allen wrench. Adjust the brake lever reach to your finger length with this wrench, as shown.*

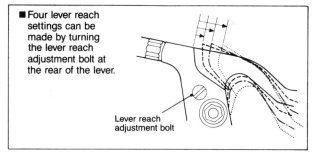

■ Four lever reach settings can be made by turning the lever reach adjustment bolt at the rear of the lever.

Lever reach adjustment bolt

Fig. 5-50. *Other brake lever reach adjusters can be turned with a screwdriver, as shown here.*

depending on your finger length. Use a 2-mm wrench for the adjuster in Figure 5-49 and a screwdriver for the adjuster in Figure 5-50. Some brake levers have a four-position adjustment (Fig. 5-50) or a two-position adjustment (Fig. 5-51).

Brake Lever Position: Loosen the brake lever clamp bolt and move the brake lever on the handlebars to a position most comfortable for you. On the new dual-lever shifter and brake combination, hold the shift lever (Fig. 5-52) out of the way so you can use a 5-mm Allen wrench on the combination lever. Tighten this bolt to 50 to 70 inch-pounds.

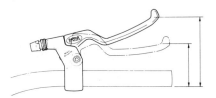

Fig. 5-51. *Maximum distance and minimum distance adjustments of brake lever from the handlebars. Maximum distance is for long fingers.*

Fig. 5-52. Hold shift lever back to get at brake lever clamp bolt on combination shift and brake levers. Tighten to 50 to 70 inch-pounds.

Fig. 5-53. Two holes are in the underside of Shimano SLR brakes (visible only when brake is removed from mounting boss). These are for setting brake spring tension.

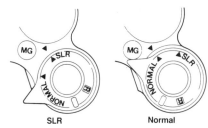

SLR   Normal

Fig. 5-54. Two spring tension adjustments are on Shimano SLR brakes.

Fig. 5-55. Spring tab on Shimano SLR brakes fit into one of the two holes in the brake body (see Fig. 5-53).

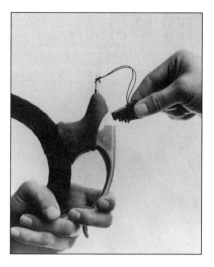

Fig. 5-56. Lock your front brake to keep bike from moving when you park it, by inserting this little plastic gizmo between brake lever and brake body. Though it's shown on road bike levers, it works equally well on ATB brake levers.

Brake Tension: Set brake tension on the SLF brakes by removing the brake from the mounting boss. Inside the brake you will see two small holes (Fig. 5-53). You should also see markings such as in Figure 5-54. For SLR brakes, insert the spring tab (Fig. 5-55) into the SLR hole. For other brakes, where more brake tension is required because, e.g., cables are routed through the frame, put the spring tab into the "Normal" hole.

Parking Brake Gizmo: Lock your front brake with the little plastic gizmo shown in Figure 5-56 on a road bike brake lever. Ths gizmo also works on ATB brake levers. With the front brake locked closed, your bike is far less likely to fall over when you park it.

The next chapter will cover derailleur adjustments, so necessary to keep you bicycle shifting smoothly, accurately and safely.

6
The Transmission System

I n this chapter you will learn how to assure smooth, accurate
and, above all, safe shifting at all times, through all gears.
Another objective is to help you transmit your pedaling energy to the
wheels with maximum efficiency. The transmission system on your bicycle consists of the rear derailleur, front derailleur, the freewheel, the
chainwheel and the chain (Fig. 6-1). Let's start with the derailleurs.

The word "derailleur" is French and means a device that derails or
moves something from one position to another. On your bike, the moving

Fig. 6-1. The transmission system includes, left to right, the freewheel, rear
derailleur, chain, front derailleur and the chainwheels.

action is on the chain. When you shift, the derailleur "nudges" the chain from one gear to the next.

Three types of derailleur systems are now on the market. One is the conventional *friction* shift system that has been the mainstay of gear selectors for at least the past 50 years. A few years ago so-called *index shifters* were introduced. This system moves the chain very precisely from one gear to the next. It eliminates the need for feeling your way with the shift levers to move the chain to the gear you have selected. Index shifting lets you concentrate on where you are going, without looking back and down to check the gear you're in. It should be a positive contribution to safe cycling. A new variation of index shifting uses dual shift levers (Fig. 6-2), one lever for shifting to a lower gear, the other to shift to a higher gear. Both types of index system work pretty much alike. One difference is that in the single shift lever index system you have the choice of switching back to a conventional friction shifting system (Fig. 6-3) if something goes wrong with the index system. The

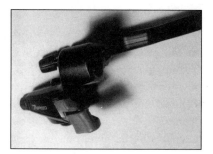

Fig. 6-2. *Dual shift lever index shifting system.*

Fig. 6-3. *Single lever index shift system has the option of changing to conventional friction system in an emergency. Twist the wing bolt as shown to go from index to friction shift.*

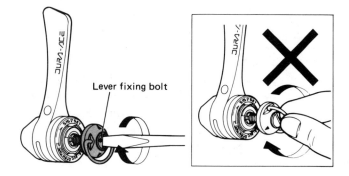

Lever fixing bolt

dual lever system does not provide this option. In the words of one such system manufacturer's technician, if something goes wrong, such as chain stretch so you cannot shift to a lower gear, "you have to get real creative." My suggestion is to study the adjustments required by the dual lever system so you can get "real creative" if need be, if you're far from a bike shop. For example, if the derailleur cable stretches (it will, it will) so you can't shift to a lower, hill-climbing gear, you need to know how to remove this cable stretch.

One problem I see with single or dual lever index systems has nothing to do with them, directly. That is where the bicycle manufacturer routes the cables through, rather than outside, the frame. Index systems need clean, smoothly working cables to work properly. When cables are routed through the frame it may be difficult to get at the cables to clear them. Also, the bends where cables enter and leave the frame tubes may create cable friction.

SHIFTING TECHNIQUES

Here's a quick review of how to shift from one gear to another. Anticipate shifting needs. Shift to a higher, hill-climbing gear *before* you hit a hill. Shifting while you muscle uphill is not always possible. If you can't shift, stop, lift the rear wheel off the ground, twirl the pedals and shift to a bigger rear cog and/or a smaller front chainwheel. Turn the bike at an angle to the trail to reduce the gradient. Straddle the bike, put one foot on a pedal at the 12:30 position. Push that pedal down hard, get up on the saddle, put your other foot on the other pedal and clomp down on it. If you still can't get going, the hill is too steep, or you're inexperienced at this maneuver (don't do it on a road, this is strictly an off-road, trail technique). Let's say the hill is too steep. I suggest you walk up the steep section until it levels out a bit. Nothing to be ashamed of, unless you're an Olympic-class rider.

If the chain makes noise after you shift, you most likely haven't moved the chain all the way onto the rear cogs. Move the rear shift lever slightly one way or the other until the noise is gone. If the chain rubs on the front derailleur cage (Fig. 6-4) *after* you have shifted the rear derailleur, turn the front shift lever slightly one way or the other until the noise is gone. This type of chain rub is caused by the chain assuming a different angle after a rear derailleur shift (Fig. 6-5), so now it rubs on the front derailleur cage. You will have to make these minor shift adjustments even with any of the new index shifting systems. Perfect they aren't.

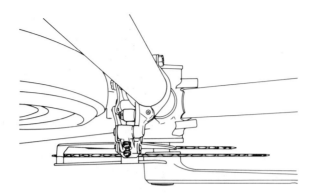

Fig. 6-4. *Front derailleur must be adjusted so the chain will not rub on either side of its cage.*

Fig. 6-5. *Chain can rub on derailleur cage when it is shifted from the big to the small rear cog, and vice versa. Prevent such rub by making slight adjustments with the front derailleur shift lever if you hear chain rub noise.*

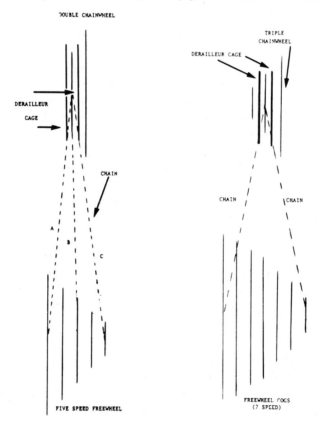

I strongly recommend you practice shifting through all the gears while pedaling on a safe surface, such as a vacant school parking lot. Once you get used to shifting it will be automatic, just like a manual auto shift system. You should not have to look down and/or back to check which gear you're on. All that matters is how you feel. Is the gear comfortable? Can you maintain a pedal cadence of at least 70 crank rpm without breathing too hard (except uphill, of course, then *any* pedal cadence that lets you reach the top is just dandy).

Some ATBs have 21 speeds, 7 cogs in the back, 3 up front. I think that's a bit ridiculous, except as a sales gimmick. The step-by-step gear shifting you need to feel comfortable at various hill gradients can be amply met with at most 18 speeds; for me, 15 is plenty. It wasn't so long ago that 10 speeds meant a derailleur-equipped bike, 3 speeds an internal rear hub shift. When there are factories full of engineering types who have to keep busy dreaming up new, or at least novel, ways of doing the same thing, 21 speeds is what you get, or, like some motorcycles, a transversely mounted 6-cylinder engine with 6 carburetors, yet. I had an old Ariel one-lunger that could go just as fast. Like the Quakers, I yearn for simplicity.

Another problem I see with the dual lever index shift system is that the shift levers are almost too conveniently located. I and other trail riders have found that it's real easy to inadvertently touch the small shift lever (Fig. 6-2), which clicks the rear derailleur down to a higher gear. When you are straining uphill, an accidental and unforeseeable shift to a higher, less advantageous gear is not the best thing that could happen to you. At worst such an accidental shift could cause a spill. So watch where you place those fingers when riding with dual shifters.

Another fairly major dual shift lever problem is that *retrofitting can be a real can of worms,* as far as I am concerned. First, you have to be absolutely sure that the chain, freewheel, derailleurs front and rear, and even the chainwheels are matched components. Using components of different makes, let alone unmatched parts of the same make, is an invitation to disaster. Some makes of shifters, for example, are designed for a specific number of freewheel gears. This is because the shifter ratchet mechanism (Fig. 6-6) has to be designed with exactly the number of freewheel cogs you use. A 6-speed ratchet shifter will not work with a 7-speed freewheel, for example.

The hangar, where the derailleur is mounted (Fig. 6-7) has to be exactly aligned with the frame, or the dual shifters will not shift accurately. Shimano makes a hangar alignment tool to check this, but it's expensive. By the time this book reaches you, I would imagine good

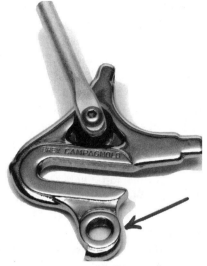

Fig. 6-6. Dual lever index shifter has an internal ratchet (arrow) designed for the number of cogs on the freewheel.

Fig. 6-7. Rear derailleur mount must be accurately aligned with the frame for dual lever index shifters to work properly.

bike shops would have this tool, though. The frame tubes must also be in alignment, along with the dropouts where the wheel is mounted. If your bike has been designed for a five-cog freewheel, a seven-cog unit might not be squeezable between the dropouts. I am also getting reports that the shifter mechanism (Fig. 6-6) has had to be replaced on some early 1990 indexing shifters. Perhaps by the time you see this book that problem will have been solved.

Then there's the cost. You will fork out at least $160 for parts alone, plus around $50 for labor. The simple, reliable friction shift system does have its appeal. At least it lets you decide where the chain will land. When you're beating along a remote wilderness trail, your steed's reliability is of paramount importance, to say the least. Walking 25 miles back to the trailhead is not the most appealing thing in the world. At 2 miles an hour, and that's fast walking on a trail, you're talking 12.5 hours. My advice to dual shift lever aficionados is to bring plenty of extra food on a long trail ride.

I would also like to point out that bike fads do come and go. A few years ago elliptical chainwheels were being touted as a sure route to more efficient, easier pedaling. Now they are passe, and today hardly a new bike has them. We are back to the good old round chainrings. The elliptical rings created an uneven pedal stroke that bothered a lot of cyclists, so they fell out of favor. There is not that much difference between the "computer-designed" elliptical rings and the round rings in any case. If your bike has elliptical chainrings, I'd leave them on. The cost and time to convert to round from elliptical is not justified from a performance standpoint, in my opinion.

For all of the above reasons, I am not going to cover retrofitting dual lever systems or even single lever index shift systems in this book. This is really and properly a shop job, and the complications can be fairly immense, including possibly a new rear hub and a new wheel building job, which can add another $80–$100 to the retrofit cost. That's because you may not be able to have the chainline aligned on your old hub (see discussion of chainline later in this chapter) if you do add a 6- or 7-speed cog. If the chainline is not correct, the chain will not seat accurately on the cogs, so you will have noisy, inaccurate shifting, at the very least.

Now, here's how to adjust your transmission system. But first a word about gearing.

GEARING

Most of us ordinary tourists need "granny" gears, a 34-tooth freewheel cog combined with a 24- or 28-tooth chainwheel. SunTour used to make a 38-tooth freewheel cog, but no more. You may, if you're lucky, find such a cog still hanging on the cog display board in your bike shop. I have one on my ATB, and hope it never wears out. With the chain on these gears you should be able to ride up most hills. However, there *are* grades over 15 percent even trained racing cyclists have to walk up.

You can change cogs on your freewheel and also replace a double with a triple chainwheel set to get wider and lower gear ratios. Please refer to the freewheel and chainwheel sections later in this chapter for gear changing instructions.

Of course, you pay a penalty for such a wide gear selection. The penalty is that you won't be able to use all gear combinations. But if you already have 18 or 21 gear selections, who cares? For example, the rear derailleur won't handle a shift to the 38-tooth cog *and* to the largest chainwheel. Well, it will if you make the chain longer. But then the chain is going to be so long it will flop around when it's on smaller gears and may jump off a cog or a chainwheel as you bounce downhill or shift inaccurately.

As noted above, there are some hills you just have to get off your bike and walk up. Because some hills are graded in degrees and others in percent grade, Table 6-1 converts from one to the other. For me, even in my lowest 24-inch gear, any hill over 15 percent grade is one I walk up.

Table 6-1 Conversion from Degrees of Grade to Percent of Grade

Degrees	Percent
1	1.7
2	3.5
3	5.2
4	7.0
5	8.8
6	10.5
7	12.3
8	14.1
9	15.8
10	17.6

Gear Ratios

For the past 100 years or so the bicycle fraternity has referred to gear ratios in "inches" of gear. The gear-inch concept is a throwback to the pre-1900 high-wheel bicycle (Fig. 6-8), when the gear ratio of a bicycle

Fig. 6-8. The gear ratio of a "high-wheeler" is simply the diameter of the wheel in inches.

was simply the diameter of the big front wheel in inches. These high-wheelers did not have gears. The pedals and cranks were attached to the front wheel. The bigger the wheel, the faster you could go. All you needed were legs long enough to reach the pedals. This concept was translated to modern multigeared bicycles by a leap of the imagination, a love of bicycle lore and some simple math.

To arrive at the "inches" of gear for any combination of front chainwheel and rear freewheel cog, use this simple two-step formula. Count the number of teeth of the freewheel cog of your choice. Do the same for the chainwheel of your choice. Find the *gear ratio* between these two gears by dividing the number of teeth in the chainwheel by the number of teeth in the freewheel cog. For example, say you counted 48 teeth in the chainwheel and 32 teeth in the freewheel cog, 48/32 = 1.5, which is the *gear ratio of this combination*. The second step in finding the gear *inches* is to multiply this *gear ratio* by the diameter of the rear wheel, which on an ATB is 26 inches. For example, 26 × 1.5 = 39 inches. That is the number of inches of this gear combination. That would be, in 1900s bike parlance, equivalent to a high-wheeler with a 3.25-foot diameter front wheel (39/12 = 3.25). At the other extreme, a freewheel 13-tooth cog and a chainwheel with 54 teeth would be a gear ratio of 54/13 = 4.2. Translated to "inches" that would be 4.2 × 26 = 109 inches. It would take a high-wheeler with a 9-foot front wheel to achieve this gear (109/12 = 9). (I have rounded the results to the nearest whole number.) This means the pedal, attached to, say, a 7-inch crank, would be about 62 inches below the circumference of the wheel when at the bottom of its stroke (109/2 + 7 = 61.5). That's an inseam length worthy of a Paul Bunyan, or maybe Bigfoot. But it does show you that technology can engineer a bike with all the speed advantages of a 9-foot direct-drive wheel in a bike a 5-foot person could ride today.

Let's go to the other extreme and find a super low, low gear, in the archaic "inch" terminology. Say you have a rear cog with 38 teeth (which is as big as they come) and a small chainwheel with 24 teeth (as small as they come). Put these two gears together and what do you have? 24/38 = 0.6 (a negative gear ratio). 0.6 × your 26-inch wheel diameter gives you an *inch* equivalent gear of 16, which is truly a wall climber.

One problem you may have in selecting your own gears is that so many combinations are either duplicates or so close as to be duplicates. I have computed a gear table (Table 6-2) for bikes with 26-inch wheels. You will see many, many repetitions: for example, a 45-inch gear appears seven times, with seven different gear combinations. In selecting gears, the idea is to arrive at a minimum of such useless combinations.

In any bicycle gear selection you are going to have duplication of gears, or gears so close together as to be useless. Table 6-2 shows the gears you get with just about any available combination of cog teeth front and rear.

Table 6-2 GEAR TABLE FOR ALL-TERRAIN BICYCLES WITH 26-INCH WHEELS*

Number of Freewheel Teeth	Number of Chainwheel Teeth										
	24	26	28	36	38	40	42	46	48	50	52
13	48	52	56	72	76	80	84	92	96	100	104
14	45	48	52	67	71	74	78	85	89	93	97
15	42	45	49	62	66	69	73	80	83	87	90
16	39	42	46	59	62	65	68	75	78	81	85
17	37	40	43	55	58	61	64	70	73	76	80
18	35	38	40	52	55	58	61	66	69	72	75
19	33	36	38	49	52	55	57	63	66	68	71
21	30	32	35	45	47	50	52	57	59	62	64
22	28	31	33	43	45	47	50	54	57	59	61
23	27	29	32	41	43	45	47	52	54	57	59
24	26	28	30	39	41	43	46	50	52	54	56
28	22	24	26	33	35	37	39	43	45	46	48
30	21	23	24	31	33	35	36	40	42	43	45
32	20	21	23	29	31	33	34	37	39	41	42
34	18	20	21	28	29	31	32	35	37	38	40
38	16	18	19	25	26	27	29	31	33	34	36

*Gear tabulations are rounded off to the nearest whole number. Differences for the diameters of 1.5, 1.75, and 2.125 inches have not been calculated because they are so small.

Workable gear combinations are, for a 15-speed ATB (triple chainwheel, 5 freewheel cogs): 26-, 36-, and 42-tooth chainwheels and 13-, 16-, 21-, 26- and 32-tooth freewheel cogs. This combination gives a low gear of 34 and a high gear of 84. For an 18-speed ATB (triple chainwheel, 6 freewheel cogs), good combinations are 28-, 36-, and 46-tooth chainwheels and 14-, 17-, 21-, 24-, 28- and 34-tooth freewheel, which gives you a low gear of 21 and a high gear of 85. If all the gear ratios on your bike are not in Table 6-2, a very simple way to compute them is to use a software program called Gearchart. The program is on a 5¼-inch floppy diskette and is for IBM personal computers. It costs about $25 from

Brian Rosenthal, 1551 Olene Avenue, Stillwater, MN 55082. To use it, just type GEAR and DOS, enter your wheel size (27 or 26 inches, e.g.) and the number of teeth on each freewheel cog and on each chainwheel.

DERAILLEUR ADJUSTMENTS

All shift systems have common adjustments. Index systems, including dual lever shifters, require a few extra refinements. Let's start with common, garden-variety derailleurs, beginning with the rear derailleur. I'll give basic adjustments, then troubleshooting tips.

Tools You Will Need

Torque wrench (inch-pound model) (Fig. 5-1)
Small Phillips screwdriver
4-, 6- and 8-mm Allen sockets for torque wrench
Park fourth-hand tool (Fig. 5-16) (optional)
Cable cutter (Fig. 6-9) (optional)

Table 6-3 TORQUE TABLE FOR DERAILLEURS*

(Values in inch/pounds)	
Front and rear derailleur cable fixing bolts	35–50
Front derailleur clamp fixing bolt	53–65
Rear derailleur mounting bolt	70–85
Shift lever fixing (clamp) bolt	35–53
Jockey and idler wheel axle nuts	50–60

*See data on torque in Chapter 5 for use of torque wrench and for torque values as they relate to safety.

Rear Derailleur Adjustment (Friction Systems)

All derailleurs have two adjusters to limit left and right movement (Fig. 6-10). They keep the derailleur from overshifting to the right or to the left.

For safety reasons it's important that the rear derailleur be adjusted so that the chain cannot be overshifted so far to the left that it falls off

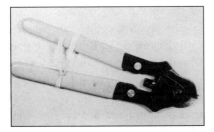

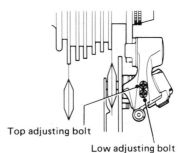

Top adjusting bolt

Low adjusting bolt

Fig. 6-9. *This cable cutter, from SunTour, does a neat, clean job of snipping off outer and inner cables.*

Fig. 6-10. *High-gear adjuster and low-gear adjuster limit derailleur travel to the right and to the left, respectively.*

the low-gear cog and jams between that cog and the spokes. Figure 6-11 shows just such a situation. Here the chain has overshifted to the left, has fallen off the low-gear cog and has caused the rear wheel to be jammed. I have also seen the chain cut off four or five spokes in a row as it rotated smack up against them when lodged between the spokes and the base of the freewheel. Either situation has caused accidents and injury in the past.

Fig. 6-11. *When the low-gear adjustment permits overshifting, the chain can fall off the large cog and get jammed between that cog and the spokes, as shown here.*

If the high-gear adjustment on your derailleur moves the chain too far to the right, the chain can fall off the small cog and jam tightly between it and the chainstay, as shown in Figure 6-12. In this case you would experience pedal lockup, as though a strong arm had suddenly grabbed the pedal and kept it from moving. You may then lose control and balance, which could lead to an accident.

Now let's learn how to adjust your rear derailleur so you can shift with ease, accuracy and, above all, safety.

1. *Check for cable slack:* In Chapter 5 you learned that brake cables stretch with use and that that stretch must be removed to maintain safe braking. Derailleur cables also stretch, and that stretch must be removed to maintain accurate shifting. Here's how: With the rear wheel off the ground (ideally, the bike should be on a stand or suspended from the ceiling), shift the chain to the small rear cog. With your finger halfway down the down tube (Fig. 6-13), lift the rear derailleur cable. If there is any slack, the cable has stretched. The slack must be removed before making any other adjustments.

2. *Remove minor cable slack:* Some derailleurs have a cable slack adjustment barrel which you can use to remove cable slack. Turn the barrel counterclockwise to remove slack, clockwise to add slack. However, if you can't remove all the slack with the barrel adjuster, turn it clockwise as far as it will go then remove cable slack at the cable fixing bolt as noted below.

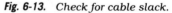
Fig. 6-12. *If the chain overshifts to the right, it can jam between the small cog and the chainstay, in the position shown by arrow A.*

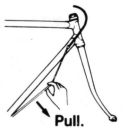
Fig. 6-13. *Check for cable slack.*

Pull.

3. *Remove major cable slack:* Shift the chain to the small rear cog. To remove the slack, loosen the cable fixing bolt (Fig. 6-14). Pull the excess cable through with a pair of pliers as shown in Figure 6-15, or with the Park fourth-hand tool (Fig. 5-16). Rotate the crank and use the shift lever to shift the derailleur all the way to the right, so the chain is on the small rear cog. If the chain won't shift to the small cog, you will need to let out a bit of cable through the cable fixing bolt. Try letting out about ⅛ inch at a time until you can get the chain to shift over to the small cog. Retighten the cable fixing bolt to 35 to 50 inch-lb.

Fig. 6-14. *Remove the cable slack by loosening cable fixing bolt.*

Fig. 6-15. *Pull the excess cable through and retighten this bolt.*

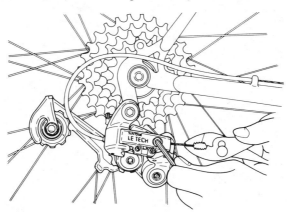

4. *Leave the chain on the small rear cog.* Now, look at the location of the top derailleur wheel. It should be directly under the small cog. Turn the high-speed derailleur limit bolt (the one closest to where the derailleur is mounted) one way or the other until the top derailleur wheel is under the small cog (Fig. 6-16). For example:

   a. If the top derailleur wheel sits to the *left* of the small cog, turn the high-speed adjuster counterclockwise until it is aligned.

   b. If the top wheel sits too far to the *right,* turn the high-speed adjuster clockwise until this alignment is obtained.

5. *Check low-speed adjuster:* While you turn the pedals, shift the rear derailleur to the big freewheel cog. If the derailleur top wheel is not aligned directly under the big cog (as in Fig. 6-17), turn the low-speed adjuster (Fig. 6-18) one way or the other until the top wheel is aligned with that cog. If the chain won't move up to the low-gear cog, there is too much slack in the cable. Shift back to the small rear cog and remove this slack as shown above.

6. *Check shifting on all rear gears:* While turning the pedals, shift up and down through all the gears to make sure the chain will seat accurately on all cogs, especially the low and high gears. Repeat this step several times. Make any fine-tuning adjustments necessary to keep the top wheel aligned directly under the high- and low-gear cogs. The chain should run smoothly and silently on both high and low gears. Any

Fig. 6-16. Align the small rear cog (high-speed cog) with derailleur wheel as shown.

Fig. 6-17. Align large rear cog (low-speed cog) with derailleur wheel as shown.

Fig. 6-18. *High-gear (small cog) and low-gear (big cog) rear derailleur adjuster bolts.*

rubbing or grinding noises on either of these gears probably means that the derailleur top wheel is not directly aligned under each gear, causing the chain to be inaccurately seated. This shortens the life of both the chain and the freewheel cog.

   7. *Check derailleur mounting bolt:* The derailleur mounting bolt (Fig. 6-19) (a.k.a. fixing bolt) should be torqued to 70 to 85 inch-lb.

   8. *Check and adjust chain wraparound:* The top wheel should be as close as possible to *all* freewheel cogs, without touching them. I like about a ⅛-inch clearance on all gears. As a general rule, as you shift through all the rear gears, the chain should fall on nearly half the teeth of each cog (Fig. 6-20). For example, on a 24-tooth cog, the chain should

Fig. 6-19. *Tighten the derailleur mounting bolt to 70 to 85 inch-lb.*

Fig. 6-20. *An example of chain "wraparound." The chain on cog no. 1 is resting on almost half its teeth, which is good, but the chain on cog no. 2 rests on fewer teeth, which can cause chain skip.*

be wrapped around at least 10 teeth; on a 34-tooth cog, around at least 15. I would not quibble about a tooth more or less, though, just so the chain is hanging on approximately half or a few teeth less than half. Anything less and you're risking chain skip and an accident. However, you can adjust the derailleur too close to the freewheel cogs. Figure 6-21 shows what can happen when the derailleur top wheel gets too close to the cog; the chain could jam between the top derailleur wheel and the right side of the derailleur cage plate, and could knock the chain off to the left, as shown. This situation can lock up the pedal motion unexpectedly and contribute to loss of control and an accident.

Check chain wraparound on all gears by shifting through them and watching how close the top wheel is from each cog. There are three simple ways to move the top wheel closer to the cogs. One is to adjust the derailleur angle with its chain tensioner bolt (if your derailleur has one, Fig. 6-22). Turning this bolt counterclockwise moves the derailleur top wheel closer to the cogs. The second is to move the wheel back farther in the dropouts, if your bike has horizontal dropouts. You won't be able to do this with vertical dropouts. The third way is to remove a link or two from the chain for the same result. See the section on chains later in this chapter for data on chain length change.

Fig. 6-21. Use the rear derailleur angle adjuster to keep the chain close to but not rubbing on the big rear cog. Here the chain is rubbing. The result, the chain is knocked off the cog, to the left, where it could jam against the spokes.

Fig. 6-22. Rear derailleur angle adjuster (arrow) adjusts top derailleur wheel closeness to large freewheel cog.

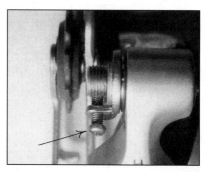

Again, Figure 6-20 is an excellent illustration of good and bad chain wraparound. Chain 1 shows good wraparound with the chain on 7 teeth of this 14-tooth cog. Chain 2 shows the chain on only 4 teeth. Obviously the chain is far more likely to skip on cog 2. Again, when the chain skips or jumps, your foot will slip if you've been pedaling hard, and you could lose balance and control.

9. *Lubricate rear derailleur pivot points* with light oil every month, more often if you ride a lot.

Changing the Front or Rear Derailleur Cable

Eventually a derailleur cable (as with all bike cables) will wear out. If you see a frayed strand any place except after the cable clamp, it's time to change to a new cable. Cables come in two parts—the spaghettilike casing tubing and the stranded steel cable that runs inside the casing. The Shimano SIS cable with casing liner is flexible, without undue compression that tends to set up resistance to cable movement inside the casing. The SIS cable is the type Shimano recommends for their index shifting system, and any bike shop should have it in stock. One more point about cables and casings: avoid "flexible" steel casings; they are stiff and add back pressure to the cable.

Before you buy a replacement cable, check with your bicycle shop to *make sure it will be compatible with your shifting system.*

a. Release the cable fixing bolt at the derailleur (Fig. 6-14). Push on the casing near the shift lever until the leaded end of the cable comes out of the shift lever.

b. Remove both casing and cable and replace with the new cable and casing. If you have cut the casing to trim off unneeded length, be sure to file off any burrs or rough edges on the cut end. I use a bench grinder for this purpose.

c. Put the free end of the cable into the shift lever, so the leaded end fits into a recessed opening in the lever.

d. Remove cable slack as discussed, above, for rear derailleurs and, below, for front derailleurs. Recheck derailleur adjustments as noted above and below.

e. Leave about one or one and a half inches of cable beyond the cable fixing bolt. Snip off excess cable. I like the cable cutter in Figure 6-9. It's from SunTour and it does a neat job of cutting without letting cable strands unravel. To keep ends from unwinding after you cut off excess cable, slip a lead cap (available from bike shops) on the cut end and melt the cap with a match or soldering iron. Or solder about an inch of the cable *before* snipping it. The solder will keep the end from unwinding.

10. *Check Derailleur Wheels:* Remove, clean and replace the derailleur wheels. Dust and dirt abrade and wear down top and idler wheels on a rear derailleur. Replace these little wheels with sealed bearing top and idler wheels (Fig. 6-23) for smoother shifting. They are made by SunTour and should be available from your bike shop. To clean and relubricate, just remove them, pry out the thin O-ring seals with a thin-blade knife, wash out old grease and dirt with kerosene and a small brush, and relube with a light grease. Then reinsert the seals and put the wheels back in the derailleur.

Rear Derailleur (Friction Shift Type) Troubleshooting

Problem: Chain skip. If the chain skips as the pedals are turned, one or more of the freewheel cogs may be worn to the point where they get little lips or overhangs, such as shown in Figure 6-24 (arrows), that catch the chain. A worn chainwheel (Fig. 6-25) also causes chain skip.

Fig. 6-23. *Sealed bearing derailleur wheels run more smoothly, last longer, and require less maintenance. Sealed ball bearing derailleur wheels are shown at the top. Conventional wheels, bottom, do not have bearings. Instead, a metal bushing, G, inside the plastic wheels rotates on steel axle bolts.*

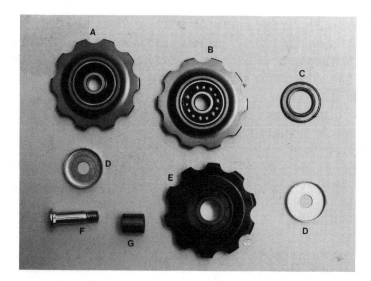

Solution: In this case the only cure is to install new freewheel cogs or a new chainwheel.

Problem: Chain skip. A worn chain will also cause chain skip.
Solution: Please see the data on how to check for chain wear later in this chapter.

Problem: Chain noise.
Solution: If the chain seems to have trouble settling down on the cog you have selected, but instead makes a grinding noise, it's telling you that you probably have not shifted accurately. A grinding noise from the freewheel (or the chainwheel) can 99 percent of the time be quieted down with a tiny adjustment of the shift lever one way or the other.

Problem: Can't shift to low rear gear.
Solution: If you have installed a new chain that's too short, the chain may not shift to the large cog. See the chain section later in the chapter.

Problem: Chain falls off gears.
Solution: If the chain is too long, it can flop around and fall off the rear cog or the chainwheel, especially when going downhill at high speed on a bumpy road when you have shifted to the high-speed gear. When riding an ATB down a rough downhill trail, keep the chain as taut as possible by shifting to the low-gear combination front and rear, or at

Fig. 6-24. *Arrows point to worn teeth on this cog which could cause chain to skip or jump. Such a cog should be replaced.*

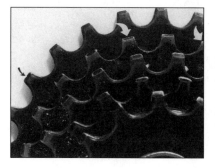

Fig. 6-25. *The chainwheel at the left is new, and does not have worn teeth. The chainwheel at the right has worn teeth on the smaller of the two rings, and is reaching the point at which replacement should be considered.*

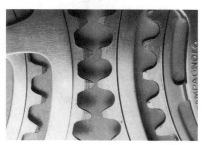

least put the chain on the largest rear cog and the second largest chain-wheel (most ATBs have triple chainwheels). You can always reshift after the downhill run is over.

Problem: Chain falls off or jams on the idler wheel (the bottom derailleur wheel).

Solution: Some rear derailleurs have a movable outer cage. This permits removal of the derailleur without having to remove the chain, as shown in Figure 6-26. If the derailleur idler wheel axle nut is not tight, this movable outer plate may slip down and permit the chain to slip off the idler (bottom) wheel. Derailleur wheel axle nuts should be tightened to 50 to 60 inch-lb.

Problem: The chain won't shift accurately to any gear.

Solution: Derailleurs do wear out eventually. Wear causes excessive free play between these parts. Check the rear derailleur by shifting the chain to the small freewheel cog. Grasp the derailleur cage at the lower (idler) wheel. Move the cage briskly from side to side. If you feel looseness, you need a new derailleur.

Problem: Index shifters to not shift accurately.

Solution: See section on index shifters later in this chapter.

Problem: Fitting chain back onto derailleur.

Solution: Figure 6-27 shows you how the chain should fit on the derailleur wheels. If you have changed the derailleur or removed the

Fig. 6-26. *Some rear derailleurs have an openable cage on the lower wheel for easy chain removal. A is the section where lip B fits when the cage is closed. C points to the axle nut which should be loosened to open the lower cage and tightened to keep it closed.*

Fig. 6-27. *This is how the chain should fit. Chain at top goes around front of top wheel. Chain at bottom goes around rear of tension wheel.*

chain for cleaning, you may puzzle for a while about which wheel and in which direction on each wheel the chain should fit. Figure 6-27 shows that the chain should be in front of the top (top) wheel and behind the lower (idler) wheel. This is also a good photo to remind you that when you are removing the rear wheel, you will need to grasp the derailleur and pull it back to let the freewheel clear the derailleur as the wheel comes out. Before removing the rear wheel, always shift to the small (high-gear) freewheel cog and to the small (low-gear) chainwheel to make it easier to move the chain out of the way as you pull the wheel out of the dropouts.

Derailleur Capacity

It's important to know how derailleur capacity is arrived at and what it means to you. For example, you may be unhappy with the gear ratios you now have. You want a lower gear, let's say, to ease your way when your bike is gear-laden and the hills are steep. To change to lower gears you will, of course, have to change your low freewheel gear to one with more teeth, or change the small chainwheel to one with fewer teeth. Or change the chainwheel setup from a double to a triple chainwheel set with a smaller chainwheel at the low end.

Select front and rear derailleurs that have the capacity to handle the larger gears you plan to install on your bike. Derailleur manufacturers give you their capacity, but it needs some interpretation. Here's how to determine what derailleur capacity you need.

To compute derailleur capacity, you simply subtract the number of teeth in the smallest rear cog from the number of teeth in the largest rear cog. Then you subtract the number of teeth in the smallest chainwheel up front from the number of teeth in the largest chainwheel. Then you add these two numbers for the total capacity of the derailleur.

For example, my ATB has a super granny freewheel gear of 13 teeth on the small cog and 38 on the big cog: $38 - 13 = 25$. The small chainwheel has 24 teeth and the big one has 48 teeth: $48 - 24 = 24$. Adding these, $25 + 24 = 49$. That's the capacity of the rear derailleur I am supposed to be using. I say "supposed" because there is not a derailleur on the market rated at 49 teeth. Not, at least, the last time I looked. The penalty I pay for this wall-climbing set of gears is that I can't use the biggest (low-gear) freewheel cog and the biggest (high-speed) chainwheel at the same time. To me, this is no penalty at all. I positively, absolutely love the hill-climbing low gear I get with this combination. Sometimes I believe I could walk up hills faster than when my chain is on the 38-tooth freewheel and on the 24-tooth chainwheel, but when I try I soon discover that, slow as it seems, *riding* uphill is a whole lot easier and more comfortable than walking and shoving the bike along, especially when the bike is loaded down with camping gear.

If you want bigger (granny) gears than your bike now has, I can recommend either the SunTour AG Tech or the SunTour MounTech (or the current version of these derailleurs). When equipped with a super-long cage, the capacity of these derailleurs is 40 teeth. Take your old SunTour derailleur to the dealer and have him fit the longer cage on it. Another excellent derailleur, also rated at 40 teeth, is Shimano's Model RD-525-SGS. The SGS indicates "super-long cage," and it too works very well indeed.

Modern top-of-the-line rear derailleur design has solved most of the shifting problems that have plagued cyclists for years. The better derailleurs, the more expensive ones, for example, have sealed mechanisms, sturdy single and double spring mechanisms and a movement that keeps the top wheel a uniform distance from the freewheel cogs.

Front Derailleur Adjustment (Friction Systems)

Like the rear derailleur, it is very important that the front derailleur be correctly adjusted for safety and ease of shifting. Here's how:

1. *Shift the front derailleur to the low-gear position* (small chainwheel).

2. *Check parallel and height position:* The derailleur cage should be positioned parallel to and from $^1/_{32}$ inch to $^1/_8$ inch above the large

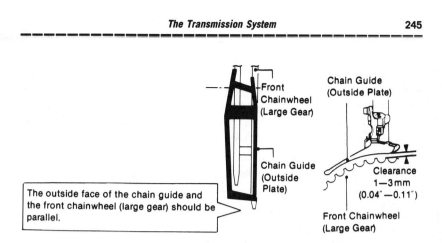

Front Chainwheel (Large Gear)

Chain Guide (Outside Plate)

Chain Guide (Outside Plate)

The outside face of the chain guide and the front chainwheel (large gear) should be parallel.

Chain Guide (Outside Plate)

Clearance 1—3mm (0.04"—0.11")

Front Chainwheel (Large Gear)

Fig. 6-28. Vertical and parallel adjustments for front derailleur.

chainwheel, as shown in Figure 6-28. Note: If you have an elliptical chainwheel, the cage should be $\frac{1}{32}$ inch to $\frac{1}{8}$ above the highest point of the chainwheel ellipse. If you have a round chainwheel with longer teeth at one section, the cage should be $\frac{1}{32}$ inch to $\frac{1}{8}$ inch above that section.

3. *To reposition the derailleur:* Loosen the derailleur clamp fixing bolt (Fig. 6-29), and move the derailleur up or down and to the right or left as necessary and tighten the clamp fixing bolt to 53 to 65 inch-lb.

Fig. 6-29. To reposition the front derailleur, loosen clamp bolt as shown.

4. *Remove cable slack:* While turning the cranks, shift the front derailleur to the small chainwheel. With a finger, lift the cable about halfway down the down tube. If there is any slack, remove it by loosening the cable fixing bolt as shown in Figure 6-30. Pull excess cable through the fixing bolt and tighten this bolt to 35 to 53 inch-lb. Leave about one or one and a half inches of cable beyond the cable fixing bolt.

5. *Adjust left and right derailleur travel:* Like a rear derailleur, the front derailleur has two adjusters—a high-speed adjuster which limits its travel to the right, and a low-speed adjuster which limits its travel to the left. Figure 6-31 shows them in close-up. You can also see that as you screw the adjuster one way or the other, it gets closer to or farther away from the stops on the derailleur which limit travel to the left and to the right.

6. *Adjust low-gear (left) travel:* While turning the cranks, shift the front derailleur so its cage is over the small chainwheel, as shown in Figure 6-32. If you can't shift the derailleur far enough to the left, turn the low-speed adjuster counterclockwise until the cage is centered over the small chainwheel. If the derailleur cage travels so far to the left that it throws the chain off the chainwheel, turn the low-speed adjuster clockwise to limit derailleur movement to the left. Shift the derailleur several

Fig. 6-30. Remove cable slack by loosening cable binder bolt, pulling cable taut, retightening binder bolt.

Fig. 6-31. High and low gear adjuster bolts limit front derailleur travel to the left and the right.

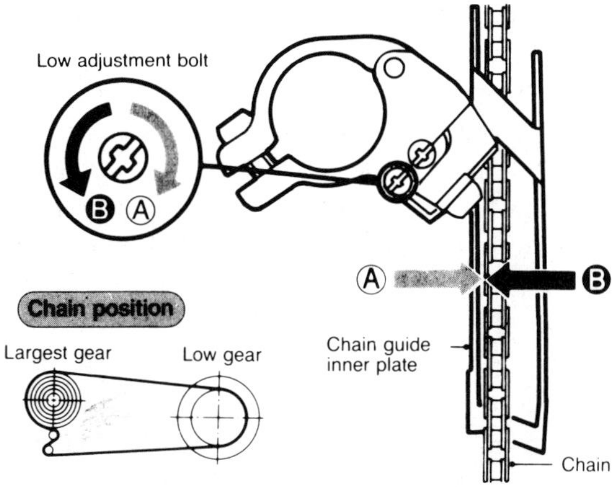

Fig. 6-32. *To adjust front derailleur left limit travel, shift to big rear cog and small front cog, then adjust low gear limit bolt so derailleur cage is close to the chain, but not touching it.*

times to make sure the chain moves accurately onto the small chainwheel, and fine-tune the low-gear limit adjuster as necessary.

   7. *Adjust high-gear (right) travel:* While turning the cranks, shift the front derailleur so the large chainwheel (high gear) is close to, but not touching, the right inner surface of the chain guide plate, as shown in Figure 6-33. Turn the high-gear adjuster clockwise or counterclockwise,

Fig. 6-33. *To adjust front derailleur right limit travel, shift chain to the smallest rear cog and the largest chainwheel. Then turn high gear limit bolt until the chain is close to but not touching the right side of the derailleur cage.*

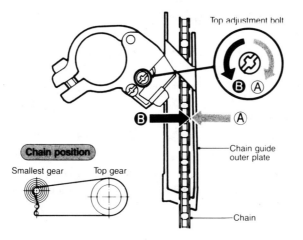

as necessary, to limit right movement of the derailleur to this location of the large chainwheel. Check both high- and low-gear adjustments by shifting the chain several times from the small to the large chainwheel, and readjust one or both limit adjusters as necessary.

Use #242 Loctite to keep the cable clamp nut, derailleur limit bolts, front and rear derailleur mounting bolts, and rear derailleur top and idler wheel bolts from working loose under road vibration.

Front Derailleur Troubleshooting

Problem: Front or rear derailleurs seem to shift by themselves, so that you find the chain on a gear combination you don't want.

Solution: Check the shift lever wing nut. Most friction-type shift levers have a wing bolt. Some use a bolt that can be tightened with a dime. In any case, the bolt works loose after a time and needs to be retightened periodically.

Problem: The chain moves too far to the left, falls off the small chainwheel and onto the bottom bracket shell (where it may jam between the fixed cup of the bottom bracket and the base of the chainwheel).

Solution: Readjust left travel as above.

Problem: The chain moves too far to the right, so it falls off the large chainwheel and down onto the crank.

Solution: Readjust right travel as above.

Problem: The chain rubs on the derailleur cage.

Solution: The derailleur cage may not be parallel to the chainwheels. Check and readjust as shown above.

Problem: Grinding noise or chain rubbing sound from front derailleur.

Solution: If you hear a grinding noise coming from the front derailleur cage, after shifting to a higher or lower *rear* cog without shifting the *front* derailleur, it's because the chain assumes an increasing angle, as shown in Figure 6-34. Here it is rubbing on the derailleur cage. Try this for yourself. With the bike on a stand or suspended from the ceiling, shift the chain to the third gear of a 5- or 6-speed freewheel, or the fourth gear of a 7-speed freewheel. With the front shift lever, adjust the front derailleur until the chain is centered in the derailleur cage. Now shift the chain to the smallest rear cog. You will see that the chain moves closer to the right front derailleur cage plate as you do so. Shift the chain

DOUBLE CHAINWHEEL

Fig. 6-34. Chain can rub noisily on the front derailleur cage if you shift from an intermediate rear cog, as shown here, to the low or high gear rear cog. Solution is to make a slight adjustment of the front derailleur shift lever to move the cage away from the chain.

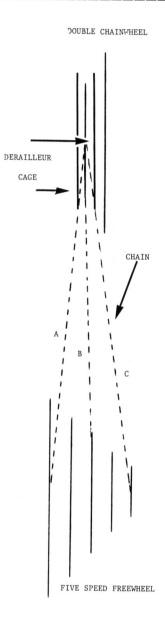

DERAILLEUR

CAGE

CHAIN

A

B

C

FIVE SPEED FREEWHEEL

to the largest rear cog. You will note that the chain moves closer to the left front derailleur cage plate. This causes an increase in chain angle in the front derailleur cage as you shift the chain from one rear cog to another. The chain then rubs on the derailleur cage, even though derailleurs are correctly adjusted. This problem is minimized with index shifting.

The solution to this chain rub and noise is simple. Move the front derailleur cage, with the shift lever, one way or the other, until the chain no longer rubs on the cage. Get into the habit of making this front derailleur shift lever micro-adjustment whenever you shift the rear derailleur. This problem is particularly acute if you have a 7-speed freewheel and a 3-speed chainwheel.

Problem: Chain jumps off chainwheel.

Solution: Another cause of chain jump is a bent chainwheel. Most chainwheels are made of aluminum. They can be bent if the bike is dropped on them, or if another bike runs into them, or by other impacts. If you suspect a chainwheel is bent, remove the chain from it, spin the cranks and eyeball the chainwheel from the rear. Mark any bent place with chalk. With a crescent wrench (Fig. 6-35) or a special straightening tool (Fig. 6-36), *gently* force the chainwheel back to true. When you do this, remember that aluminum is a lot more brittle than steel. It won't take much bending to break it. Try to make only one bend back to true.

Problem: You can shift the chain to the large chainwheel, but have trouble shifting back down to the small chainwheel.

Solution: The derailleur is too high above the chainwheel. Readjust as shown above.

Fig. 6-35. Straighten a bent chainwheel with a crescent wrench.

Fig. 6-36. Use this special tool for straightening a bent chainwheel.

Problem: Cannot shift up to the large chainwheel.

Solution: The derailleur is positioned too low above the large chain-wheel, where it rubs on the large chainwheel. Readjust as shown above.

INDEX SHIFTING SYSTEMS

Index shifting systems take the guesswork out of accurate shifting from one gear to another. Originally developed so racing cyclists could shift quickly and accurately during a race, these systems are now on the market as original equipment on some makes of bicycle.

Properly adjusted, index shift systems are a safety device as well as a convenience for fast and precise shifting. It takes practice to shift with a conventional derailleur system as you try to move the chain to the correct gear. Inaccurate manual shifting may leave the chain partly on a cog. Such shifting not only wears out the cog and the chain faster, it can contribute to chain skip, loss of control and an accident. This type of accident can be avoided, of course, by learning how to shift smoothly and accurately. Index shifting automatically gives you smooth, accurate and safe shifting to the gear you want. It moves the chain precisely onto the cogs of the freewheel and chainwheel without guessing or fiddling with shift levers. You always know which gear you're in. You won't ever have to look down and back at the rear cogs to see which gear the chain is on, or down at the chainwheel for the same reason. All of which means *safety,* because you can concentrate on traffic, road or trail conditions.

Even uphill shifting is easier, because you can get the chain to a lower gear quicker than with a conventional system. With index shifting, the chain moves fast, precisely and without any further need to fine-tune where you have placed the chain. The system is self-tuning, if it's adjusted correctly in the first place.

How to Adjust Single Lever Index Shifting Systems

The first commercially available index shifting system was the single lever design, introduced to the U.S. market in 1984. Since that time index systems have been refined to the point where they are pretty foolproof. Latest versions use two levers each for front and rear shifters. I'll review adjustments for the single lever index system first, then cover the newer double lever systems.

First, if the index feature won't work, you can quickly and easily shift to old-fashioned friction shifting. Do this by turning the dial on the shift lever from "index" to "friction" (Fig. 6-37). For example, if the cable stretches while you're out on a ride so the index shift goes on strike on some gears, just switch to friction and pedal on. Earlier single lever index shifting systems operate with a definite "click" which you hear each time you shift the chain on the freewheel cogs or on the chainwheels.

These are the steps in adjusting single lever index shifting systems:

1. *High-speed adjustment.* Shift to the small freewheel cog. Eyeball the derailleur top wheel and this cog. The top derailleur wheel should be aligned just under the right edge of the small freewheel cog. If not, turn the high-speed adjuster clockwise or counterclockwise until the derailleur wheel is lined up as above.

2. *Low-speed adjustment.* Shift the chain to the big freewheel cog (low gear). The derailleur top wheel should line up with that cog. If not, adjust the low-speed adjuster clockwise or counterclockwise until the top wheel is lined up with that cog.

3. *Remove excess cable slack.* Maintaining correct cable tension is critical for all index systems. If the cable is too slack, the chain won't shift from the high (small cog) to the next cog. If it's too tight (too much cable tension) the chain may skip a gear as you shift to a lower gear. Move the rear derailleur shift lever wing bolt to the friction mode, as shown in Figure 6-37. Be sure to turn the little ring back down flat again after you switch from one mode to the other. If the ring is not flat, the derailleur system can switch from one mode to the other, which may be a bit disconcerting.

Shift to the high (small rear cog) gear. Pull excess cable through the derailleur cable fixing bolt and tighten it to 35 to 53 inch-lb. Fine-tune cable tension with the derailleur's *inner cable tension barrel,* as you make the following adjustments.

Fig. 6-37. *If you can't shift a single lever index shifter, turn the wing bolt to friction, so you can use the derailleur.*

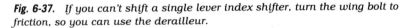

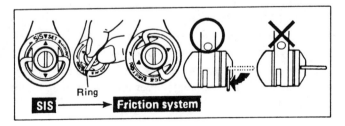

Cable Tension Adjustment

1. *Turn the shift lever wing bolt so the system is in the index mode,* as shown in Figure 6-37.

2. Now shift from the small freewheel cog to the next biggest cog. If the chain won't move to this gear, turn the cable slack adjuster (Fig. 6-38) counterclockwise one or two turns. Try shifting again. If the chain overshifts and moves to the third gear, turn the cable slack adjuster clockwise a half to one turn and continue this fine tuning until the chain falls exactly on the second gear.

3. With the chain resting on the second gear, turn the inner cable tension adjuster counterclockwise while you turn the pedal forward, as if you were cycling. As you turn the adjuster, watch the rear third cog and the chain. As the chain just begins to approach the third cog, stop twisting the adjuster.

4. Shift back to the small rear cog. Repeat step 6 below on each of the freewheel cogs, fine tuning with the cable tension adjuster on the derailleur as necessary. You could also remove cable slack with the cable adjuster on the shift lever (Fig. 6-39).

5. Put the chain on the smallest chainwheel and the largest freewheel. Turn the rear derailleur angle adjustment screw (screwdriver points to it in Fig. 6-40) to bring the derailleur top wheel as close to the big rear cog as possible, without touching it.

6. For the final adjustment step, crank in reverse (backpedal). If the chain rubs as you're backpedaling, the top wheel is too close to the large rear cog. Turn the angle tension adjustment screw (Fig. 6-40) clockwise until you can backpedal without having the derailleur top wheel rub on the big (low-gear) rear cog.

Fig. 6-38. *This cable slack adjuster on the derailleur, arrow, can remove minor cable stretch.*

Fig. 6-39. *Another place to remove minor cable stretch is the slack adjuster on the shift lever (arrow).*

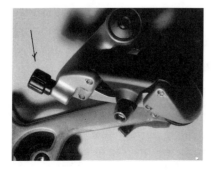

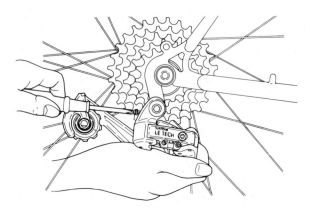

Fig. 6-40. *Turn the angle adjuster on the rear derailleur to bring the top derailleur wheel as close as possible to the big cog, without letting the chain touch that cog.*

7. Adjust the front derailleur as noted in the section above, "Front Derailleur Adjustment." Front derailleur adjustments for single lever index shifters are the same as for conventional shift systems.

DUAL LEVER INDEX SHIFTING SYSTEMS

In this system, introduced in 1990, both front and rear derailleurs are controlled by dual levers. However, the rear derailleur set of levers operates somewhat differently than the front set. I will describe each set individually, starting with the rear derailleur levers.

Rear Derailleur Dual Shift Levers

The shift levers on the right side of the handlebars operate the rear derailleur. Use the big lever ("2" in Fig. 6-41) to shift from a small freewheel cog to a bigger one. Use the small lever ("1" in Fig. 6-41) to shift from a big freewheel cog to a smaller cog. Here's how:

1. *To shift from a smaller rear cog up to the next largest cog:* Press lever 2 (Fig. 6-41) one click. You can start with the smallest rear cog and shift up one cog at a time. For example, if you have six freewheel cogs, you can start shifting from the small one, one cog at a time, all the

Fig. 6-41. *On rear derailleur dual index shifters, the big lever, 2, moves the chain from smaller to bigger rear cogs. Use the small lever, 1, to shift from a bigger to a smaller rear cog. On front derailleurs, use the levers the same way.*

way to the biggest (slow-speed) cog. You can shift the big lever to each cog, sequentially, or all the way to the biggest rear cog.

2. *To shift from the smallest rear cog all the way to the biggest rear cog:* Press lever 2 (Fig. 6-41) all the way. Press the big shift lever *all* the way to shift the chain to the biggest rear cog from any smaller cog. For example, if the chain is on the third cog and you want to shift to the biggest cog as you approach a hill, you press the big lever all the way.

3. *To shift from a bigger to a smaller rear cog:* Use the small shift lever ("1" in Fig. 6-41). Each time you press the small lever the chain moves from one large cog to the next smallest cog.

Both shift levers are spring-loaded and thus return to the original position as soon as you remove finger pressure.

Front Derailleur Shift Levers

The shift levers for the front derailleur look like the levers for the rear derailleur, but they work differently. The big lever ("2" in Fig. 6-41) moves the chain from a small to a larger chainwheel. The small lever ("1" in Fig. 6-41) moves the chain from a larger to a smaller chainwheel.

1. *To shift from the smallest to the largest chainwheel:* Press the big lever ("2" in Fig. 6-41) a full stroke.

2. *To shift from the smallest chainwheel to the middle chainwheel, or from the middle chainwheel to the largest chainwheel:* Press the big lever ("2" in Fig. 6-41) a half stroke. If you hear noise when shifting from the smallest to the middle chainwheel, gently press the small lever ("1" in Fig. 6-41). This corrects a slight overshift by moving the front derailleur cage slightly toward the small chainwheel.

3. *To shift from the largest to the smallest chainwheel:* Press the small lever ("1" in Fig. 6-41) a full stroke.

4. *To shift from the largest chainwheel to the middle chainwheel, or from the middle to the smallest chainwheel:* Press the small lever ("1" in Fig. 6-41) a half stroke, from the initial position.

How to Adjust Dual Lever Index Shifting Systems

Adjustments for front and rear dual lever indexing shift systems may seem the same as for conventional friction shift systems. However, there are important differences. So please review the data that follow if you have a dual lever index system on your bicycle. The same bolt and nut torque specs apply to both friction and index systems, however. Adjustments and troubleshooting are combined below.

Troubleshooting the Rear Dual Lever Index Shift System

Problem: Chain won't shift smoothly to the largest freewheel cog.

Solution: Check and adjust for cable stretch as shown earlier in this chapter on friction shift systems. Note: You can remove minor cable stretch at the cable tension barrel on the shift lever (Fig. 6-39) and/or at the derailleur (Fig. 6-38), if these adjusters are on your components.

Problem: Chain won't move up from the smaller to the next larger rear cog.

Solution: Adjust the cable tension barrel on the derailleur (Fig. 6-38) counterclockwise a quarter turn; repeat as necessary.

Problem: Chain moves past the second gear as you attempt to shift to it.

Solution: Turn the cable tension barrel (Fig. 6-38) clockwise a quarter turn; repeat as necessary. Then shift the chain to the next smallest rear cog. Turn the crank so the chain moves the rear wheel. Turn the tension barrel counterclockwise until you hear the chain make noise against the third cog (up from the smallest cog).

Problem: Chain moves past the small cog and jams between it and the chainstay.

Solution: Align the derailleur top wheel under the small cog or slightly to its right. See section on friction and single lever index shifters above.

Problem: Chain skips while you pedal or as you shift.

Solution: Shift the chain so it is on the smallest chainwheel and the largest rear cog. While turning the crank backward (backpedal), turn the cage tension bolt (Fig. 6-38) counterclockwise to bring the rear derailleur upper pulley almost but not quite to where it touches the big rear cog. Now shift to the next smallest rear cog, then back to the big cog. Should the top derailleur pulley touch the big cog, turn the cage tension adjuster (Fig. 6-40) clockwise to bring this pulley to just below the big cog.

Problem: Chain skips or is noisy as you pedal.

Solution: Chain or cog teeth, or both, may be worn. See sections on friction shifting, above, and on chain wear later in this chapter. Replace worn cogs and chain.

Troubleshooting Chainwheel Dual Lever Index Systems

Problem: Can't shift from a smaller to the largest chainwheel.

Solution: The cable has stretched. Shift to the smallest chainwheel. Remove minor cable stretch with the cable adjuster barrel at the shift lever (Fig. 6-39), if your shifters are so equipped. Remove major cable stretch as described in the section above on friction front shifters.

Problem: Chain overshifts off the small chainwheel. Chain falls off to the left.

Solution: Shift the chain to the smallest chainwheel and to the largest freewheel cog. Adjust the low-gear limit bolt (Fig. 6-42) until the clearance between the chain and the front derailleur chain guard inner plate (Fig. 6-43) is around $^1/_{64}$ to $^1/_{32}$ inch. Check shifting and readjust the low-gear limit bolt as necessary.

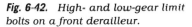

Fig. 6-42. High- and low-gear limit bolts on a front derailleur.

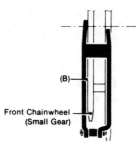

Fig. 6-43. *As for friction systems, adjust the front derailleur travel to the left, with the low-gear bolt, so the cage is close to but not touching the chain.*

(B)

Front Chainwheel (Small Gear)

Problem: Chain overshifts and falls to the right off the large chainwheel.

Solution: With the chain on the big chainwheel and smallest freewheel cog, turn the high-gear limit bolt (Fig. 6-42) on the front derailleur so there is a bare minimum clearance between the chain and the inside of the outer front derailleur cage plate (Fig. 6-44). Check to make sure the chain does not rub on the cage plate.

Problem: Can't shift accurately to the center chainwheel. Chain seems to jump or skip off this gear.

Solution: Turn the high-gear limit bolt (Fig. 6-42) one or two turns counterclockwise. Check shifting and readjust this bolt as necessary.

Problem: Difficulty in shifting from the center to the big chainwheel.

Solution: Adjust the high-gear limit bolt (Fig. 6-42) counterclockwise a quarter turn or so.

Problem: Difficulty in shifting from the center to the small chainwheel.

Solution: Turn the low-gear adjuster bolt (Fig. 6-42) a quarter turn counterclockwise. Check shifting; readjust this bolt as necessary.

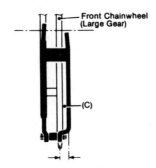

Front Chainwheel (Large Gear)

(C)

Fig. 6-44. *On index systems, adjust the right limit bolt (high-gear) so the chain does not touch the cage.*

Problem: When chain is on big chainwheel it rubs on the outer (right) side of the derailleur cage plate.

Solution: Turn the front derailleur clamp bolt (Fig. 6-45) two or three turns to loosen it. Move the front derailleur up or down until the outer cage plate clears the chain $^1/_{32}$ to $^1/_8$ inch (Fig. 6-46). Tighten the clamp bolt to 35 to 52 inch-lb.

Fig. 6-45. *Loosen index shifter front derailleur clamp bolt so you can align it as shown in Figure 6-46.*

Fig. 6-46. *Move the derailleur up or down so right cage plate is about $^1/_{32}$ inch from the highest point on the big chainwheel, and parallel to it.*

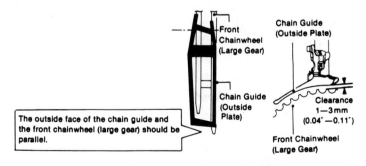

Problem: After solution above, chain now rubs on inner or outer cage plate.

Solution: Shift the chain up to the big chainwheel. Loosen the front derailleur clamp bolt as in the solution above. Pivot the derailleur until its outer cage plate is above and parallel to the large chainwheel (Fig. 6-46).

On All Dual Lever Shifters

Problem: None of the above problems can be solved on either front or rear shifters.

Solution: The ratchet mechanism is defective. Have your dealer replace it. This is a shop job.

How to Replace a Cable on Dual Lever Index Shifters

Replacement of the cable on the front or rear of these shifters is similar to cable replacement of single lever index shifters and friction shifters, with one small difference. The difference lies in how you snake the cable end through the shift lever body.

To change a derailleur cable:

a. Remove the small plastic plate under the short shift lever, with a small Phillips screwdriver (Fig. 6-47). (If your shifters do not have this piece, as on some models, continue with the steps below.)

Fig. 6-47. Some dual lever index shifters have a small plate that must be removed to install a new cable. Screwdriver points to the plate bolt.

b. Shift the chain to the small rear cog if you are changing a rear derailleur, or to the small chainwheel if you are changing a front derailleur cable.

c. Turn the cable binder bolt (Fig. 6-48) at the derailleur counterclockwise until you can pull out the old cable.

d. Remove the old cable from the spaghetti tubing, and push the leaded end out of the shift lever (Fig. 6-49).

e. Push the end of a new cable (be sure to use the same make cable; check with your bicycle shop) through the shift lever. This is a bit tricky, as you may have discovered at this point. It's almost impossible to see the tiny orifice the cable has to go through. Start the cable insertion just under the small shift lever (Fig. 6-49), and poke and prod until it comes out the other side, through the cable slack adjuster. This can be a stinker of a procedure, I know. Stick with it, you'll get there. It helps if you remove the cable slack adjuster from the shift lever. Be sure to replace it later.

f. Pass the new cable through the spaghetti tubing, through the frame mounted cable stops, the rear derailleur cable slack adjuster and into the cable binder bolt.

g. Pull up hard on the new cable, about halfway down the down tube, to prestretch the cable.

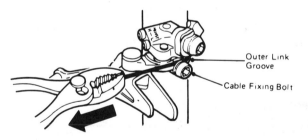

Fig. 6-48. Removing cable slack on index shifters, at the front derailleur.

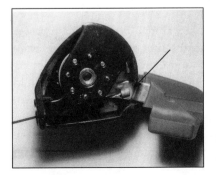

Fig. 6-49. Shift cable leaded end can be pushed out as shown to remove old cable. Note that slack adjuster barrel has been removed, left, to make new cable installation easier.

h. Hold the cable taut with a fourth-hand tool or pliers (Fig. 6-48) and tighten the cable binder bolt to 35–52 inch-lb.

i. Recheck all shift adjustments. Review the troubleshooting procedures above for rear and front derailleurs and readjust as necessary.

j. Replace the plastic piece you removed in step "a" above.

Shift Lever "Reach" Adjustment

Some dual lever index shifters have a "reach" adjustment to tailor their distance from handlebars to fingers. Locate this adjuster by looking *underneath* the shift lever body. Use a screwdriver to turn the adjuster one way or the other until the shift levers fit your finger length. There are three such adjustments.

CHAINS

More than any other part of your bike, the chain is exposed not only to abrasives such as dirt, sand and mud, but to water as well, which washes away protective lubricants. It's the one part of your bike that wears out fastest and needs the most maintenance. All-terrain bicycle chains need more frequent maintenance if ridden on sandy trails or through water. A new chain should last 2,000 to 3,000 miles; if exposed to abrasives without maintenance, it can wear out in only 500 miles. A worn chain, as I said earlier, can jump or skip off gear teeth and cause an accident.

Steps to Keep Your Chain Healthy

Clean your chain any time it looks dirty and before every long trip. A dirty chain not only wears out faster, it also wears down the teeth of your freewheel and chainwheels, and their replacement costs a bundle. Clean your chain while it's on the bike, or remove it for a more thorough cleaning.

On the bike, clean it with a chain cleaner (Fig. 6-50). The chain passes over brushes which dip in kerosene in the unit as you turn the crank counterclockwise. The cleaner is small and light enough to carry along on your trip; if your cookstove uses kerosene you can use the same fluid in the cleaner. Or you could spray the chain with a degreaser, which flushes out dirt and cleans the chain.

Off the bike, you'll need a "chain breaker" tool (Fig. 6-51) to push one of the pins out of the chain so you can remove it. Put the chain

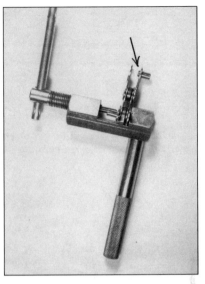

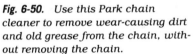

Fig. 6-51. *Use this "chain breaker" tool (a.k.a. rivet remover) to push out a chain rivet part way to remove the chain.*

Fig. 6-50. *Use this Park chain cleaner to remove wear-causing dirt and old grease from the chain, without removing the chain.*

breaker on a chain pin and turn the handle five and a half to six turns, just far enough to push the pin almost all the way out the other side of the chain. Leave about $^1/_{32}$ inch of the pin *inside* the cage plate (arrow in Fig. 6-51), so you can snap the chain back together. Some makes of chain require their own special chain breaker tool, so make sure you buy the one that's made for your chain. Clean the chain by agitating it thoroughly in a pan of kerosene. Use a brush to clean out old grease and remove sand and grit. Do not use highly flammable solvent, such as gasoline or naphtha, to clean your chain!

Check for chain stretch. While the chain is off, check it for stretch, which is an indication of chain wear. A worn chain can skip and jump off cogs front or rear and may cause loss of control and an accident. Check chain wear this way: Remove the chain, lay it flat and count off 24 links. Since link pins are a half-inch apart (Fig. 6-52), 24 links should measure 12 inches. If they measure much more, say $12^1/_{16}$ inches, replace the chain. Another way to check chain wear is to bend the chain and compare it with a new chain, as shown in Figure 6-53. The chain at the bottom is worn and should be replaced.

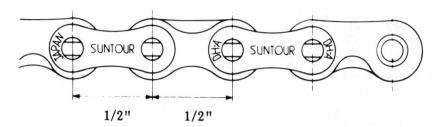

1/2"   1/2"

Fig. 6-52. *Check for chain wear by counting off 24 links. If this distance is greater than 12¹/₁₆ inches, chain is worn and should be replaced.*

Fig. 6-53. *Another way to check for chain wear is to bend it as shown. Chain at bottom is worn and should be replaced.*

Relube a clean chain by laying it on newspapers, on the garage floor, side plates vertical. Spray the chain with a good lubricant in a spray can, one containing molybdenum in a petroleum base. This type of lubricant is thin enough to minimize abrasive pickup from the road yet provide excellent lubrication. After spraying one side, turn the chain to the other side and spray it. If possible, let the lubricant penetrate for a couple of hours, or overnight, before reinstalling the chain. When you are ready to reinstall the chain, pick it up, wipe off excess lubricant and put it back on the bike this way:

a. Pass the chain over a rear cog, in *front* of the upper pulley over the *rear* of the lower pulley.

b. When you are through with these steps, the chain should be positioned as shown in Figure 6-27.

c. To ease chain fastening, give it as much slack as possible by dropping the chain down off the small chainwheel and letting it lie on the bottom bracket shell. A Quick-Link tool (Fig. 6-54) helps to hold the chain.

d. You should have the rivet sticking out one end of the chain. So the chain will run the same way, the rivet should face the way you pushed it out. If you pushed the rivet out toward the left side of the bike, push it back with the chain tool from the right side. It's a bit more pain this way, but it's better for the chain because it keeps the same wear pattern.

Fig. 6-54. Use this Quick-Link tool to hold the chain while you rivet it back together with the chain breaker tool.

e. Start with the end of the chain without the rivet. Thread it through the front derailleur cage, then back over the small freewheel cog.

f. Pass the chain over the *top* of the upper pulley, so it comes out the *front* of that pulley.

g. Now snap the two ends of the chain together. If you had left about $1/32$ inch of the rivet inside the side plate, that much of it you should be able to force (snap) into the chain.

h. Push the rivet the rest of the way in with the chain tool (Fig. 6-55) until the same amount of the rivet shows on both sides.

Fig. 6-55. With the chain breaker tool, push the rivet back into the chain until the same amount of the rivet is showing on both sides of the chain. Twist the chain at this link to remove stiffness.

i. The chain will most likely be stiff at this point. Remove the stiffness by grasping the chain links on both sides of the section you reriveted, and twisting the chain from side to side until it feels loose. If you don't free up this stiff link, you will have chain jump.

j. Put the chain back on the small chainwheel.

Installing a New Chain

a. *The new chain should be the same length as the old one.* Lay them side by side on the floor. Remove unneeded links with the chain tool; save them for emergency road repair if the chain breaks. Then install the chain as shown above, except in this case it makes no difference which side the rivet is on.

b. *Make this check to be sure the chain is the correct length.* Chains come in 112-, 116-, or 120-link sizes. The chain should be long enough so you can shift to the large freewheel cog, short enough so it won't skip or jump off a gear. If the chain is too long, it will be too slack when it is on smaller gears and may jump off. If it is too short, you may be able to shift to the big rear cog but not to the biggest chainwheel or even to the middle chainwheel.

c. Shift the chain so it's on the largest freewheel sprocket and the largest chainwheel. The rear derailleur should now be almost parallel to the chainstay (Fig. 6-56). If you can't shift the chain to the biggest

Fig. 6-56. With the chain on the big rear cog and big chainwheel, chain is correct length when the cage is nearly parallel to the chainstay, as shown.

freewheel cog and to the largest chainwheel, you may have a super-low-gear setup, such as a 34 or 38 rear cog, for which the chain is too short. In this case don't add links to the chain, because if you do, the chain will be dangerously loose when you shift to the smallest freewheel sprocket. Console yourself that you have a super-low granny gear for steep hills. If, on the other hand, your biggest freewheel cog has 32 teeth or less, you should be able to shift so the chain is on that sprocket and on the large chainwheel. If not, add chain links as needed.

　　d. Shift the chain to the smallest freewheel sprocket and the smallest chainwheel. The rear derailleur should be about vertical to the ground (Fig. 6-57). If not, remove one or two links.

　　e. Check and adjust chain wraparound as described above.

　　f. Always carry the chain remover tool and spare links in your tool kit. The day I left my chain tool home was, of course, the day the chain broke on a rural road in Wisconsin. I pounded the broken link pin out with an old nail and a rock I found nearby. I removed the broken link and pounded the pin back into the now shorter chain, using the nail and the rock. What a pain!

　　g. I recommend installing a chain guard on your chainstay, to prevent occasional chain rub from damaging its finish. The guard self-adheres to the stay. Clean the stay before installing the guard.

　　On a trip, I recommend you carry a can of chain lube. At day's end, wipe or brush off accumulated gunk from the chain (Fig. 6-58), and spray it with the lubricant. *Keep lubricant from the brake shoes and the tire!*

Fig. 6-57. *With the chain on the smallest rear cog and smallest chainwheel, the chain is the correct length when the cage is close to vertical from the chainstay, as shown.*

Fig. 6-58. Use this Park Tools brush to remove gunk from the derailleur wheels, freewheel cogs and chainwheels.

Daily chain lubrication is especially important if you have biked through water or over abrasives such as sand. Adequate chain lubrication also reduces wear on gear teeth, and as I said earlier in this chapter, a new chain is a lot cheaper than a new cog or chainwheel.

New Chain Designs

One not so recent and two relatively new makes of chain require special installation consideration. SunTour Superbe Pro chains have "high-arch" inner links (Fig. 6-59). A conventional chain design is shown for comparison in Figure 6-59. When you replace the SunTour chain, be sure the arched part of the outer link goes over the gear teeth, as shown in Figure 6-60.

For index systems, it is especially important that you use the same make and model chain that came on the bike. Some chains are narrower than others. For example, a 7-speed freewheel usually requires a narrow-design chain. A normal width chain will just not work.

The new Shimano Hyperglide chain takes a special pin every time you take it apart. These pins are available in bike shops. The manufacturer recommends a shop-type chain rivet remover to remove or install the special pin. However, I can report that my standard, garden-variety chain tool worked just fine with this chain. If you elect the special

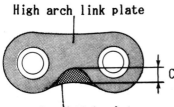

High arch link plate

Conventional link plate

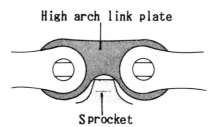

High arch link plate

Sprocket

Fig. 6-59. *SunTour high-arch link plate, compared with conventional chain link plate.*

Fig. 6-60. *When replacing a high-arch chain, be sure the high-arch side goes over the cog teeth, as shown.*

tool, you will have to take your bike to the shop or spend around $60 for the shop tool. You must cut (remove the rivet) from a new Hyperglide chain at only a black rivet. If you cut it any other place, you damage the chain. This also holds true for newer Regina chains and, I suppose, eventually, for many other makes. Check instructions that come with your new chain.

Chainline Adjustment

The principle in chainline is that the center cog of the freewheel cluster be in line with the center chainwheel of a triple chainwheel setup. For a dual chainwheel setup, the center freewheel cog should be aligned exactly between the two chainwheels. If the chainline is not correct, the angles and the wear and tear on all components of the transmission system will be greater. In Figure 6-61, for example, the chain is on a single chainwheel and the third gear of a 5-speed freewheel. In Figure

Fig. 6-61. *Correct chainline for a single chainwheel and 5-speed freewheel.*

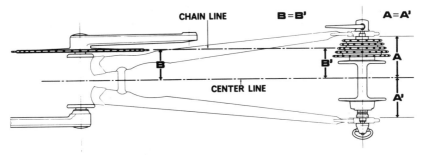

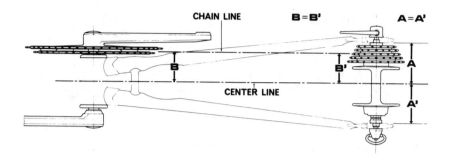

Fig. 6-62. *Correct chainline for a dual chainwheel and 5-speed freewheel.*

6-62, you will see that the chain is centered between the double chain-wheels and on the third cog (center) of a 5-speed freewheel. In Figure 6-63, the chain is centered on the center chainwheel of a triple chain-wheel and the third cog of a 5-speed chainwheel. In Figure 6-64, the chain is centered between a double chainwheel and between the third and fourth cogs of a 6-speed freewheel. In Figure 6-65, it's centered on the center chainwheel of a triple chainset and between the third and fourth cogs of a 6-speed freewheel; in Figure 6-66, between a double chainwheel and on the fourth gear of a 7-speed freewheel; and in Figure 6-67, on the center of a triple chainwheel and the fourth gear of a 7-speed freewheel.

Chainline adjustments are limited, for the most part, to what you can do with the rear hub. As you will see in the section on hubs in Chapter 7, there are spacing washers on both sides of the hub axle. Within limits, you can transfer these washers from one side of the axle (hub) to the other to adjust the chainline. However, be careful. If you move the freewheel over too far to the right, the small cog can rub on the chainstay.

Fig. 6-63. *Chainline for triple chainwheel and 5-speed freewheel.*

ALIGNMENT

TRIPLE CHAINWHEEL

FIVE SPEED FREEWHEEL

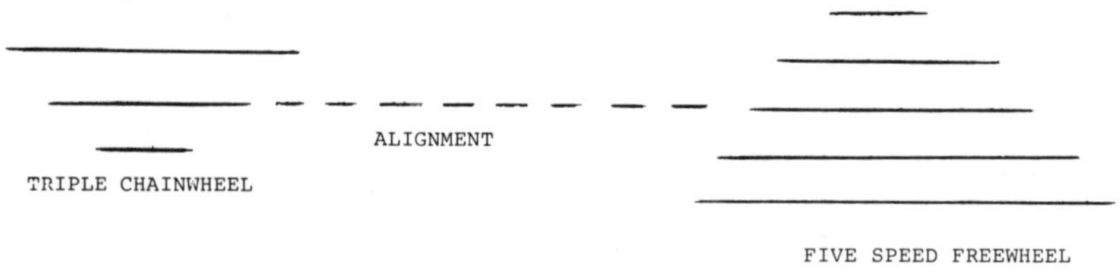

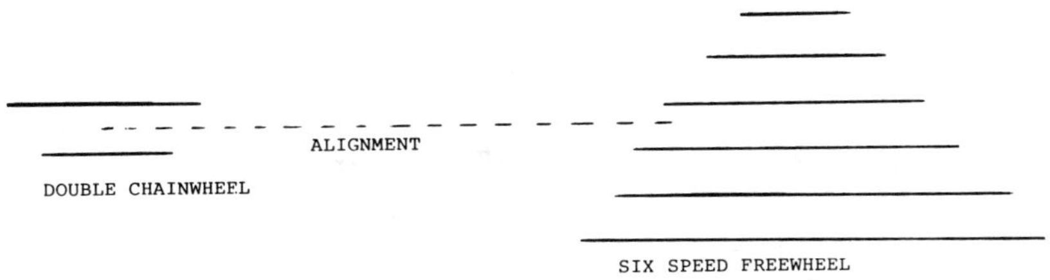

Fig. 6-64. *Chainline for dual chainwheel and 6-speed freewheel.*

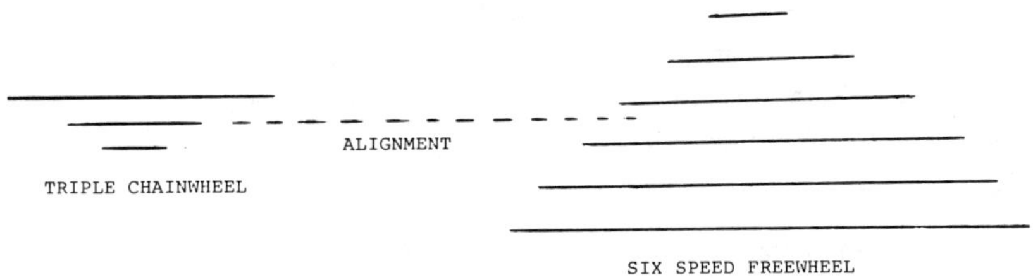

Fig. 6-65. *Chainline for triple chainwheel and 6-speed freewheel.*

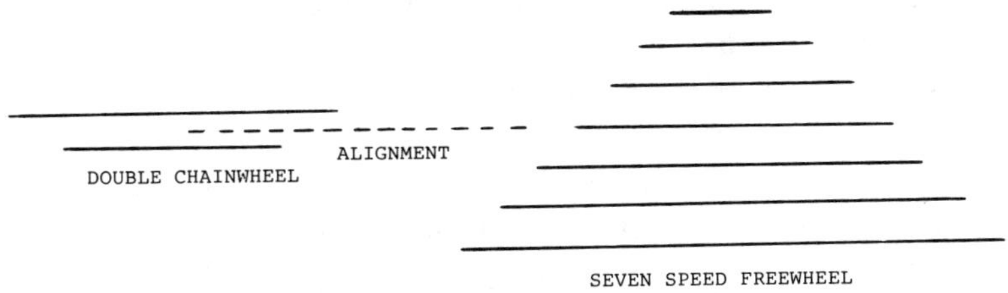

Fig. 6-66. *Chainline for dual chainwheel and 7-speed freewheel.*

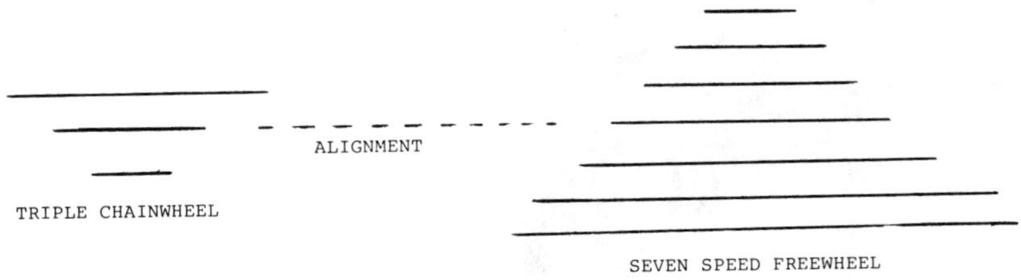

Fig. 6-67. *Chainline for triple chainwheel and 7-speed freewheel.*

FREEWHEEL

Here's what to do to keep your freewheel happy:

1. Squirt a little *light* oil (such as sewing machine oil) into both sides of the freewheel every four or five months.

2. If a dirt particle holds freewheel pawls open so cranks freewheel in both directions, pour a little solvent, such as diesel oil or campstove kerosene, into both sides of the freewheel while spinning the wheel rapidly, first in one direction, then in the other. Do this without removing the wheel from the bike. Relube with light oil as noted above.

3. When you clean your chain, also clean off accumulated dried dirt, old oil, etc., from the freewheel cogs. Gunk accumulates on the freewheel cogs (Fig. 6-68) and should be removed periodically.

Changing Freewheel Cogs

If you are not happy with the gear ratios that came with your bike, you can change individual freewheel cogs (also chainwheels, discussed later in this chapter). There are two basic types of freewheels, the separate freewheel (Fig. 6-69), which unscrews from your rear hub, and the cassette type (Fig. 6-70), which is integral with the rear hub. I'll cover the separate freewheel first.

To change cogs on a separate freewheel:

1. *Tools:* You will need a special tool which fits your freewheel. There are a great many freewheels, and each has its own special tool that fits.

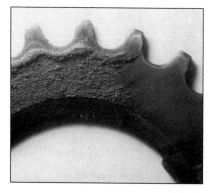

Fig. 6-68. *Gunk like this can accelerate wear on cogs, chainwheels, chains and derailleur wheels.*

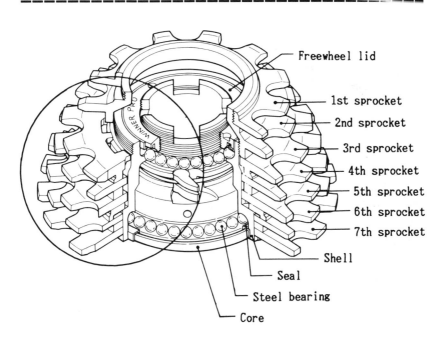

Freewheel lid

1st sprocket

2nd sprocket

3rd sprocket

4th sprocket

5th sprocket

6th sprocket

7th sprocket

Shell

Seal

Steel bearing

Core

Fig. 6-69. *Use light oil to lubricate freewheel bearings.*

Fig. 6-70. *Freehub cogs can be removed by turning smallest, threaded cog counterclockwise.*

Figure 6-71 shows just a few of the dozens of freewheel removers on the market. I will note here that if you break a spoke on the freewheel side you will have to remove the freewheel to change that spoke, so it's a good idea to be able to remove the freewheel even if you don't want to change cogs. Here's how:

2. Remove the wheel.

3. Remove the quick-release unit by holding the lever with one hand while you loosen the skewer adjuster nut with the other hand. Don't lose the little springs on the quick-release skewer (Fig. 6-72). When you replace the quick-release unit, remember that the little springs go on

Fig. 6-71. *To remove a freewheel you will need one of these special tools. See your bicycle shop for the right one.*

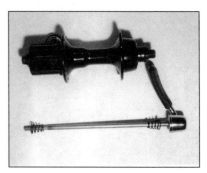

Fig. 6-72. *Watch that you don't lose the little springs on the quick-release skewer. Replace them with the small side toward the hub.*

with their small side facing toward the wheel. Please refer to Chapter 3 on quick-release use and adjustment. If the hub axle uses nuts, remove both.

4. Hold the freewheel remover tool on the freewheel while you insert the quick release and tighten it against the tool, leaving it slightly loose. Or snug an axle bolt up against the tool and back it off one or two turns (Fig. 6-73).

5. With a wrench, turn the freewheel remover tool counterclockwise until the freewheel just breaks loose, no more. If the freewheel is stubborn, hold the remover tool in a vise and twist the wheel counterclockwise a half turn.

6. Remove the quick release. You should be able to unscrew the freewheel by hand. If not, repeat steps 4 and 5 above. Be very careful

Fig. 6-73. *With quick release holding freewheel remover tool, turn the tool with a wrench, counterclockwise a half turn, just enough to break it loose from the hub. Then remove the quick release and turn the remover tool by hand to remove the freewheel.*

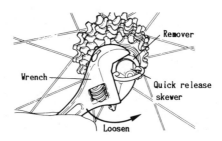

as you unscrew the freewheel. The hub threads are aluminum (Fig. 6-74); freewheel threads are steel and could easily damage the more fragile aluminum threads. Be especially careful when you replace the freewheel; it's easy to cross-thread it on. If you feel resistance, you have probably cross-threaded. If so, back the freewheel off carefully and start again.

7. Clean the freewheel cogs. Dunk and agitate the freewheel in kerosene to clean its innards. Do not take the freewheel itself apart. There's no need for this.

8. While the freewheel is off, check the spokes next to the freewheel, where they enter the hub. Look for signs of metal fatigue such as cracks. Look for gouges in the spokes (Fig. 6-75) where the chain had fallen off the freewheel down onto the spokes and cut them. Replace any damaged spokes. See Chapter 9 for spoke replacement help.

How to Change Freewheel Cogs

If you want to replace a worn freewheel cog, or change to a bigger Alpine hill-climbing cog, follow these steps:

1. If the freewheel is on the hub, you can use two cog removers (Fig. 6-76). One tool keeps the freewheel from turning, the other will remove the small cog (Fig. 6-77), after which remaining cogs can be removed.

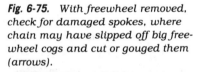

Fig. 6-75. With freewheel removed, check for damaged spokes, where chain may have slipped off big freewheel cogs and cut or gouged them (arrows).

Fig. 6-74. Hub threads (arrow) are aluminum, freewheel threads are steel, so be careful not to cross-thread and strip hub when replacing the freewheel.

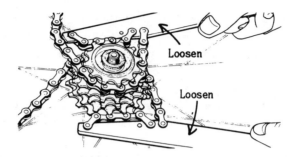

Fig. 6-76. *Use two cog pullers to remove a cog from a freewheel without removing it from the wheel.*

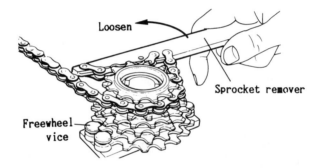

Fig. 6-77. *Removing the small freewheel cog. Freewheel is held in special vise.*

2. If the freewheel is off the hub, put it in a freewheel vise (Figs. 6-78 and 6-79), and put that vise in a bench vise. Or do what I do. Drill two holes in your wood workbench to hold two bolts, spaced to fit the holes in the large freewheel cog (Fig. 6-80), which will hold it while you remove the small cog.

3. Use the cog remover (Fig. 6-81) to turn the small freewheel cog counterclockwise. Remove it. On most freewheels only the small cog is threaded on. If the second cog is also threaded on, remove it the same way. Now you can slide off the remaining cogs and their spacers. As you remove these parts, make a note of which spacers go where, because some may be thinner than others (Fig. 6-82). If the space between any two cogs is too wide or too narrow, the chain may slip when you shift and cause an accident.

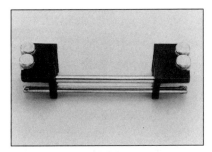

Fig. 6-78. *Freewheel vise that makes it easier to remove cogs from freewheel.*

Fig. 6-79. *Freewheel is held in freewheel vise.*

Fig. 6-80. *An alternative to the freewheel vise is, simply, two bolts in a workbench.*

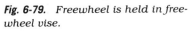

Fig. 6-81. *Turn the cog remover counterclockwise to loosen and remove a cog from the freewheel.*

Fig. 6-82. *Freewheel body, upper left. Note spacers between cogs. When replacing cogs, be sure to replace spacers between them to provide chain clearance.*

FREEHUB MAINTENANCE

Freehubs combine the hub and the freewheel in one piece. As you can see in Figure 6-70, the cogs are mounted on splines and held in place by the small freewheel cog, which is threaded on. The freehub permits a stronger wheel because the rim does not have to be "dished" much, as it does for a conventional hub (see Chapter 9 for an explanation of dishing). Also, a freehub axle is stronger because it extends all the way out to the end of the freewheel. This means that the bearings are at the extreme right-hand side of the hub, rather than at the right side of the hub body. Hub bearing surface wear is less and hub strength is greater. In fact, many makes of top-line all-terrain bikes now come with the freehub. Racing cyclists also prefer it. Note: Hollow rear hub axles (equipped with a quick release) are bendable under wheel impact. Freehubs minimize this problem. Solid bolt-on axles minimize it still further.

To maintain a freehub you will need special tools. There are many models and makes of these hubs. New models, requiring new special tools, seem to be announced monthly. I can only give general maintenance data. For your specific make and model hub, I suggest you see your bicycle dealer for information on what special tool(s) you will need. In this section I will cover only cog changes. Please refer to the section on hubs later, in Chapter 7, for bearing maintenance.

To change a freehub cog:

1. Remove the small freewheel with the cog tool (Fig. 6-76). The smallest cog threads on and holds the other cogs on the splines.

2. With the small cog removed, slide the other cogs, with any spacers (remember where they go for reassembly), off for replacement.

Note: The cassette hub is removable, but that does require special tools and expertise, which I recommend be done at the bike shop. There really is no reason why the cassette needs removal in any case, unless after many, many thousands of rough miles it should wear out.

CHAINWHEEL

Table 6-4 CHAINWHEEL TORQUE SPECIFICATIONS

	(in inch-lb)
Crank binder bolts	300–325
Chainwheel binder bolts	70–100

Maintenance Tips for Long-lived Chainwheels

1. *Abrasives such as sand and road dirt can wear out the aluminum-alloy teeth of a chainwheel.* Use a small brush, such as an old toothbrush, and kerosene to remove gunk from the chainwheel every time you clean the chain. I know it's not easy to reach behind the chainwheels, especially the middle of a triple chainset (Fig. 6-83), but it's important you get both sides of all the teeth clean to prevent premature wear and costly replacement.

2. *If chainwheel teeth are worn* it's time to replace the chainwheel. Most ATB cyclists use the smaller of a double chainwheel or the middle of a triple chainwheel on slow-speed off-road rides. Inspect those chainwheels closely for wear after every 200 miles of cycling.

3. *Look for a bent chainwheel.* A bent chainwheel can cause chain skip. See data above, and Figures 6-35 and 6-36, for correcting a bent chainwheel.

4. *Check for loose chainwheel binder bolts.* I was ride-testing a new bike for a magazine article a few years ago. When I shifted the chain from the small to the large chainwheel, the pedals suddenly locked and I almost lost control. I found that the chainwheel binder bolts either had not been sufficiently tightened or had worked loose, which allowed the two chainwheels to spread apart. When I shifted, the chain fell down between them. These bolts *can* work loose, so check them after every long trip or every few months. You'll need a 5-mm Allen wrench and a slot wrench (Fig. 6-84). A double chainwheel set has five binder bolts,

Fig. 6-83. Clean chainwheel teeth when you clean the chain. Use light grease on the cables where they pass under the bottom bracket shell, if your bicycle cables are routed this way.

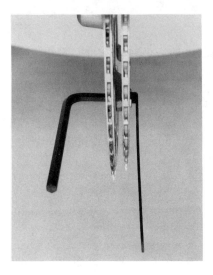

Fig. 6-84. *Periodically check tight-*
ness of chainwheel binder bolts. If
they work loose, the chain can slip
down between them and cause an
accident. See text for details.

and a triple chainwheel set has ten binder bolts. To tighten these bolts, use the slot wrench to hold the binder bolt nut, and the 5-mm Allen wrench to tighten the binder bolt. Tighten each bolt to a torque of 70 to 100 inch-lb.

The Chainwheel Approach to Lower Gears

To change gear ratios you could change freewheel cogs, as discussed above. You could also change chainwheels. For example, elliptical chain- wheels come with only a 28-tooth small chainwheel. You could keep the two larger elliptical chainwheels, but replace the 28-tooth ring with a 24-tooth round chainwheel. Look at the gear table (Table 6-2) to find the lower gear you'd be in with this and other freewheel combinations. Note: Bring your old chainwheel to the bike shop to make sure any new ones you buy are compatible with the old chainwheel and crank. If you go so far as to change cranks as well, again, bring the old cranks to the shop for a replacement that fits your axle. If you go from a double to a triple chainwheel, you will need a longer axle so the inner chainwheel will clear the chainstay. See Chapter 7 for axle change instructions. Be sure the new axle is compatible with your cranks.

Here's how to remove the chainwheels and replace a chainwheel. (Note: In Chapter 7, I will discuss bottom bracket bearing maintenance. The chainwheel and its crank and the other crank must be removed to service bottom bracket bearings, so please keep these crank instructions in mind for Chapter 7.) Crank removal goes like this:

1. Remove the dust cap (Fig. 6-85).

2. With a 14- or 15-mm socket wrench, turn the crank binder bolt counterclockwise (Fig. 6-86). Remove it and its washer.

3. Thread in a crank puller tool (Fig. 6-87). Before installing this tool in the dust cap threads, hold it in one hand by the side that threads into the crank, and with the other hand turn the other section counterclockwise as far as possible. Thread it in carefully so as not to strip the soft aluminum threads. Be sure the tool uses *all* the dust cap threads; otherwise the tool will pull right out and you will have a costly shop job to rethread the crank.

Fig. 6-85. *Remove dust cap with Allen wrench, or use a screwdriver, depending on type of cap.*

Fig. 6-86. *Turn the crank bolt counterclockwise to remove it.*

Installation/removal of crank fixing bolt

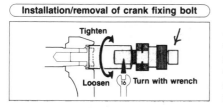

Fig. 6-87. *Insert a crank puller in the dust cap threads. To make sure it goes in as far as possible, turn the center bolt (arrow) counterclockwise as far as possible before inserting the tool.*

4. Turn the crank puller clockwise with a wrench (Figs. 6-88 and 6-89) until the crank is loose on the bottom bracket axle. If you meet a lot of resistance and can't get the crank to break loose, tap the end of the crank puller briskly with a hammer a few times, then keep turning. Repeat as necessary.

5. Some makes of crank use an Allen bolt, and have, in effect, a built-in crank puller. Be careful when using an Allen wrench to loosen this bolt. It's easy to slip and skin knuckles. Turn the Allen bolt counterclosewise with a 6-mm Allen wrench (Fig. 6-90) until the crank is loose enough to pull off the axle. The Allen bolt is integral with the crank and remains in it when the crank is removed from the spindle. The Allen bolt crank was a great idea because it was so easy to remove. Thieves agreed; soon after they were introduced, a lot of $110 chainwheels and cranks, along with attached pedals, disappeared.

6. After cleaning the chainwheel and doing bottom bracket maintenance (see Chapter 7), replace the crank and chainwheel on the axle. *Do not apply any lubricant to the axle shaft or to the crank.* This is a press fit! Tighten the crank binder bolt to 300 to 350 inch-lb.

7. A word of warning about elliptical chainwheels. When reinstalling chainwheels on the crank, make sure the topmost part of the chainwheel (the apex of the ellipse) is in line with the crank (Fig. 6-91). As you replace the crank/chainwheel combination on the axle, make sure the top of the ellipse is about $1/32$ inch from the outer front derailleur cage plate and vertical to the ground. Otherwise you negate any benefit the

Fig. 6-88. *Tighten the crank puller center bolt flush against the axle, top. Then turn the crank puller with a wrench.*

Fig. 6-89. *Crank puller is being turned with a wrench to force the crank off the bottom bracket axle.*

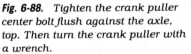

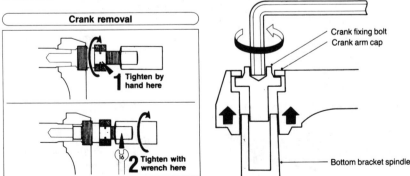

Fig. 6-90. *When chainwheel and crank have integral Allen wrench crank puller, use a 6-mm Allen wrench to remove the crank from the axle, as shown here.*

Fig. 6-91. *When reinstalling the crank and chainwheel, be sure the highest part of an elliptical chainwheel, and its crank, are parallel to the seat tube, as shown here.*

Fig. 6-92. *This "Rock Ring" helps protect your valuable chainwheels from being ground up by rocky terrain.*

oval ring imparts. This warning also goes for some makes and models of 1990 chainwheels where the teeth are slightly higher in one area than in others.

8. Retighten the crank bolt(s) every 50 miles for the next 200 miles. This is an important step. If the aluminum squared and tapered shank works loose, it can move and destroy itself on the steel axle.

9. Replace the dust cap(s).

10. If you plan on riding over rough, rocky terrain, a Rock Ring (Fig. 6-92) will help prevent gouges in your expensive aluminum chainwheel. Costs about $34 from your bike shop. Add $3 for shipping if you order from the manufacturer, VF Technology, Inc., Box 1476, Route 25B, Center Harbor, NH 03226, or Visa order 1-800-451-5326.

11. Grease cables where they pass under the bottom bracket (Fig. 6-83).

This covers the transmission system. Now let's go to those parts that use ball bearings: hubs, pedals, bottom bracket and headset, parts that go around and around, in the next chapter.

7

Bearings: Maintenance, Adjustment, Lubrication, Replacement

.....**B**earings—those tiny, round, precision-ground pieces of steel in your *hubs, pedals, headset and bottom bracket*— have common maintenance and adjustment characteristics, which is why they are grouped in this chapter.

SEALED VS. NONSEALED BEARINGS

All modern bearings have some degree of seal. My definition of a true sealed bearing, however, is one that uses sealed cartridge bearings (Fig. 7-1), as opposed to those using ball bearings either loose or in a retainer (Fig. 7-2). Cartridge bearings are removable, but only with special tools, though they do have an effective seal against water and abrasives.

Fig. 7-1. *Sealed bearing hub. Left to right: high-flange hub, sealed bearing (standard industrial cartridge), low-flange hub.*

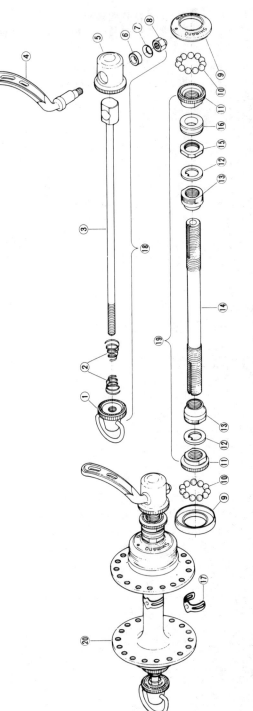

Fig. 7-2. *Exploded view of loose ball bearing hub. 1, quick-release adjustable nut; 2, quick-release springs; 3, quick-release skewer; 4, quick-release lever; 5, 6, 7 and 8, lever parts; 9, dust shields; 10, balls; 11, axle locknut; 12, locknut washer; 13, adjustable cone; 14, axle; 15, adjustable cone; 16, locknut on freewheel side; 17, oil hole cover; 18, quick release, complete; 19, axle components; 20, hub body.*

I suggest you relube cartridge bearings every 1,000 miles, noncartridge more often, depending on use, as noted below. I like the kind of grease that resists washing out by water, such as boat trailer wheel bearing grease. It's available in any marine supply store. I use this grease in wheel hubs, both sealed and nonsealed, in headsets, in bottom brackets and even in pedal bearings.

Here is how to maintain these parts. Let's start with nonsealed bearing hubs.

HOW TO KEEP HUBS ROLLING SMOOTHLY, LONGER

Clean and relube conventional nonsealed bearing hubs after every extensive trip or every two weeks on a road or trail trip if you have biked through water or over sandy trails. This two-week maintenance frequency for nonsealed bearing hubs may seem a pain. If so, here's a suggestion, based on my experience.

I was on a road trip in Vermont. We had pedaled over dirt and sandy roads to get into state parks at night. One evening, after dinner, I decided to check my hubs. Spinning a bike wheel, I heard a grinding noise coming from my precision-machined, costly Campagnolo rear hub, a gritty sound that penetrated to the very depths of my wallet. Sand had worked its destructive way into the bearings. Fortunately I had a set of hub wrenches (Fig. 7-3) along, and grease. When I disassembled the hub, I did indeed find sand, but no damage. I was lucky.

So, my suggestion is to make the following daily check on a bike trip, or make it at least monthly if you do more casual day riding. Turn the bike upside down. Spin each wheel. Feel for grinding with your fingertips on the hub body (careful you don't catch fingers in the spokes); listen for grating sounds from the hub. Relube by following the instructions below. If all seems okay, you may be able to get by for a longer period.

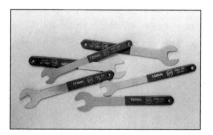

Fig. 7-3. Thin-bladed wrenches for hubs.

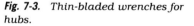

But if you have forded streams or cycled over sand a lot, I do urge you to up the relube frequency. These instructions apply to freehubs (with an integral freewheel) as well as to conventional hubs.

Tools and Supplies You Will Need

1. Thin hub cone wrenches, 13-, 14-, 15-, 16- and 17-mm (depending on size of hub locknuts and adjustable cones) (Fig. 7-3).

2. 13-, 14- or 15-mm socket, for an inch-pound torque wrench (see Fig. 5-2) if hubs have axle bolts instead of a quick release.

3. Axle vise to protect axle threads (Fig. 7-4) (optional). Note: This vise also fits pedal axles, as discussed in the pedal section in this chapter.

4. Water-resistant grease.

5. Torque wrench (see Figs. 5-1, 5-2 and 5-3. Also please review use of a torque wrench in Chapter 5).

Maintenance Steps

1. Remove the wheel from the bicycle (see Chapter 5).

2. If the wheel is held by axle bolts, remove them. Or remove the quick-release mechanism. Hold the quick-release adjusting nut (Fig. 3-55) while you turn the quick-release lever counterclockwise until the adjusting nut comes all the way off the skewer threads. Grasp the quick-release lever and pull the skewer out of the hollow axle. Catch the little springs ("2" in Fig. 7-2) so you don't lose them. Put the springs and the adjusting nut back on the skewer for safekeeping. On a rear wheel, remove the freewheel, as described in Chapter 6, so you can get at the bearings on the freewheel side. You do not have to remove the freewheel on freehubs, though, because the bearings on the freewheel side are reachable once the axle is withdrawn.

3. From here out, you can simply lay the wheel on the bench and remove the bearings. However, the axle vise (Fig. 7-4), held in a bench vise as shown, makes life a lot easier. The axle vise holds the axle by its threads, so they won't strip. Or hold the locknut in a bench vise.

4. Hold the adjustable cone with one cone wrench, and turn the locknut counterclockwise with the other cone wrench (Fig. 7-5). Remove the locknut and the spacing washer.

5. With the cone wrench, turn the adjustable cone a few turns counterclockwise. You should now be able to unscrew it by hand. Remove it from the axle.

6. Lay a rag out on the workbench next to the wheel. Hold the axle end facing you with one hand, and loosen the vise just enough to remove

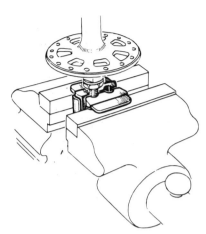

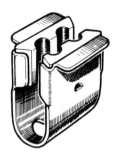

Fig. 7-4. *Hub and pedal vise.*

Fig. 7-5. *Use of two hub wrenches. One holds the adjustable cone while the other, at top, tightens or loosens the locknut.*

the wheel. Still holding the axle securely in the hub, carefully lay the wheel on the rag.

7. Lift the wheel off the rag enough so you can pull the axle out. You should still have an adjustable cone, washer and locknut on one end of the hub axle. Leave them on the axle. Be ready to catch loose ball bearings as they fall out of the hub.

8. With a screwdriver, carefully pry off both dust caps ("9" in Fig. 7-2).

9. Remove any bearings still in the hub.

10. Roll the loose balls around in a cup of kerosene to remove old grease and dirt. Carefully spread them out on the rag and dry off the kerosene.

11. Clean both hub cups, the adjustable cones, the dust caps and the axle.

12. Examine the hub cups (Fig. 7-6) and the adjustable cones (Fig. 7-7) for signs of galling and brinelling. The grooves worn in the adjustable

Fig. 7-6. Inspect hub cups for grooves and other signs of wear damage.

Fig. 7-7. Check hub cones for wear. This cone has grooves worn into it and should be replaced.

cone in Figure 7-7 are an example of such wear. Replace such worn cones. If the hub cup(s) are worn, it's time for a new hub.

13. Examine the loose ball bearings for wear. If you've had the bike for three or four years, I recommend you replace them. Take a sample ball bearing to your bike shop to make sure you get the right size. Buy a couple of extra balls in case you drop one and lose it.

14. Hold the axle in the axle vise (this is where the vise helps). Hold the other adjustable cone with the cone wrench, and remove the remaining locknut, washer and adjustable cone.

15. Check the axle alignment. Roll it on a smooth, flat surface, such as an old piece of plate glass. Replace it if it's bent. Take the axle to your bike shop for an exact replacement.

16. Cover the loose balls in grease. Layer in grease in both hub cups and on the adjustable cones.

17. Thread the adjustable cone, washer and locknut on one end of the axle to about where they were before you removed them. Hold the adjustable cone with a hub wrench, and tighten the locknut with another hub wrench. Then look at both ends of the axle. About ¼ inch of threads should be left where the axle fits into the dropouts. If not, adjust the cones and locknuts as necessary. If you are working on the front wheel, both ends of the axle should show the same number of threads when you replace the other adjustable cone.

18. Insert the ball bearings in one side of the hub. Layer more grease on top of the balls.

19. Replace the dust cap on that side.

20. Insert the axle with adjustable cone, washer and locknut into the hub side that has the bearings in place. Be careful not to dislodge bearings.

21. Hold the axle up while you turn the wheel over and lay it down on the bench.

22. Replace bearings in the other side of the hub, cover with more grease.

23. Replace the dust cap.

24. Thread on the adjustable cone, replace the washer, thread on the locknut. Again, check to make sure the same number of axle threads show on both sides of the hub. On a rear hub, the same number of threads should show outside the freewheel as on the other side of the hub.

25. Hold the adjustable cone with one wrench while you tighten the locknut with another wrench. The cone and locknut on the facing side of the hub should still only be hand-tight.

26. Hold the adjustable cone you tightened in step 25 above with one wrench. Tighten the other adjustable cone just barely snug. Back the cone off, counterclockwise, a half turn. Now hold that cone with one wrench and tighten its locknut with another wrench.

27. Here is the critical step in adjusting not only hub bearings but all nonsealed bearings in the bottom bracket, headset and pedals:

    a. Insert the quick-release skewer in the hollow hub axle. Be sure the small side of the little springs face toward the hub.

    b. Adjust the quick-release lever (please review these instructions in Chapter 3 and see Figs. 3-51 to 3-57, and 3-60, 3-61, 3-62). Turn the release lever to the closed position.

    c. Or if you have a solid axle, thread on the bolts and tighten them to 300–350 inch-lb.

        (Note: When you tighten the axle in the bicycle frame dropouts, hub adjustable cones will tighten up due to thread play.)

    d. Twist the axle. If it feels tight (you feel turning resistance), loosen the quick release or the axle nut, loosen the locknut with one wrench and loosen the adjustable cone a quarter turn with another wrench. Hold the adjustable cup with one wrench, tighten the locknut with the other wrench. Close the quick release or tighten the axle nuts again. Repeat this step until the axle spins smoothly.

    e. Grasp the tire. With quick, sharp jerks, move the wheel from side to side. If you feel sideplay, the cone adjustment is too loose. Readjust cone as above.

Sealed Bearing Hubs

Lubrication of cartridge, sealed bearing hubs is simple:

1. Follow steps 1 and 2 above (remove the wheel, quick release or axle bolts).

2. *Carefully* pry off the fragile seal (Fig. 7-8 and Fig. 7-9) with a thin-bladed knife.

3. With your fingers, force grease into the bearing cartridges. Be generous.

4. Replace the seal. Remember, the seal is fairly fragile. If bent, it won't seal well. Press it back evenly all around the edges.

Eventually cartridge bearings wear out and need replacement. As I said earlier, this requires special tools and should be a bicycle shop job. However, on some sealed hubs, such as SunTour and Mavic, you could, in an emergency, tap the axle out through the hub with light use of hammer. Then, with a carefully placed screwdriver, inserted through the hub onto the inner steel edge of the cartridge, tap the pressed-in cartridge bearing out of the hub. Install new bearings by reversing this procedure. Or you could order the special tools for your particular hub from your dealer. Be sure to use an exact cartridge replacement. You may also be able to find a clone cartridge from a bearing supply house, since these are the same bearings used in small electric motors, e.g.

Note: The quick release is just that. It's quick for you, and quick for crooks. One way to have the benefits of a quick release without the hazard of theft is to install a Qwik Cam (Fig. 7-10). It replaces the lever with a standard Allen wrench. If you lose the wrench, you can always buy another in any hardware store.

Fig. 7-8. *Bearing seals can be pried off, carefully, with a thin-blade knife.*

Fig. 7-9. *Sealed bearing, with seal removed.*

Fig. 7-10. Replace quick-release lever with this security device to reduce possibility of wheel theft. See text.

Bottom Bracket Maintenance

The bottom bracket (Fig. 7-11) consists of ball bearings, usually in a retainer, a fixed cup on the right side of the bicycle, a plastic seal inside the bottom bracket shell, an adjustable cup and a lockring. Some bottom brackets use sealed cartridge bearings which *are not* removable except with an arbor press. However, some types of sealed bearing bottom

Fig. 7-11. Bottom bracket. A, axle; AA, axle flats; B, fixed cup; C, adjustable cup; D, lockbolts that hold cranks on axle; E, locknut (a.k.a. lockring); F, ball bearings in retainers; G, washers to go under lockbolts D.

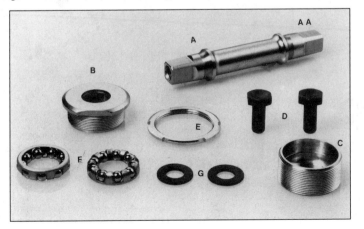

brackets can replace conventional units, as noted below. But on Fisher and Klein ATBs, e.g., the bottom bracket unit is not removable except with shop tools, a job for the bike shop. I'll discuss these later on in this section. Let's start with the nonsealed ball bearing type bottom bracket.

Tools You Will Need

1. A locknut remover to fit your locknut. See your bicycle dealer for the type you need.

2. Pin wrench for the adjustable cup (Fig. 7-12). Although a pin wrench will fit any hole *spacing,* not every manufacturer's holes are the same *diameter.* Make sure the pin wrench you buy will fit the holes in your adjustable cup.

Disassembly

1. Remove the cranks. See Chapter 6 for instructions.

2. Remove the lockring counterclockwise (Fig. 7-13).

3. Remove the adjustable cup counterclockwise (Fig. 7-14).

4. Remove the outer set of bearings, the axle, the inner set of bearings and any plastic seal (Fig. 7-15). The bearings in older bikes may be loose instead of in a retainer, so be ready to catch them.

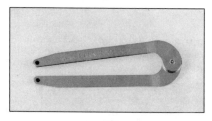

Fig. 7-12.   Pin wrench for removing bottom bracket adjustable cup.

Fig. 7-13.   Removing bottom bracket lockring.

Fig. 7-14.   Removing and/or adjusting bottom bracket adjustable cup.

Fig. 7-15. *With lockring and adjustable cup removed, bearings and axle can be removed from bottom bracket shell.*

5. Clean dirt and old grease from cups and bearings with kerosene.

6. Inspect the bearings for wear. If your bike is relatively new and hasn't had much use, chances are that all you will need to do, after cleaning the bearings, cups and spindle, is to repack the bearings with grease and replace them. If the balls are in a retainer, I recommend scrapping the old balls along with their retainer (Fig. 7-16) and replacing them with loose balls. This will give you 11 instead of 9 balls per bearing set, so the bottom bracket spindle will run more smoothly, and the additional balls will add to both bearing and cup life. Most modern bottom brackets use ¼-inch balls, but take your old ones to the bike shop to make sure you get the same size replacements.

7. Inspect the cups (Fig. 7-17) for signs of galling or brinelling, indicated by pitting or grooves worn in the race, and replace them if necessary.

Fig. 7-16. *When replacing bottom bracket bearings, be sure their curvature matches that of the axle curved bearing surfaces.*

Fig. 7-17. *Fixed cups removed. Arrows show where to look for damage. Note: If this cup is worn, most likely the adjustable cup and all bearings are too and should be replaced.*

Reassembly

Now that you have cleaned your ball-and-cup type bottom bracket and replaced any worn parts, you are ready to grease and put it back together. I recommend boat trailer wheel bearing grease. It adds a bit more pedaling drag but won't wash out as fast as ordinary grease when you run through water or mud. Here are the steps for reassembly:

1. Roll the loose balls in grease until they are thoroughly covered.
2. Put a layer of grease on both cups.
3. Put the loose balls in the cups. The grease will hold them in place.
4. Insert the spindle (a.k.a. axle) in the bottom bracket. Make sure the longer spindle end goes in first, because that's the spindle side for the chainwheels. If your bottom bracket did not come with a plastic protective cover, it's a good idea to install one (Fig. 7-18) to keep away abrasives and water that get into frame tubes and work down into the bottom bracket shell.
5. Thread the adjustable cup clockwise into the bottom bracket shell, and turn it by hand as far as possible. Use the pin wrench to continue turning it until it's snug. Back the cup off a half turn.
6. Thread the lockring onto the adjustable cup by hand. Hold the adjustable cup with the pin wrench so it can't turn, and tighten the lockring firmly with the lockring wrench.
7. Check bearing adjustment for tightness. Twirl the spindle with your thumb and a finger. It should rotate smoothly. If it feels rough or is hard to turn, loosen the lockring and turn the adjustable cup counterclockwise about a quarter turn, and tighten the lockring. Check the adjustment and repeat this step as necessary.
8. Install both cranks. See instructions in Chapter 6.
9. Check the bearing adjustment for looseness. Place the crank at the 12 o'clock position and move it sharply from side to side, toward

Fig. 7-18. *Complete bottom bracket assembly. Protective plastic shield, bottom, helps keep out water and dust that might drip down the seat and downtubes into the bottom bracket shell and increase bearing wear.*

and away from you. If you feel looseness, turn the lockring counter-clockwise until it's loose, and turn the adjustable cup clockwise about a quarter turn. Hold the adjustable cup with the pin wrench and tighten the lockring. Check this adjustment and repeat this step as necessary. The cranks should rotate smoothly and stop gradually.

Replacing the Bottom Bracket Unit

If the adjustable cup bearing surface is worn, pitted or grooved, it should, of course, be replaced. Replace the fixed cup also because it, too, will be shot. However, if you have to go this far, I recommend you replace the old bottom bracket assembly with a sealed bearing unit, such as one made by SunTour (Fig. 7-19). When you buy the cartridge type, make sure you get one with a long spindle if you have a triple chainwheel. Here's how to replace it:

1. Remove cranks and adjustable cup and its lockring as described above.
2. Remove the fixed cup. The fixed cup has flats for a special wrench. Use the one that fits your fixed cup. I recommend that you not invest in this tool for only this one-shot purpose, though. It's a tough job and you can damage the frame if you are not careful. Most fixed cups, particularly on older bikes, are on so tight it takes a lot more torque (turning energy) than you can apply with this tool. Have the fixed cup removed by a bike shop, which has special tools for this operation. As I noted, the only reason to remove the fixed cup is to change to another make or model bottom bracket assembly. You could remove the fixed cup by holding the cup flats in a machinist's vise and turning the entire bike. Your vise should have undamanged jaws for this operation, oth-erwise the fixed cup flats will slip out of the vise. If the bike was made in the United States, France or Italy, turn the bike clockwise. If it's made anyplace else, chances are the cup is right-hand threaded, so turn the bike counterclockwise.

Fig. 7-19. Sealed bearing bottom bracket unit.

3. Replace the new bottom bracket assembly. See instructions above. Or install a sealed bearing unit (Fig. 7-19). You will most likely need special tools for the lockrings. However, one advantage of a sealed bearing unit, the kind that replaces conventional bearing units, is that the sealed unit can be adjusted left or right to meet your chainline needs. Please refer to the discussion on chainline in Chapter 6.

Sealed Bearing Bottom Bracket Maintenance, Cartridge Type

1. Remove both cranks for access to bearing seals.

2. Look at your bottom bracket seals. Do they have snap rings (Fig. 7-20)? If so, please go on to the instructions for snap ring bottom brackets, below.

3. If not, use the special wrench that fits your bottom bracket adjustable locknut to remove it.

4. Remove the bottom bracket unit.

5. Pry off all bearing seals with a thin-bladed knife.

6. Stuff grease into the bearings.

7. Replace the seals.

8. Replace the bottom bracket unit. This is a good time to check your chainline, since, as I noted, the bottom bracket unit can be moved left or right as necessary to correct a misaligned chainline. See Chapter 6 for chainline data.

9. Replace the cranks. See Chapter 6.

Fig. 7-20. *This type of sealed bearing bottom bracket unit can only be removed with special tools, a shop job. To grease bearings, simply remove snap ring, pry out shield and stuff in grease.*

Sealed Bottom Bracket Maintenance, Snap Ring Type

1. Remove both cranks for access to bearing seals.

2. This type of bottom bracket unit (Fig. 7-20) cannot be removed except with an arbor press. This is definitely a shop job. However, you can certainly relube these bearings, as follows:

   a. Remove both snap rings with a pair of snap ring pliers.

   b. Pry off both O-ring seals with a thin bladed knife.

   c. Use a small grease injector (Fig. 7-21) or your finger to push grease into the bearings.

   d. Replace the seals and replace the cartridge in the bike's bottom bracket shell.

   e. Replace the cranks.

HEADSET MAINTENANCE

The headset (Fig. 7-22) takes a terrific beating, especially on rough roads. The lower set of balls is under thrust stress, the upper set is under radial stress. Thrust stress is force applied toward or away from an object, like

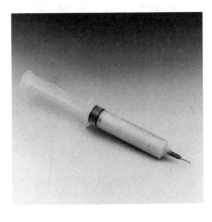

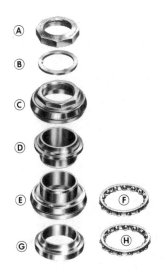

Fig. 7-21. Use a grease injector to get grease into sealed cartridge bearing.

Fig. 7-22. Headset components. A, locknut (a.k.a. lockring); B, washer; C, adjustable cup; D, top fixed cone; E, bottom fixed cup; F and H, ball bearings in retainers; G, bottom fixed cone.

the reactive force on the springs of a car on a rough road or when you strike a nail with a hammer. Radial stress is force spread outward, like the ripples a pebble makes when it's dropped in a pond. Road shock tends to flatten bearings. The bottom set takes most of the beating. Road shock will also wear grooves in the headset cups and cones.

Loose headsets will cause wheel shimmy, loss of control, and an accident. Please see Chapter 3 for a review of the hazards of wheel shimmy, which are very real and very definite. There is also more information on this subject later in this chapter.

Make these two checks for headset adjustment every few months if you ride a lot:

1. Straddle the bike, squeeze the front brake lever hard, rock the bike back and forth (Fig. 2-21), and watch the headset locknut as you do so. If you feel looseness, if the locknut moves in any direction, or if it's so loose you can turn it by hand, readjust the headset bearings, as shown below, to prevent hazardous wheel shimmy.

2. Raise the front brake lever, lift the front wheel off the floor and turn the handlebars from side to side. The handlebars should turn or move without binding. Readjust headset bearings if necessary, as shown below.

Disassemble, clean and readjust the headset every four to six months, and install new bearings every year. Here's how to do it:

Tools You Will Need

1. Pair of headset wrenches (Fig. 7-23) that fit Campagnolo, SunTour and older Shimano headset locknuts and adjustable cups. The new larger headsets take a 36-mm wrench, the older ones a 32-mm. Mavic headsets

Fig. 7-23. Use one wrench to hold the adjustable cone while, with the other, remove the locknut.

take *two* sizes, one wrench for the locknut, a bigger one for the adjustable cup. These wrenches (Fig. 7-24) are very special, won't fit anything else. Shimano has special headset wrenches (Fig. 7-25), but standard 32-mm wrenches will also fit their newer headsets.

2. A 5- or 6-mm Allen wrench or a 10-mm open end wrench to fit your stem binder bolt (Fig. 7-26).

Steps for Headset Maintenance

1. Remove the front wheel.

2. With chalk, mark the stem where it comes out of the locknut, so you can replace it at the same height. This is important, because if you change the stem height, you will have to readjust the front brake-shoe-to-rim clearance, as I noted in Chapter 3 and Chapter 5.

3. Loosen the stem binder bolt with a 6-mm Allen wrench or 10-, 11- or 12-mm wrench (Fig. 7-26), but do not remove it all the way. The expansion bolt has a nut that expands against an angle cut in the stem

Fig. 7-24. Mavic headset wrenches.

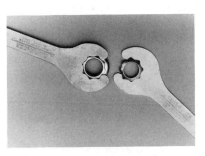

Fig. 7-25. Shimano headset wrenches. However, you can also use 32-mm headset wrenches.

Fig. 7-26. Loosen the stem binder bolt to remove the stem.

(Fig. 7-27). As it's tightened, it wedges the stem tightly inside the fork steering tube. The stem bolt must be tapped down to break the wedge lock. Tap this bolt down with a hammer over a block of wood (Fig. 7-28). One tap should break it loose.

4. Remove the handlebars and stem (Fig. 7-29). Drape them over the top tube, out of the way.

5. Remove the locknut. Hold the adjustable cup with one wrench while you loosen the locknut with another wrench (Fig. 7-23). Remove the washer under the locknut.

6. Loosen the adjustable cup until you can turn it by hand. Hold the fork in the bike with one hand while you remove the adjustable cup (Fig. 7-30). Carefully remove the fork. Catch loose bearings if they're not in a retainer. Or put a rag on the workbench, put the bike on it, and catch loose balls as you withdraw the fork.

7. If the headset has a dust shield (Fig. 7-31), remove it so you can remove the ball bearings.

8. Remove the bearings. Clean off old grease. If the bearings are in

Fig. 7-27. The stem binder bolt uses an expansion nut that when tightened presses against the steering tube to hold the stem firmly in place.

Fig. 7-28. With the stem expansion or binder bolt loose, tap it down to break the bond between the bolt and the steering tube, so the stem can be removed.

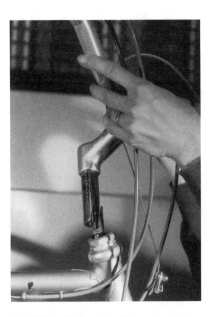

Fig. 7-30. Hold the fork with one hand while you remove the adjustable cup and top set of bearings. Carefully pull the fork out. Be ready to catch any loose bearings that may fall out of a worn retainer. In some cases, balls may be loose, not in retainers.

Fig. 7-29. Stem, handlebars and cables can be removed and draped over the top tube so you can remove the headset.

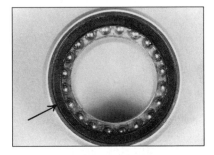

Fig. 7-31. Remove the seal (arrow), so you can remove the balls in their retainer.

a retainer, check retainer and bearing wear. If the bearings easily fall out of the retainer, it's time to replace them.

9. Clean old grease out of the adjustable cup and the top and bottom cones and cup.

10. Examine cups and cones for grooves, rust or wear. If you see grooves or dents in the cups or cones, take your bike to the bike shop and have them replaced. Don't do this yourself. This job requires special tools and skills. Have your bike shop check the seats where the cones and cups fit to make sure the factory has accurately machined them. If not, have them remachined so that cups and cones seat accurately. This permits the bearings to absorb road shock evenly and wear uniformly. Uneven bearing wear can loosen the headset and cause wheel shimmy.

Headset Reassembly

1. Headset bearings are inexpensive. But they can play a major role in safe bicycle handling, and in wheel shimmy avoidance. My advice is to install new balls. Forget the retainer. Buy enough of the same size to replace the number of balls in the retainer plus two or three more. As you can see in Figure 7-32, you can get more balls, at least two more, in the same space. More balls mean greater headset life and improved protection against bearing wear.

2. Reassemble the headset. Grease the bearings, cups and cones. Replace any seals. Note: If you leave the bearings in the retainer, be sure you replace the retainer correctly. The curvature of the retainer must be matched to the curvature of the cone.

3. Place the bottom set of bearings in the bottom cup with enough grease to hold them in place.

4. Put a lot of grease in the adjustable cup. Fill the cup with the ball bearings (Fig. 7-33).

5. Replace the fork. Be careful not to knock any balls off the bottom cup. Hold the fork in place while you thread on the adjustable cup by hand, as far as possible.

6. Tighten the adjustable cup with a wrench until it is snug, then back it off a quarter turn.

Fig. 7-32. *Replace headset balls when you take the headset apart. The balls are tiny, their beating is big, their cost is small. Use loose bearings; you get two extra balls to absorb road shock that way, as you can see. Buy extra balls to replace those you drop that, with a life of their own, take refuge where you will never, never find them.*

Fig. 7-33. *Be generous with grease, a cost-effective route to longer bearing life.*

7. Install the washer over the adjustable cup.

8. Thread on the locknut. Hold the adjustable cup with one wrench and tighten the locknut with the other wrench.

9. Replace the handlebars. The stem should be at the height marked earlier. Remember, if you don't replace the stem at the original height, you will have to readjust brake shoe clearance, for which please see Chapter 5. Also, and this is very important, at least 2½ inches of the stem *must be inside the steering tube* (Fig. 7-34)!

10. Tighten the expander bolt to 180 inch-pounds.

11. Replace the front wheel.

12. Check the headset adjustable cup setting:

   a. Check for looseness. Mount the bike. Hold the front brake lever tightly closed. Rock the bike back and forth (Fig. 2-21). If the fork feels loose, hold the adjustable cup with one wrench and turn the locknut counterclockwise one turn. Turn the adjustable cup clockwise a quarter turn, hold it with the wrench, and tighten the locknut. Repeat until the fork has no free play.

   b. Check the headset for tightness. Lift the front wheel off the ground and turn the handlebars in both directions. Tilt the bike so the handlebars move freely by gravity, without binding or tightness. If the handlebars stick or bind, hold the adjustable cup with a wrench, loosen the locknut, then loosen the adjustable cup a quarter turn and hold it with a wrench while you tighten the locknut. Repeat until the fork turns freely.

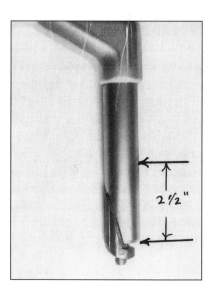

Fig. 7-34. *Keep at least 2½ inches of the stem inside the head tube.*

A Word About Wheel Shimmy

I've mentioned the dangers of wheel shimmy several times so far in this book. Once started, shimmy is difficult or impossible to stop. You can easily lose control and go for a spill. Loose headsets are the cause of many wheel shimmy accidents. Headsets work loose more often in all-terrain bicycles than in other bike types. This is because trail shock ultimately flattens the headset just a fraction of a thousandth of an inch. The flattening effect comes sooner if the headset is loose. It always creeps up on you, gradually, unnoticeably. Sometimes, the headset locknut and adjustable cup work loose as bearings wear down. Sometimes, the adjustable cup is loose to begin with, right out of the bike factory. Then, one day, at speed, down a rough, steep hill, the front wheel assumes a quick left-right-left life of its own.

I have even found five balls missing from the retainer in one ATB accident I investigated, an accident involving wheel shimmy and serious, permanent injury to the rider. This particular ATB was an el cheapo, part of a stable of similar inexpensive (spell that under $200) bikes for loan to guests of this mountain resort inn. We can glean two lessons here. First, loaner bikes may be dangerous. Two, cheap bikes have poor metallurgy, steel parts that wear down fast on repeated impact. In the case of this accident, the bike involved had a headset with grooves worn in cups and cones, *plus* missing ball bearings.

Even expensive bikes may have loose headsets. For example, a few years ago, on a bike trip in Puget Sound's San Juan Islands, I made a random check of headsets of bikes parked on the ferry en route from island to island. Many of these bikes had been rented from bike shops on the mainland or had been provided by a bike tour agency. I must have checked a hundred bikes during these island-hopping ferry rides. About one in every four bikes I checked had dangerously loose headsets.

A good way to keep the headset from working loose is to install a SunTour headset clamp (Fig. 7-35 and Fig. 7-36). This unit prevents the locknut from loosening. Or install a Max System Bulldog Brace head and stem lock (Fig. 7-37 and Fig. 7-38). This headset lock has a set-screw lock plus tapered prongs and a clamping ring that locks the prongs against the handlebar stem. If your bike shop does not have this set, write to Cariberia Imports, Nevada 306, San Gerardo, Rio Piedras, Puerto Rico 00926, or phone 1-809-764-8422.

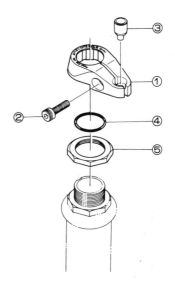

Fig. 7-35. *Use a headset lock device to help prevent the locknut from working loose and causing wheel shimmy and an accident.*

Fig. 7-36. *Another view of the head- set locking device in Figure 7-35.*

Fig. 7-37. *Another type of headset locking device. Note grip prong washer at bottom.*

Fig. 7-38. *Lockrings of the device in Figure 7-37, which expand and grip steering head when tightened down. Set screw also locks these lockrings in place.*

PEDAL MAINTENANCE

The pedals on your bike sit closer to the ground than any other part except tires, so they take heavy wear from dust, dirt and water. Their tiny ball bearings are subjected to pressure of 50 pounds in moderate pedaling, 170 pounds when racing, and 350 pounds by strong riders straining uphill. So pedals require periodic cleaning and lubrication, especially after hard riding over trails and through water. Here's how to maintain your ball bearing type pedals (for cartirdge type bearings see separate instructions later in this section):

Tools You Will Need

1. 8-, 10-, 11- and 15-mm wrenches.
2. Special wrenches for your pedals if they don't take the tools above. See your bike shop.

Maintenance Steps

Maintenance is pretty straightforward. It simply involves getting access to the bearings, removing, cleaning and replacing them. Here's how:

1. Remove both pedals. Most pedal axle flats take a 15-mm wrench. A few makes use a 6-mm Allen wrench on the inside end of the axle. I don't want to get you all bogged down with right- and left-hand thread instructions. Just remember this: *pedals always thread on in the direction of crank rotation and, of course, thread off opposite crank rotation.* If you keep this in mind you can't go wrong. Also remember that most pedals have an "R" and an "L" stamped on the axle.
2. Put the threaded end of the pedal axle in a pedal vise (Fig. 7-4), and put that vise in a bench vise. (Note: this pedal vise has a small-diameter hole for the pedal axle, a larger one for the hub axle.) Now you are ready to work on the pedal. You could skip the pedal vise and just hold the pedal by the axle flats in a bench vise, the part you turn with a wrench. But the axle vise is much handier and eliminates the potential for thread damage.
3. Remove the dust cap (Fig. 7-39). You may need a special tool for this, thanks to those busy little engineer types. To even get at the dust cap on some pedals you have to remove the cage. Most take a 2-mm Allen wrench.
4. With a 9-, 10- or 11-mm wrench, turn the axle locknut counterclockwise, and remove it and the washer under it.
5. Remove the pedal from the axle vise, and lay the pedal on a rag on the workbench, ready to catch the small loose ball bearings.
6. Turn the adjustable cone (Fig. 7-40) counterclockwise and remove it.
7. Pull the axle out of the pedal body. Remove all the bearings.

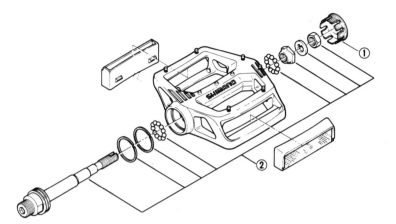

Fig. 7-39. *Exploded view of typical ATB pedal. 1, the dustcap; 2, the component group.*

Fig. 7-40. *Pencil points to pedal adjustable cone.*

8. Clean the bearings, cones and axle bearing faces.

9. Put a generous layer of grease on both cups in the pedal body.

10. Replace the balls in both pedal body cups.

11. Insert the axle in the pedal body. Be careful not to knock balls out of the cups as the axle goes in.

12. Thread on the adjustable cone, hand-tight, as far as possible.

13. Replace the pedal in the axle vise.

14. Replace the washer and thread on the locknut.

15. Tighten the locknut while you hold the adjustable cup from turning.

16. Remove the pedal from the vise. Twist the axle between thumb and forefinger. If it feels tight, loosen the locknut, back the adjustable cup off a quarter turn and retighten the locknut as in step 15 above. Now push the axle in and out from side to side. If you feel play, loosen

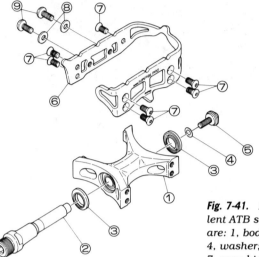

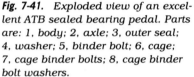

Fig. 7-41. *Exploded view of an excellent ATB sealed bearing pedal. Parts are: 1, body; 2, axle; 3, outer seal; 4, washer; 5, binder bolt; 6, cage; 7, cage binder bolts; 8, cage binder bolt washers.*

the locknut, tighten the adjustable cup a quarter turn and retighten the locknut. Repeat these steps until the axle turns smoothly, without binding or looseness.

    17. Replace the pedal cages.

    18. Replace the pedals on the cranks.

Cartridge Type Bearings

These bearings use standard industrial cartridge bearings, available from a bearing supply house or from a small electrical motor repair shop (in case your bike shop doesn't stock them).

    1. Remove the pedals.

    2. Remove the cage.

    3. Remove the axle bearing retainer bolt ("5" in Fig. 7-41).

    4. Carefully tap the axle out of the pedal body.

    5. Carefully pry off bearing seals with a thin-bladed knife.

    6. Stuff lots of grease into the bearings and press the seals back in place.

    7. Carefully tap the axle back into the pedal body.

    8. Replace the pedals on the cranks.

    In the next chapter we will cover the saddle, seat post and handlebar adjustments.

8

Tire Repair, Saddles, Seat Posts and Handlebars

H ere are quick, easy and effective ways of avoiding flats, repairing punctured tubes, adjusting handlebars and saddles, and some new products that can make your rides easier and less fatiguing.

First, tire repair for when, not if, you get a flat. Start by improving the odds against a puncture.

TIRE CARE

1. *Reduce impact on your tires* and the chance of a blowout as you come to an obstruction, such as a pothole. Pull back on the handlebars as the front wheel comes to a tire-threatening obstacle. Move forward on the saddle as the rear wheel does the same.

2. *Protect your tubes from punctures by street debris.* Install a heavy-duty plastic tire liner, such as Mr. Tuffy, between the tire and the tube. This liner comes in sizes to fit most tires. In areas where barbed thorns can cause many flats, such as the Southwest, use thicker thorn-resistant tubes (Fig. 8-1). You could also switch to a semisolid tire called the Poly-Air. It has no inner tube so it is immune to punctures. If you can't find it at your bike shop, write Poly-Air Tires, Inc., 205, 259 Midpark Way S.E., Calgary, Alberta, Canada T2X 1M2, phone 403-256-9562. I can

Fig. 8-1. Use a thorn-proof tube, left, in cactus country.

report that these tires offer the same, or nearly the same, comfort as pneumatic tires.

3. *Remove anything stuck in your tires,* such as glass shards, nails, thorns and small stones in the tread, before each ride.

4. *Replace worn tires and those with weather-cracked sidewalls.* The cost of new tires is a small price to pay to avoid accident-causing tire failure.

5. *Alternate braking between front and rear wheels* on long downhill runs, to avoid heat buildup that could cause a blowout.

6. *Match a new tire to your rim width.* ATB tire tread widths vary from 2.25 inches to 1.5 inches. Bead widths of these tires can vary even within the same sizes. Please review tire-to-rim sizing data in Chapter 3. As a general rule, use the wider tires with the wider rims. If you put a wide tire on a narrow rim you risk a bead pop-out and a blowout.

7. *Keep tires inflated to the correct pressure.* For trail, off-road rides, keep at least 35 psi in the tire. For road use increase the pressure to 50–75 psi, depending on the make of tire. Tire sidewalls usually give safe pressure ranges. An underinflated tire can bottom out and puncture, an overinflated tire can pop the tire off the rim.

8. *Scan the road ahead.* Watch for anything on the road immediately in front of your bike that could cause a puncture. Be ready to take evasive action.

Always carry a tire pump. Pumps come in different lengths to fit specific frame sizes. Take your bike to the shop to make sure the pump fits your bike. Better yet, if you are buying a new bike, buy a pump, patch kit and tire levers at the same time, along with a couple of spare tubes. One company, Odyssey, even makes a seat post that doubles as a tire pump. You remove the saddle and seat post as a unit to pump up your tire. I like this idea, because bumpy trails or projecting limbs can knock a frame-mounted pump off your bike. Another pump folds into a small size for carrying in the bike bag (Fig. 8-2).

Fig. 8-2. *Collapsible pump, shown collapsed, takes up little room in your bike bag.*

Of course, always carry a patch kit and tire levers. Bring a roll of duct tape (ask your hardware store clerk). Use it to patch slits and large holes in the tire that would result in a cut in the tube or a puncture. The duct tape can get you home, where you can replace the tire.

Spare tubes keep you on the move. Patch the punctured tube later, around the campfire. Fold-up knobby tires spell security. Stow them in your bike bag or strap them on your carrier or under your seat. If you destroy a tire on a razor-sharp rock, the spare tire will keep you going.

HOW TO FIX A FLAT

Tools and equipment you will need: (a) patch kit, (b) tire levers and (c) duct tape.

1. Release remaining air from the tube by holding down the valve core. Use a twig or pencil on a Schraeder valve or unscrew its core (Fig. 8-3). Unscrew a Presta valve core and hold it down (Fig. 8-4).

2. Remove the wheel from the bicycle.

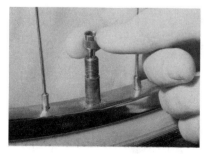

Fig. 8-3. *Remove air from a Schraeder valve tube by removing the valve core or pushing down on the core with a pencil, thin screwdriver or twig.*

Fig. 8-4. *Remove air from a Presta valve tube by unscrewing and pushing the valve core down. Screw the core down when the flat is fixed or after you have pumped air into the tube.*

3. Squeeze both sides of the tire all the way around to break the bond between tire bead and rim.

4. Remove the tire from the rim, starting on the side opposite the valve (Fig. 8-5). If the tire is really stubborn, use two tire levers, one to hold the tire off the rim, and the other to separate the tire bead from the rim. Once you get about 10 inches of the bead off, you should be able to remove the rest of the bead with one lever or with your fingers.

5. Remove the tube from the tire.

6. Pump air into the tube so you can find the leak (Fig. 8-6).

Fig. 8-5. *Use one, or if the tire is stubborn, two tire levers to pry the tire off the wheel. Start across from the valve.*

Fig. 8-6. *Pump air into the tube to find the puncture.*

7. Use one of these three ways to find the leak:
   a. Dunk the tube in water, and watch for the source of air bubbles (Fig. 8-7).
   b. If water isn't available, try listening for the hiss of escaping air (Fig. 8-8).
   c. Put the tube next to your cheek to feel escaping air (Fig. 8-9).
   d. Circle leak(s) with chalk, a pen or anything that will leave a mark on the tube (Fig. 8-10).

Fig. 8-7. Dip the tube into water. Bubbles show the location of the puncture.

Fig. 8-8. If water isn't available, try listening for the hiss of escaping air to find the puncture location.

Fig. 8-10. Circle the puncture with chalk, a pen or pencil.

Fig. 8-9. Put the tube next to your cheek to feel the rush of escaping air through the puncture.

8. Roughen the area around the puncture with the sandpaper that came with your patch kit (Fig. 8-11). Don't use a metal scraper; it can weaken the tube.

9. Put a few drops of patch rubber cement around the puncture area (Fig. 8-12). Spread it out with the nozzle of the glue tube and wait a minute until it gets tacky.

10. Peel the backing paper off a patch (Fig. 8-13). Put the patch on the puncture and press it down firmly with your fingers (Fig. 8-14).

11. Pump up the tube and check it again for punctures and leaks as above. Moisten the top of the valve to make sure the valve core is seated. If you see bubbles, tighten the valve core. If the valve still leaks on a Schraeder valve, buy a new valve core from your bike shop or a service station. Presta valve cores aren't replaceable.

Fig. 8-11. *Gently abrade the tube around the puncture with sandpaper.*

Fig. 8-12. *Apply a few drops of patch cement and spread it around the puncture.*

Fig. 8-13. *Peel the backing off a patch.*

Fig. 8-14. *Wait till the patch cement is tacky, then apply the patch over the puncture.*

12. Thoroughly inspect the inside tire casing, sidewalls and tread for whatever caused the puncture. Remove all foreign embedments. If you find a slit in the tire casing, roughen the cut area on the inside of the tire with sandpaper. Cover that area with patch cement. When the cement dries, cover the cut with a canvas patch from your patch kit or with a piece of duct tape. Otherwise the slit can puncture the tube. Replace a slit tire as soon as possible.

13. If you have a major cut in the tube and no spare tube, put multiple patches over the slit, then apply duct tape around the patches. If you're lucky you may have a slow leak but can make it home.

14. If you don't have a tire lever, remove the quick-release unit from the hub and use its lever. It works.

15. Check your patch kit every so often to make sure an opened tube of rubber cement hasn't dried out. Keep a couple of extra patch kits in your bike bag.

16. Remove the rim strip (Fig. 8-15). Snip off any spokes that protrude from the nipples and could puncture the tube. Install a new rim strip if necessary.

REASSEMBLING THE TIRE AND TUBE

1. Lay the tire on a flat surface and put the tube in it (Fig. 8-16).

2. If the tire has a directional tread (see sidewall), make sure it faces the direction of wheel rotation.

Fig. 8-15. Remove the rim strip. Check underneath for protruding spokes that could puncture the tube, and cut them off above the nipple.

Fig. 8-16. On a flat surface, replace the tube in the tire. But first check inside the tire tread, interior and sidewalls, for cuts, breaks and whatever caused the puncture.

3. Place the tire and tube over the rim, and push the valve stem through the rim hole (Fig. 8-17).

4. Place one side of the tire on the rim, fitting the tire in both directions from the valve (Fig. 8-18). Continue until one side is fitted completely in the rim.

5. Turn the wheel over and finish fitting the tire in the rim, again working evenly from both sides of the valve (Fig. 8-19). You should be able to work by hand (Fig. 8-20). If you have trouble, use the tire lever but be careful not to squeeze and puncture the tube between the tire lever and the rim.

6. Make sure the tire seats evenly in the rim, especially at the valve area. Push the valve down into the tire about an inch, then squeeze the tire walls until the tire is seated in the rim. Otherwise the tire wall will protrude.

Fig. 8-17.   Push the valve out through the valve hole in the rim.

Fig. 8-18.   Start the tire replacement at the valve area.

Fig. 8-19.   With your fingers, push the tire bead in the rim.

Fig. 8-20.   Finish up tire replacement with your fingers. If you must use a tire lever, be careful not to squeeze and puncture the tube against the rim.

7. Pump the tire up. If you have Presta valves, remember these are fragile and easily broken if you don't hold the pump steady as you use the plunger (Fig. 8-21) (if you use a frame-mounted pump). Hold the pump on the valve as shown in Figure 8-21. Remove the pump from a Presta valve with a sharp downward blow from the side of your hand (Fig. 8-22). Don't try to wiggle it off; that's a good way to bend and break the valve stem.

8. Inspect the tire sidewalls to be sure the bead is evenly seated, all the way around, in the wheel rim. If not, deflate, reseat, and pump the tire up.

SADDLES

What you sit on and what you steer with are both major contributors to cycling comfort or pain. Frankly, when it comes to saddles, I prefer one made of leather, preferably one with springs that absorb road shock. A leather saddle will have "give," and the leather shapes and molds itself to your anatomy (Fig. 8-23). As it conforms to you, the leather saddle offers support where you need it most. A plastic saddle, on the other hand, will never shape itself to you. The plastic has little "give" or

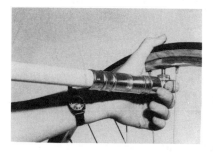

Fig. 8-21. *Hold the pump as shown. This is specially important with a more fragile Presta valve.*

Fig. 8-22. *Remove the pump with a sharp downward blow. If you wiggle it off you could break a Presta valve.*

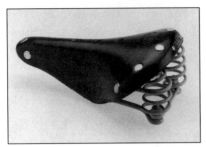

Fig. 8-23. This leather saddle will break in and conform to your body contours.

bounce. Even gel-filled plastic saddles or saddle covers cannot, in my opinion, begin to challenge the comfort of a leather saddle. Ask any cowpoke, equestrian or mounted cop.

Excellent high-quality leather saddles have been made by Brooks since the early 1900s. The Brooks Conquest two-wire dual spring saddle (Fig. 8-23), costs around $40 from any good bike shop. This is the rugged, comfortable model I recommend for trail or road riding. It weighs 30.3 ounces. A 16.7-ounce version, the Brooks Team Professional, without springs, costs the same. I prefer the spring-loaded comfort of the Conquest, which reduces fatigue on long, bumpy rides.

Leather Saddle Selection and Care

Keep your fine leather saddle (I'll cover other saddle materials below) in shape for years of riding comfort. Here's how:

1. **Break-in:** Time and miles are the only way to break in a new leather saddle. It takes at least 500 miles of riding to make a new saddle pliable enough to fit your anatomy. It's worth it. You could also ride your leather saddle on a bike exerciser, which is how I broke in one leather saddle.

Don't try to break in a new leather saddle by soaking it in neat's-foot oil. This will oversoften the leather, so that it will be swaybacked.

2. **Leather Preservation:**

a. First, brush the saddle with a soft, dry cloth.

b. For a new saddle, apply a light coat of a good leather preservative, such as Brooks Proofide, to the top portion of the saddle. Use a soft cloth.

c. Let the preservative dry, preferably overnight, so it soaks into the leather.

d. Polish the saddle with a soft cloth.

e. Apply the preservative after every ride through rain. This is especially important if your bike does not have fenders to keep water and dirt off your saddle.

f. Never apply heat to the saddle to dry the preservative. If the saddle is water-soaked, dry it at room temperature before applying preservative. Note: Some leather saddles, such as the Brooks Team Pro Special ($44.95, 15.3 oz, no springs), are prestretched and dressed with preservative, so the initial dressing is unnecessary.

3. **Saddle Adjustments:** A leather saddle will stretch. If you can depress the saddle by pushing hard on it, it's time to take out the stretch. Remove this stretch by turning the stretch adjuster, located at the nose of the saddle (Fig. 8-24).

Four-Wire Adapter

If you have one of the older Brooks saddles, the kind with four wires (Fig. 8-25), you should install an adapter (Fig. 8-26) to keep the wires from bending. Modern seat posts are made for two-wire saddles. The new two-wire model (Fig. 8-23) can be installed on any standard seat post. If you install a four-wire saddle on a seat post built for two wires, the wire can bend, especially if you are a heavyweight. When the saddle wire bends, the saddle will tilt off-center. The adapter costs around $10. Insert the adapter so the two-wire seat-post clamp grips all four saddle wires (Fig. 8-26). The adapter comes with a longer seat-post clamp bolt because the four wires are wider. The adapter fits Campagnolo Gran

Fig. 8-24. Remove saddle stretch by adjusting the stretch nut at the nose of the saddle.

Fig. 8-25. Do not use a four-wire leather saddle in a seat post designed for a two-wire saddle, as is shown here. See Fig. 8-26.

Fig. 8-26. *Use an adapter to grip a four-wire saddle in a two-wire seat post.*

Sport and Nuevo Record, Sugino and S.R. twin bolt, LaPrade, and many other makes of seat posts.

Wider saddles are available for women. The women's version is slightly broader in the beam than the men's saddle.

Nonleather Saddles

Plastic saddles, even foam-filled models, will never shape to your anatomy. On the other hand, they don't need breaking in, won't stretch, are immune to water, dust and dirt, and require little or no maintenance. Because they're lighter, as low as 9 ounces for the Selle San Marcli Condor ($25), in contrast to 15.3 ounces for the Brooks Team Pro, racing cyclists like them. Plastic saddles for women, such as the Avocet GelFlex ($30), are wider to accommodate the female pelvic area. If you like your saddle but it's a pain on long rides, you could cover it with a Spenco elastic polymer pad that more evenly distributes pressure and absorbs road shocks. It costs around $23.

Automatic Saddle Height Adjuster for All-Terrain Bikes

As I noted in Chapter 3, the safest way to ride an all-terrain bicycle downhill is to lower the saddle and put as much of your weight as far back over the rear wheel as possible. Then, when you reach the flat or start the next hill, raise the saddle to your normal riding position.

Raising the saddle up and down a lot is a bother. You nearly always have to stop, dismount, open the seat post quick-release binder bolt (Fig. 8-27), adjust the saddle height, tighten the quick-release bolt, mount the bike, and pedal off.

A solution is a Breeze Hite-Rite adapter. It comes with all the necessary washers, nuts and bolts to install on your quick-release binder

Fig. 8-27. *Seat post quick-release binder bolt.*

bolt and seat post. Install it with your saddle at your normal riding height (Fig. 8-28). When you want to lower the saddle, just open the seat post quick release, hump your butt down on the saddle and close the quick release to move the saddle down (Fig. 8-29). When you want the saddle back up to your normal riding height, just open the quick release, lift your weight off the saddle, and it will spring back to the original position. If you are not sure about the correct saddle height, it should be just high enough so your knee is slightly bent when the pedal is parallel to the seat tube (Fig. 2-6 and Fig. 2-7). If the saddle is so low you can't get

Fig. 8-29. *Here the saddle is at its lowest. When the seat post quick release is opened, the saddle springs back to the high position, as shown in Fig. 8-28.*

Fig. 8-28. *Use a Hite-Rite saddle adjuster when moving the saddle up or down for fast descents or climbs.*

full leg extension at the bottom of the stroke, you put excess pressure on the knee. Long hours of pedaling with a saddle that's too low is just asking for knee damage. Ask your orthopedic surgeon.

Saddle Adjustments

The first cardinal rule about saddle height is *always make sure that at least 2½ inches of the seat post is inside the seat tube* (Fig. 8-30). Otherwise you risk breaking off the seat post or the seat post cluster. If the seat post is too short, install a longer one (Fig. 8-31).

Saddle tilt: Adjust saddle tilt by loosening the saddle clamp bolt (Fig. 8-32 and Fig. 8-33) (these bolts differ in size according to make of seat

Fig. 8-30. Always keep at least 2½ inches of the seat post inside the seat tube, for safety.

Fig. 8-31. If the seat post is too short, install a longer one.

Fig. 8-33. An older model seat post clamp bolt is a bit hard to reach.

Fig. 8-32. Adjust saddle tilt by loosening the seat post clamp bolt.

post). Move the nose of the saddle up or down and retighten the clamp bolt to 175–350 inch-lb. Most people seem to find a comfortable saddle tilt to be just slightly nose down, about 10 degrees from horizontal. If the saddle is tilted too far down, your body is thrust forward and too much weight is placed on the arms: the result, sore arm muscles and pain in the palms of your hands. If the saddle tilt is too far upward, you tend to slip backward on the saddle and have arm strain, due to holding onto the handlebars to avoid this slip. You also can have NCP, a.k.a. numb crotch pain. No, that's not a contradiction. Numbness can be a form of pain.

You can also move the saddle closer to or farther away from the handlebars to suit your upper torso and arm length. However, this is a very limited option. If your bike is badly sized to you (see Chapter 2), moving the saddle in any direction won't compensate. But if the bike fits you, back and forth saddle adjustment may make the difference between arm strain and comfort. The ideal saddle position is when the noise of the saddle is directly above a plumb line intersecting the middle of the bottom bracket. Don't worry too much about this adjustment. All that counts is that the saddle-to-handlebar distance is comfortable to you. And that's a decision only you can make. Make this adjustment by loosening the saddle clamp binder bolt and moving the saddle farther from or closer to the handlebars. Do this in increments of a half inch until you find the position most comfortable for you.

SEAT POSTS

High-quality all-terrain bikes have a precision seat tube that allows the seat post to smoothly slide up and down in when you wish to readjust saddle height. Grease the seat post to make saddle height adjustments easier, with or without the Hite-Rite. Have your bike shop ream out your seat tube if the seat post won't slide easily inside it.

Install a longer seat post if the one that came with your ATB won't get you up high enough. Seat posts come 300 mm long, and 25.4, 25.8, 26, 26.2, 26.4, 26.6, 26.8, 27 and 27.2 mm wide (to convert mm to inches, multiply mm by .03937). For fat tube aluminum bikes there's a 25-mm × 250-mm seat post.

Do not force a seat post that seems like it should fit, or use one that fits loosely! Hammering down an oversize seat post only destroys the bike frame, or requires major bike shop surgery to remove it. Too small a seat post may not be held securely by the seat post quick release. The result, the saddle may move down when you least expect it. The seat post must slide snugly, but smoothly, up and down in the seat tube.

A recent innovation, a hydraulic seat post (Fig. 8-34), is claimed to reduce road shock to your upper body, make unnecessary a change of rider position or style when meeting rough terrain, improve braking and handling on descents. Called a HydraPost, it comes in the stock sizes noted above, weighs 25 oz and costs about $75. A titanium version weighs 18 oz, but the price is not available at this writing. It's available from your bike shop, or write Knapp Engineering, 1081 Graham Ave., Kent, Ohio 44240, or call 1-800-343-7951. A spring-loaded seat post is made by Sakae (Fig. 8-35).

MORE NOTES ABOUT HANDLEBARS

I discussed handlebars at some length in Chapters 2, 3 and 5. All I can add to that discussion are the pros and cons of flat vs. downturned handlebars. The flat bars permit a more upright riding stance and a better road view, which is a safety factor in city cycling. The wide, flat bars also provide high leverage for muscling the front wheel straight while traversing stubborn rocky and pitted terrain which tries to wrest steering control from you.

Fig. 8-34. A seat post with a built-in hydraulic shock absorber.

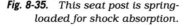

Fig. 8-35. This seat post is spring-loaded for shock absorption.

The downturned bars give you four places to rest your hands. You can put your hands in two places on top of the bars, halfway down the curve and at the bottom end of the curve where it aims back at you. Downturned bars seem favored by some ATB racing cyclists. The problem seems to be that if you have to grip the bars in just one location for hours on end, the nerves in the palm of your hand protest. The result, POYHP (palm of your hand pain). If you can move your hands to different places on the bars, you can set up different pressure points on your palms. This is true. However, I still prefer the flat bars. If my palms start to hurt I just hang out a wrist and wiggle my hand until the pain subsides. The flat bars let me sit more upright when I choose to or need to. Unless you are into racing, I see no need for the downturned bars on an ATB, personal preference aside. If you are used to downturned bars, plan to use your ATB pretty much as a road bike. If you ride on rough terrain, flat bars give more leverage control.

You can tailor flat bars to your reach, to some extent, by twisting them in the stem, if you have a separate stem and bars. Or you could install a handlebar extender (Fig. 8-36). Or install a downturned handlebar adapter on your flat bars (Fig. 8-37 and Fig. 8-38). Or install a

Fig. 8-37. Add these downturned grips to your flat bars for more hand positions.

Fig. 8-36. If you want bar extenders, try these Moots add-ons.

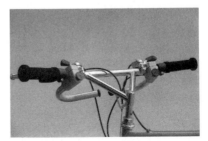

Fig. 8-38. The same grips as in Fig. 8-37, except turned in, out of the way.

handlebar with a curvature to match your reach (Fig. 8-39) or "Tour de France" type racing bars (Fig. 8-40 and Fig. 8-41).

Stems come in different "rises." If you have to bend over too far to reach the bars, with the saddle at the correct height, you probably need a stem with a higher "rise" that gets the bars up closer to your body.

While on the subject of bars and comfort, don't overlook the advantage of padded bicycle gloves, and the comfort of good bar end grips (Fig. 8-42).

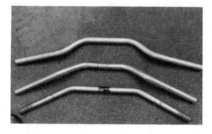

Fig. 8-39. Flat ATB bars come in a variety of configurations. Here are just a few, to give you an idea of the options.

Fig. 8-40. ATB racing goes "Tour de France" with these bars.

Fig. 8-42. A padded handlebar grip helps reduce road shock and hand pain.

Fig. 8-41. Another variety of "Tour de France" bars. Note the elbow rests. Do not use this type of bar in traffic. You need to see where you and the traffic are going.

Fig. 8-43. This Odyssey steering damper is a hydraulic actuated device that fastens to the frame and to the fork. It helps you keep steering control, especially on a rough trail.

A word about steering control. Automobiles and some motorcycles have a steering damper, a hydraulic control which keeps the front wheel(s) from being thrust from side to side when encountering a bump. I have found such a steering damper handy on an ATB—the hard way. I was traversing a winding, rocky, pitted trail. Such a trail, in ATB parlance, is called "technical" for want of a better word. "Technical" means you better know how to leverage your body to stay upright as you hit one obstacle after another which try to thrust the front wheel in different directions within seconds. On my ride, I guess I wasn't "technical" enough, because an unseen rock came up and hit my front wheel and tore the handlebars right out of my grip. I went over the bars and landed on my nose, which seemed to cut a groove in the ground until I stopped moving forward. I was momentarily stunned. Fortunately my only damage was a bit of skin off my nose, and hurt pride. Then and there I thought a steering damper would have kept me from losing control. Not long after that mishap, Odyssey did come out with just such a steering damper (Fig. 8-43), and I can report that it does work. It's adjustable for the amount of turning resistance you need for the trail you're on. See your bike dealer or write Odyssey, 17101 S. Central Ave., #G, Carson, CA 90746.

9
Wheel Truing and Building, Frame Checks and Finishing

..... Y our wheels will eventually become untrue. Even the best professionally built wheels will, after miles of pounding, go off center. Brand new bikes, right out of the factory, may have unevenly tensioned spokes. Proper spoke tensioning is an exacting, time-consuming process. Even experienced wheel builders take upward of an hour to build a wheel. Here's what happens when wheels go out of true, and why they do so:

1. An untrue rim cuts braking ability (see Chapters 3 and 5 for details). A wobbly rim means one or more spokes are loose.

2. A loose spoke can break. When it does, the wheel will be badly out of alignment and could cause shimmy and loss of control.

3. Unevenly tensioned spokes, where some are tighter than others, causes spoke stretch. As spokes stretch, the wheel goes out of line. When spokes are loose, spoke nipples are also loose and can become looser under road shock.

Check your wheels for alignment this way: Put your bike on a bike stand, hang it from the ceiling, or lift it up and spin the front wheel. Do the same with the rear wheel. Watch each wheel rim as it passes a brake shoe. If the wheel moves closer to, then farther from the rim, it is untrue and should be realigned.

There are two degrees of wheel truing. The first is the simple type of truing you will probably have to do two or three times a year until you have removed spoke stretch and put each spoke under the same or nearly the same tension. The second and more difficult and time-consuming type of wheel truing is when you have built a completely new wheel from scratch, with new spokes in a new rim. In this chapter I will show you how to do the casual kind of wheel truing first, because that's the kind you'll do most often. Then I'll get into wheel building, and after that show you how to true a newly built wheel so it stays truer longer.

SIMPLE WHEEL TRUING

Tools you will need:

1. A spoke wrench (Fig. 9-1).
2. A simple truing fixture (Fig. 9-2). A low-cost stand is made by Minoura, and costs around $35 from The Third Hand tool people; or use your bike as shown below.
3. A bike workstand (optional).

Using Your Bike as a Truing Fixture:
1. Put your bike in a workstand, hang it from the ceiling or turn it upside down.

Fig. 9-2. This wheel truing stand is inexpensive and a time saver in accurate wheel truing.

Fig. 9-1. Three of the styles of spoke wrenches you could use. Be sure your spoke wrench fits the spoke nipples. Otherwise you could round them off as you tighten them.

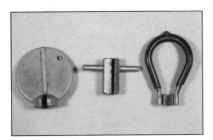

2. Remove both wheels. Remove the tires, tubes and rim strips.

3. Look at the rim. If it is badly dented, stop here. The rim should be replaced. If you wish to do this work yourself, please refer to the section below on wheel building. You can, of course, use the old hub. But I advise new spokes. Look at the spokes, particularly where they come out of the hub. If you see cracks or if the spokes have been cut by the chain (rear wheel), replace them. Do not cut the spoke. Simply unscrew the nipple, pull out the bad spoke(s) and install new ones. On a rear hub, you will have to remove the freewheel, as shown in Chapter 6. Turn the spoke nipples on any new spokes to bring the wheel approximately back in line, then follow the procedure below to finish truing the wheel.

4. Remove all four brake shoes (see Chapter 5).

5. Replace both wheels, sans tubes, rim strips and tires. Make sure the rear wheel is as far back in the dropouts as possible and that the front wheel is as far up in the fork dropouts as possible.

6. Put an Allen wrench in each brake arm (Fig. 9-3).

7. Spin the wheel slowly. Find a place where each side of the rim is the same distance from the seat stays or fork blades (Fig. 9-4). Mark that spot with crayon, on each side of the rim.

8. Find the spot(s) you marked in step 7. Adjust the Allen wrenches so each one touches the rim at these spots. The spot areas are your basic measurements. You need to true the wheel to them.

Fig. 9-4. *A quick way to check wheel trueness is to hold a ruler on the chainstay (or fork blade) to find wheel wobble or untrueness.*

Fig. 9-3. *You could use Allen wrenches in your brake arms, instead of a wheel truer.*

9. Spin the wheel. If the rim moves to the left, tighten the spoke nipple on that left side of the rim clockwise a half turn, to pull the rim to the left. Figure 9-5 shows how the rim moves left or right as you adjust spoke tension. If the rim moves to the right, tighten a nipple on that side. If you want to move the rim to the left, but the nipple on that side is already so tight the spoke wrench slips, loosen the nipple on the right side, counterclockwise, a half turn. You may have to adjust spoke tension on two or even three spokes if the rim is way out of line.

If You Use a Truing Fixture:

(These steps are for existing wheels. For truing instructions for newly built wheels, see below.)

1. Remove both wheels, tires, tubes and rim strips and the freewheel (see Chapter 7).

2. Put a wheel in the truing fixture.

3. Adjust the truing fixture indicators as you spin the wheel slowly until you find a spot on the rim where the indicators are the same distance from each side of the rim. Mark this spot on both sides of the rim with crayon.

Follow This Truing Procedure Whether You Use Your Bike or a Truing Fixture:

1. Put a drop of light oil, such as WD-40, on the top of spoke nipples in the rim. Wipe off excess oil so it won't damage the rim strip or tube when you replace them.

2. Check the spokes, especially on the freewheel side, where they curve up from the hub, and replace any that are bent, twisted or cut.

3. Pluck each spoke, starting at the tire valve. Tighten loose spokes by turning the nipple clockwise until the spoke is about at the same tension as the rest of the spokes. If the nipple keeps turning but the spoke won't tighten, the nipple is stripped. Replace that spoke and nipple, and tighten it until it's at about the same tension as the rest of the spokes.

4. Study Figure 9-5. Note that tightening a left spoke nipple (clockwise) pulls the rim to the left, and tightening a right spoke nipple pulls the rim to the right. Loosening a left-side spoke moves the rim to the right, and loosening a right-side spoke nipple moves the rim to the left. The "right and left" sides of a rim are arbitrary. If you're working on the side of the wheel that's on the left side for you, then that's the left side.

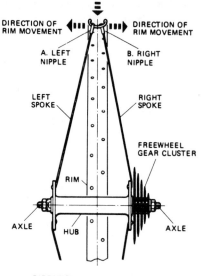

DIRECTION OF RIM MOVEMENT

Fig. 9-5. Tighten a left-side spoke to pull the wheel to the left, vice versa for the right side. Or loosen a right-side spoke to let the wheel move to the left, and vice versa for the left side.

5. Make sure the truing indicators (on the bike or in the truing fixture) touch the side of the rim you marked with crayon. That mark is where the rim is true laterally, from side to side, and that's your starting point.

6. Rotate the rim until one side moves as far away as possible from the truing indicator. Mark that spot with crayon.

7. Tighten a nipple a quarter turn on a spoke that will pull the rim toward the indicator. If the rim is too far to the left, tighten a right-side nipple.

8. Make rough truing adjustments, a quarter nipple turn at a time, until the rim is almost true.

9. Make final touch-up truing adjustments one-eighth nipple turn at a time until the rim is true from side to side.

10. If you can't true the rim by tightening a spoke, loosen a spoke on the opposite side a quarter turn. For example, if the rim is too far to the right, and you can't tighten a left-side spoke to pull it back, loosen a right-side spoke a quarter to an eighth turn.

11. With side-to-side (lateral) untrueness removed, now check for concentric (roundness) trueness. With the truing indicator on top of the rim (B in Fig. 9-6), note the average concentric trueness and mark any place the rim moves up or down from that average.

12. Correct concentric untrueness by tightening adjacent left-side/right-side spoke nipples an eighth turn at the high place, or loosening

Fig. 9-6. _This Preci-Ray Belgian made wheel truer makes the wheel alignment process easier and quicker._

one right and one left-side nipple an eighth turn at the low place. _Use two adjacent spokes to pull the rim up or move it down. That way you keep the wheel laterally true while you correct concentric untrueness._ Repeat this step until you have removed all high and low spots and the rim is concentric.

   13. Check the rim once more for side-to-side trueness, and if necessary true it up as shown above.

   14. When the rim is true, make sure spoke nipples do not protrude above the nipple inside the rim, where they can pierce the tube and cause a flat. File down or snip off protruding spoke ends.

   15. Prestretch each spoke. Squeeze a pair of spokes by hand. This is an important step when you have built a new wheel, with new spokes. Do this during the wheel building process.

   16. Turn each spoke another eighth turn to remove spoke stretch. If you build a lot of wheels, it pays to use a good spoke tensionometer, such as the Hozan (Fig. 9-7), which costs around $180. This is a terrific instrument, individually calibrated, extremely accurate and easy to use. If you build wheels for racing especially, this is the tensionometer to use. Instructions are easy to follow, and come with the unit. The Wheel-smith is another quality tensionometer (Fig. 9-8). At $80, it's ideal for building accurately tensioned wheels. Both instruments are available from good bike shops, or from The Third Hand (see Appendix).

   17. Check the wheel for lateral and concentric trueness, and true it again if necessary. Again squeeze pairs of spokes together to relieve tension, recheck trueness and true up as above.

Fig. 9-7. Use a spoke tension indicator, such as this dial indicator by Hozan, if you do a lot of wheel truing. Evenly tensioned spokes add to wheel life and impact resistance.

Fig. 9-8. Another excellent spoke tension indicator is this model from Wheelsmith.

18. Replace the brake shoes and, if necessary, readjust brake shoe clearance, as shown in Chapter 5.

19. Replace the rim strip, tube and tire. See Chapter 8.

20. Put the wheels back in the bike.

HOW TO BUILD A WHEEL

If you have dented a rim beyond repair, want to upgrade your hubs, bought a new frame and want to add your own components, or want an extra set of wheels for your ATB—one set for the trail, one for the road—you have a choice of having a professional wheel builder lace (spoke) the wheels or doing it yourself. It takes three to six hours if you're not used to it. With practice you should be able to cut this time to an hour.

Bike shops charge about $45, including the spokes, to build and true a wheel. This does not include the cost of spokes, a new hub, of course, or a new rim. Every bicycle enthusiast should build his or her own wheels at least once to understand what it takes to create wheels that will see you through hell and high water. You'll appreciate your newfound skill if you ever get stuck in the boonies and have to replace a busted spoke(s) or if you live where bike shops are scarce. If you tour in third world countries, wheel building ability is a *must*.

Steps in Wheel Building

Tools you will need:

1. Wheel truing fixture (A in Fig. 9-9) (you could use your bicycle as above).
2. Caliper ruler (B in Fig. 9-9) or accurate straight ruler.
3. Spoke wrench (C in Fig. 9-9)
4. Push screwdriver (D in Fig. 9-9) (an ordinary screwdriver will do but it's slower).
5. "Dishing" tool (E in Fig. 9-9) for centering a front wheel and "dishing" a rear wheel. You could make your own out of a straight piece of 2 × 4 with offset blocks at each end. Use a 10-inch bolt with two

Fig. 9-9. Tools for lacing (spoking) and truing a newly built wheel: A, truing stand; B, caliper ruler; C, nipple wrench; D, push screwdriver; E, "dishing" tool.

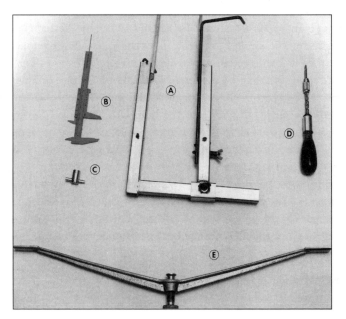

nuts and lock washer for the center indicator. The homemade version is cumbersome. A Park dishing tool can be used on any size wheel, costs around $25 and worth it. You can buy a Minoura dishing tool for about $12 that fits 26 wheels.

About Spokes: Spokes for 26 inch ATB rims come in eight different lengths, as shown in Table 9-1.

Table 9-1 AVAILABLE SPOKE LENGTHS FOR ATB RIMS*

Inches	Millimeters
10.236	260
10.314	262
10.354	263
10.393	264
10.433	265
10.472	266
10.629	270

*Have your bike shop select spokes to fit your combination of hub, spoke crossing and rim diameter. If you need special-length spokes, some bike shops have a spoke cutter/threader machine.

Spokes come in three gauges: 14, 15 and 15 double-butted. The lower the gauge, the thicker and so the stronger the spoke. For example, a 14-gauge spoke is 2 mm thick, a 15-gauge spoke is 1.56 mm thick, so the 14-gauge spoke is about 2.8 percent thicker. The 15-gauge double-butted spokes are 14-gauge thickness for about 50 mm (2 inches) at the spoke head end, the part that goes into the hub. Use 14 gauge if you want a strong, durable wheel, 15 gauge double-butted for some sacrifice in strength to save a few ounces in weight and 15 straight gauge for lightness at the expense of strength.

I prefer Swiss precision-made D.T. stainless steel 14 gauge double-butted spokes. They are the strongest spokes you can buy, in my opinion. The few ounces 14-gauge spokes add to your wheels might concern a racing cyclist, but for the average cyclist these ounces are unimportant.

Four-Cross vs. Three-Cross Lacing

You can lace your wheels with spokes crossed every third spoke (Fig. 9-10) or every fourth spoke (Fig. 9-11). You get a stiffer wheel with

Fig. 9-10. *Example of a three-cross spoking pattern. Spoke A crosses under spokes B and C and over spoke D.*

Fig. 9-11. *A four-cross spoking pattern. Spoke A crosses over spokes B, C and D and under spoke E.*

three-cross spoking. The stiffer wheel more efficiently translates muscle power to go power. But the stiffer wheel also sends road shock back into the frame, which can be fatiguing on a long ride.

Four-cross spoking requires longer spokes, which soak up road shock better than the stiff three-cross pattern. Use three-cross for racing and four-cross for casual and long-distance riding and touring.

Steps in Building Four-Cross Wheels

1. Select the correct spoke length. There are far too many combinations of spoke crossings, rim diameters, rim widths, hub flange diameters, spoke hole drillings in hub and rim to generate one table that gives the correct spoke length for all of them. New hub and rim designs hit the market frequently, so even if I could come up with a comprehensive spoke-length table it would be obsolete in short order. Have your bicycle dealer select the correct length spokes for you when you buy a new hub and rim, or take an old spoke to the bike shop for a replacement.

2. Note that *rim* holes are staggered so that every other hole is closer to one side of the rim than the one preceding it or the one following it (Fig. 9-12 and Fig. 9-13).

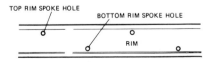

Fig. 9-12. *An exaggerated view of rim hole placement. Note that holes are offset.*

Fig. 9-13. *An actual rim, still showing spoke hole offset.*

3. Note: Some hubs have one side of every other hole chamfered so the spoke bends gradually, instead of at a sharp angle (Fig. 9-14). Insert spokes in the hub as noted in step 7 below, so the spoke bend follows the curve of the chamfer. If you don't, the spoke bends sharply and can break where it angles up out of the hub. Most modern hubs have a slight chamfer on both sides of all holes.

4. Poke a spoke through the rim hole to make sure it's big enough to accept the spoke, but not so big the spoke can bounce around in the hole under the stress of road shock and break. For example, some hubs are drilled for 15-gauge spokes and are too small for 14-gauge spokes, and vice versa. Exchange hubs rather than drill out holes that are too small, or use 14-gauge spokes instead of 15-gauge if the holes are too big. If you drill out rim spoke holes you probably won't get them at the right angle.

5. Note that hubs have holes in one flange that are offset to the holes in the facing flange (Fig. 9-15).

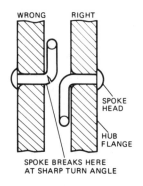

WRONG   RIGHT

SPOKE
HEAD

HUB
FLANGE

SPOKE BREAKS HERE
AT SHARP TURN ANGLE

Fig. 9-14. *Hub spoke holes are chamfered. Be sure to put the spoke so the spoke head is opposite the chamfer. Otherwise the spoke makes a sharp bend. Metal fatigue at the sharp bend can cause spoke breakage.*

Fig. 9-15. Note that rim spoke holes are offset in opposite flanges.

6. Drill a half-inch hole in your workbench or in a 12-inch square of 2-inch planking to hold the hub while you lace up the wheel. Remove the quick-release skewer or the axle nuts.

7. Put a spoke down every other hole in both flanges, so the spoke heads face upward (Fig. 9-16).

8. Sweep the spokes up, turn the hub over and insert spokes as in step 7. The hub should look like Figure 9-17, so every other spoke hole has a spoke head facing up.

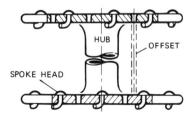

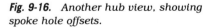
Fig. 9-16. Another hub view, showing spoke hole offsets.

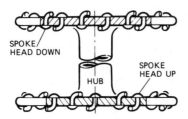

Fig. 9-17. Spoke head position should alternate. Every other spoke head should be on the opposite side of the flange from its neighbor.

9. Sweep both sets of spokes up, and put the hub in the hole in your workbench or block of wood (see step 6).

10. Lay the rim over the hub on the workbench.

11. Locate the valve hole in the rim (arrow, Fig. 9-18). Look at the first hole to the *right* of the valve hole. If it's a *top* rim hole, take any spoke in the *top* flange of the hub that has its spoke head facing *up,* and insert it in this rim hole and thread on a nipple four turns. If the first hole to the *right* of the valve hole is a *bottom* hole, insert this spoke into the first hole to the *left* of the valve hole.

12. Count off four empty rim spoke holes to the *right,* not counting the valve hole. This should be a top rim hole. Take the next spoke with its spoke head facing up in the top hub flange and put it into this fourth rim hole.

13. Put every spoke with its head facing up in the top hub flange into every fourth top rim hole, working to your right. You should now have nine spokes in the rim, each with a nipple threaded on four turns. There should be three empty rim holes between each spoke.

14. Hold the hub so it can't turn, and *twist* the rim to the right so the spokes are at an acute angle, just grazing the outside of their adjacent

Fig. 9-18. Start the first spoke to the right of the valve hole, arrow.

empty *hub* spoke holes. If a spoke crosses over the *rim valve hole,* twist the rim to the *left* instead of to the right.

15. Take any *head-down* spoke (a spoke with its head *under* the hub flange) in the top hub flange (Fig. 9-17), and going in the *opposite* direction from the first nine spokes, cross it *over* three and *under* the fourth spoke (Fig. 9-11 and Fig. 9-19). For example, in Figure 9-19, spoke A goes to the left and crosses *over* spokes B, C, and D and *under* spoke E. Continue this spoke lacing pattern until the wheel looks like Figure 9-19, with one empty spoke hole between each pair of spokes and with each spoke going in an alternate left-right direction, with nipples threaded on four turns.

16. This is the most critical step in wheel lacing. Turn the wheel and hub over. Sweep all but one of the unlaced spokes out of the way. Refer to Figure 9-15 and note that the top and bottom hub flange spoke holes are offset, so that if you poke a spoke straight down in a top flange hole it stops midway between two of the bottom flange spoke holes. Now look closely at Figure 9-15. Find spoke A and note that its spoke head, facing up in the top hub flange, is just to the right of spoke head B and is centered midway between spokes B and C in the bottom hub flange.

Fig. 9-19. *Spokes are in twos after the first steps in wheel building.*

17. Put any spoke with its head up on the top hub flange into the position shown by spoke A in Figure 9-20, starting in a top rim hole. Note that this spoke goes to the right.

18. Put all the remaining head-up hub flange spokes into the rest of the top rim holes (every other empty spoke hole), working to the right. Spokes should now be in groups of three (Fig. 9-21).

19. Pull any top hub flange head-down spoke to as sharp an angle to the *left* as possible, so it's almost touching a head-up spoke in the top hub flange, and put it in the only bottom rim hole it will reach. If it sticks out more than half an inch from the rim spoke hole, move the spoke to the next left bottom rim hole. If it won't go that far, go back one bottom rim hole to the right.

20. Continue lacing the remaining head-down spokes to the left, crossing *over* three spokes and *under the fourth spoke*. When you are finished, the spokes should be in groups of four and look like Figure 9-22.

21. Tighten each spoke two turns at a time, then one turn at a time, then a half turn at a time until spokes are about evenly tensioned and the wheel looks almost straight. It won't be, but you will correct and true up the wheel as noted earlier in this chapter, except for the rear wheel, which will need to be "dished."

Fig. 9-20. Beginning spoke crossing pattern. See text.

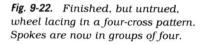

Fig. 9-21. *Spokes are now in groups of three.*

Fig. 9-22. *Finished, but untrued, wheel lacing in a four-cross pattern. Spokes are now in groups of four.*

Three-Cross Wheel Building

If you prefer a stiffer wheel, build one with spokes crossed over three instead of the four described above. Lacing a three-cross pattern (Fig. 9-10) is essentially the same as four-cross, with a few important exceptions:

1. Place the first nine spokes into every other hole in the top of the flange, as described in the four-cross instructions.

2. This is the crucial step. Put another nine spokes into the bottom flange, spoke head up, exactly as you would in lacing a four-cross wheel. But this time, offset the first spoke in the lower flange one hole to the right of the spoke above it in the upper flange.

3. Now, take one spoke from the upper flange and poke it through the first spoke hole to the right of the valve stem hole. This should be a hole on the upper side of the rim—that is, on the side of the rim toward you. Put a nipple on the threaded end of the spoke and turn it about two complete turns. Skip the next three spoke holes to the right of the one you just put the spoke in. Take hold of the next spoke to the right of the first one on the upper flange, and place this spoke into the fourth hole. This hole should also be on the upper side of the rim. Continue to the right all the way around until all the spokes in the top flange are laced into the rim. Check to make sure they are evenly spaced and are in holes on the upper side of the rim.

4. Take hold of the hub, with the same side still facing up, and twist the rim so that the spokes make an acute angle to the rim. They should nearly touch the holes adjacent to them in the flange. Locate the first spoke you laced, the one immediately to the right of the valve hole. Look down at the lower flange. Take hold of the unlaced spoke that is offset directly the right of the first spoke you laced. Put this spoke in the right of that first spoke and screw a nipple on it. Skip the next three holes, and put the next spoke to the right into the fourth. Go all the way around the rim until all nine spokes on the lower flange are laced into a hole. These holes should be on the lower side of the rim, the side farthest away from you.

5. Now, proceed just as you would for a four-cross wheel. However, you are making a three-cross wheel, so you should only cross over the first two spokes to the right and under the third. Be sure that every spoke from the upper flange is laced into a spoke hole on the upper side of the rim. Keep holding the rim as you have throughout, placing the last set of spokes from the lower flange into the remaining holes, passing over two spokes and under the third. This last set should, of course, be in holes on the lower side of the rim.

How to True a Newly Built Front Wheel

It's easier to true a freshly laced front wheel because it doesn't have to be "dished" like a rear wheel. I'll explain the "dishing" process in the section below on truing a rear wheel. Follow these steps in truing a front wheel:

1. Assemble the tools shown in Figure 9-9. You can use your bike as a truing fixture, as described earlier in this chapter, but a wheel truing fixture is more accurate, easier and quicker to use.

2. The hub and rim measurements used below in the sample truing process are examples only. They may not apply to the hubs and rims you use. However, follow the measure process shown here on your own hubs and rims, and consider the measurements given as illustrative only.

3. Measure the width of the rim. In Figure 9-23 it's 23 mm, or about 1 inch.

4. Measure the space between hub locknuts. In Figure 9-24 it's 100 mm, or about 4 inches. This is shown graphically in Figure 9-25.

5. Subtract the rim width, 1 inch, from the width between the axle locknuts, 4 inches. You get 3 inches.

6. Divide the figure obtained in the preceding step, 3 inches, by 2

Fig. 9-23. Measure width of rim.

which equals 1½ inches, which is the distance each side of the rim should be from each hub axle locknut in this example (Fig. 9-25), *when the rim is trued.* Again, these measurements apply to one make of hub; make your own measurements on the hub/rim combination you are using.

7. Put the centering tool on a flat surface. Turn the measuring bolt until its bottom is 1½ inches from the flat surface (Fig. 9-26).

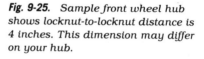

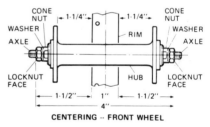

Fig. 9-25. Sample front wheel hub shows locknut-to-locknut distance is 4 inches. This dimension may differ on your hub.

CENTERING -- FRONT WHEEL

Fig. 9-24. Measure distance between hub locknuts.

Fig. 9-27. Put the dishing tool on one side of the wheel, on a flat surface. This tool, once set, determines correct centering of the rim over the hub.

Fig. 9-26. Set dishing tool. See text for measurement data.

8. Lay the wheel on the workbench, and put the rim centering tool on it (Fig. 9-27). Use the dishing tool on both sides of the wheel (Fig. 9-28).

9. Study Figure 9-5 and review the truing instructions given earlier in this chapter.

10. Adjust the group of four spokes nearest the rim valve hole and the four spokes across the valve hole—on the opposite side of the rim— until the rim centering tool flat ends (arrows, Fig. 9-27) touch each side of the rim. Wiggle the centering tool to make sure both flats lay evenly on each rim side. If not, adjust the spokes until they do.

11. Turn the wheel over and repeat step 10. Mark both sides of the rim where the centering gauge shows the rim is centered. Review Figure 9-25, which shows the rim centered between both the hub flanges and the axle lockouts.

12. Put the wheel in the truing fixture (Fig. 9-29).

13. Adjust the side-to-side (lateral) truing fixture indicators until they touch both sides of the rim where you marked it in step 11. This is your beginning guide to truing the newly laced wheel.

14. Finish truing the wheel as shown earlier in this chapter. Remove the wheel from the truing fixture and check side-to-side adjustment with the centering gauge a few times to make sure the rim is centered between the hub flanges and axle locknut (Fig. 9-25).

Fig. 9-28. *Use the dishing tool on both sides of the wheel.*

Fig. 9-29. *This professional wheel truer checks both lateral (side-to-side) and concentric (roundness) alignment simultaneously.*

Fig. 9-30. Measure locknut-to-locknut distance on a rear hub. Note that the rim is "dished" or moved closer to the right hub flange. Actually, the wheel rim is centered between the locknuts, when properly dished.

Fig. 9-31. Maintain accurate rear wheel dishing by measuring locknut-to-locknut distance as shown here.

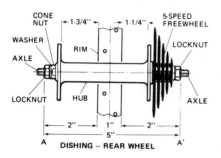

Truing the Rear Wheel

You trued up the front wheel so the rim is centered between the axle locknuts. Do the same with the rear wheel, except "dish" it so the rim is centered between the locknuts (Fig. 9-30). "Dishing" keeps the chain from rubbing on the spokes when the chain is on the large rear freewheel cog. "Dishing" will be automatic as you follow steps 1 through 13 above. Just repeat the measurements of the rim (Fig. 9-23) and hub locknut to locknut (Fig. 9-30 and Fig. 9-31), subtract those two measurements, divide them by two and set your wheel dishing tool accordingly. Dishing puts the rim closer to the right hub flange than to the left hub flange.

Before we go into frame alignment and frame scratch touch-up, let me tell you a true story about a class in bicycle maintenance I taught at a city college in Chicago. I had asked the group to bring their bikes to class. My plan was to have them completely disassemble, clean, re-lube, readjust and reassemble their bikes. All the students but one brought in very nice, fairly costly bikes. The exception was an older lady, who wheeled in a decrepit, rusty, old, ladies' model coaster brake junker. I'm afraid the class could see the expression on my face, which said that I did not want to cope with this $50 bike or her efforts in bringing it back to some semblance of life. What happened the next week I richly deserved. At the end of the first class, I gave the students a list of tools they would need. At the second class, this sweet lady wheels in a huge tool chest, from which you could rebuild a Rolls, let alone a bike. Before I could stop myself, because I had a hunch what was coming, I asked her what she did. Her reply: "I'm a tool and die maker." Which meant that she had forgotten more than I would ever know, or want to know, about tools and machinery. After the class's laughter, at my expense, for my chauvinism, we got down to work. This nice lady had her bike apart, reassembled and running good as new before anyone else. Moreover, she did a great job of removing her old corkscrew rims, and building new rims around her old hubs (Fig. 9-32). Served me right.

FRAME ALIGNMENT

If your bike needs a lot of balance and steering correction to keep it going straight, you may have a bent frame or fork that can cause wheel shimmy and an accident. If your index shifters won't index any more, particularly the rear derailleur, you may have bent the rear derailleur mounting ear or damaged the derailleur. In previous books I have instructions on how to check frame alignment yourself. Since that time bicycles and their components have become immensely more complex.

Fig. 9-32. This lady was a star, Grade AAA student in the author's bike maintenance class. Her background as a tool and die maker helped.

I just can't recommend you do your own alignment checks. This is a process that requires special tools and knowledge. The hazards of a misaligned frame or a rear derailleur that shifts erratically are too great to risk anything but the most professional frame work. Besides, if you did find a bent fork blade or frame tube, you would still have to take the bike to a bike shop that knows how to realign these parts. Better yet, take your bike to a frame builder, a person who builds custom frames. He or she will have the tools and the skills to bring your bike back to true.

If you hit a rock hard, you may have bent a fork blade. If your front brakes locked up because the brake shoe rubbed on the tire instead of the wheel rim, and you dumped the bike, you may well have bent the down tube, where it joins the steering tube and top tube. If you ran into a tree, God forbid, your frame may be a candidate for scrap. All I want you to remember is that any damaged part of your bike frame can cause wheel shimmy and loss of control or dangerously defective braking. So take your steed to the bike shop, and let an experienced mechanic check the bike over if you even *begin* to suspect something is bent, somewhere, on your frame. After all, if you have a really severe bellyache and an intact appendix, it's wise to have your doctor check you over, no? A ruptured appendix, like a ruptured bike frame, could send you to the deep six.

KICKSTANDS

Only inexpensive bikes come with kickstands. A kickstand is an unstable way to keep a bike upright. A passing child, even the wind, can knock the bike over, with possible damage to the derailleur, brake levers and the paint finish. This is why expensive bikes are not equipped with kickstands. The kickstand can also loosen. When you tighten it, it's easy to squeeze and damage the chainstays. Remove the kickstand if it's bolted on the chainstays, and check these stays for damage caused by overtightening the kickstand mounting bolt. You can't do much about such damage except to throw the kickstand away.

NICKS AND SCRATCHES

Repair minor nicks and scratches with matching paint you can buy from the bike shop. Feather the edges of the area to be retouched with fine sandpaper. Follow directions on the pressurized spray can. Make a quick circular spray in the air and then quickly spray the feathered area. Apply at least three coats, letting each coat dry before spraying the next and sanding with fine sandpaper between coats.

The next chapter goes into the ATB bicycle racing scene and describes the various kinds of races and competitive events. If you want to race, you'll also find data on how to get started.

10

Racing Your ATB and the History of ATBs

I..... asked Sara Ballantyne to write about the world of racing ATBs. What follows comes from her. Sara is a member of the Specialized Stumpjumper Team. Her three-year dominance of the NORBA (National Off-Road Bicycle Association) World Championship makes her the number-one female mountain bike racer in the world today. She is a multitalented athlete who enjoys mountain climbing, snow skiing and mountain running during the off-season. Sara has been the NORBA World Champion in 1987, 1988 and 1989, European World Champion in 1988 and 1989.

WORDS OF WISDOM FROM SARA

"Ten seconds riders! . . . 5, 4, 3, 2, 1, GO!" Tensions and heart rates are high as the racer tries strenuously to be the first to lock into his pedals and maintain the lead. Sometimes I wish I had a "normal" 9-to-5 job when I wake up for the umpteenth time in the morning, my stomach a ball of knots, nervous energy flowing through my body in preparation for another day of mountain bike racing. But all it takes is jumping onto my mountain bike and riding off into the cool breeze of the early morning, spinning effortlessly through the gorgeous surrounding mountains, to realize why I do what I do. I can't think of any other job I'd rather have.

I love mountain bike racing and feel fortunate that I can make a living at it. It enables me to travel to many parts of the United States as well as Europe, New Zealand, Australia, Japan and who knows where else. I find ever increasing numbers of people are discovering how much fun ATB racing can be. I love the feeling I get from competing and pushing myself to new limits all the time. I'm continually meeting new and interesting people. It's exciting to have an influence on other novice riders while at the same time helping the sport grow.

I can't quite figure out exactly what it is about mountain biking that turns so many people on. Is it that primitive desire to be a kid again and get all muddy out in the wilderness? Is it the continual obstacles we encounter out there while riding, and whatever creativity it takes to get around or over them? Is it those "out-of-body" experiences we may get on all-day rides? I only know that the bug has hit me hard and is here to stay awhile.

Today there are many choices of mountain bike races. The sport has grown tremendously, both from a standpoint of participation and in its technology. In the early days, on single-speed bikes, the objective was to get downhill the fastest. Weight was little consideration. In fact, the heavier the bike, the better. Bikes today are much lighter, have steeper frame angles, shorter chainstays and shorter wheelbases. This new geometry lets the ATBs of today go faster and negotiate sharper turns and obstacles at speeds impossible with the single-speed clunker of yesteryear. Now you can choose a combination of 21 gears, instead of no gear at all.

A WORD ABOUT NORBA

Before I get into racing techniques, I would like to comment briefly on a recent change in the governing body of off-road racing. Up to 1989, NORBA was owned by the American Bicycle Association. Today the United States Cycling Federation (USCF) owns NORBA. The USCF now oversees both road racing and off-road racing. I see no major change in off-road racing from this switch in ownership. However, this change is a sign that the growing sport of mountain bike racing will have the guidance and the requirements for orderly conduct the USCF has long brought to bicycle racing events.

NORBA rules and guidelines, however, remain virtually unchanged. Self-sufficiency and individual ability are still stressed. In other words, the rider must know how to change a flat tire, piece back a busted derailleur, reconnect a broken chain, or handle whatever other problems may arise while racing. This translates into carrying a spare tube, pump, patch kit, chain tool, Allen wrenches and good karma. It is guaranteed that no one will come along driving a support vehicle. In fact, if a racer does take outside assistance for any kind of mechanical problem, or changes bikes during the race, he will be disqualified. A racer must know his bike intimately. He must be prepared to deal with whatever mishap may occur. I know of stories where sticks or rocks got caught up in the drive train and demolished a racer's rear derailleur, forcing the rider into creating a single gear because he no longer had shifting capability.

This self-reliant rule is what separates mountain bike racers from road racers. In fact, mountain bike racing is a much more individual sport than road racing. There is little, if any, of team tactics in mountain biking. The terrain doesn't allow for this. Changing continuously from a dirt two-wheel drive road, riding through stream beds, back to a narrow single track, is not uncommon. Having to negotiate rocks and fallen trees in your path makes a "pack" situation (where riders in a team help each other beat other team riders) difficult if not impossible. The surrounding aspens and pine trees dictate where the rider's path will be, rather than the team tactics of road racing. So the rules for traveling through these areas may be single file. The racer must always be prepared for anything or anybody on the course. It makes life very exciting for both racer and spectator. Each rider seems to have his own style.

A racer may have a two-minute lead on the rest of the pack and surely seem to have the race in the bag when he hits a rock a little too hard, and "uh-oh" . . . next thing you know the lead racers are passing you by! It's all part of mountain bike racing.

RACE CATEGORIES

As of 1989, the categories of racing include

1. Beginner (formerly known as Novice), a first-timer
2. Intermediate (formerly Sport), experienced amateur riders
3. Expert (remained the same), very advanced amateur riders
4. Super (formerly Pro/Am), elite top-level amateurs

TYPES OF RACES

1. The Hill Climb

These races are often massed start with your category (as designated above). Men and women are in their own class. Every race promoter decides on the distance of the hill climb. I have seen them as long as 13 miles (e.g., Whistler, B.C., elevation gain 5,280 feet!) and as short as a quarter mile. Racers tend to spread out quickly as each rider battles for more oxygen as the elevation increases. Promoters may decide to have a "time-trial" hill climb, where each racer pushes himself to the limit against the clock. Some say, "If you can still stand at the finish line, you haven't pushed hard enough!"

Hill Climb Techniques: The rider's position on the bike varies with the grade of the climb. For instance, to prevent the rear wheel from slipping, it may be necessary to remain seated on the bike (Fig. 10-1). Over loose, rough sections, the rider should keep her momentum up while concentrating on a smooth, round pedal stroke to maintain forward power. Bikes with shorter wheelbases and steeper angles tend to climb better but lose comfort downhill. Be prepared for a much friskier ride and quicker responses from your bike. Compare it with a Jaguar cruising on a mountain road vs. a Lincoln Continental on the same road. The Jag will have a quicker response, the Lincoln will be comfortable, more laid-back, not as aggressive.

2. The Downhills

These races are done in a time-trial fashion. Each racer has his own start. The quickest time to the bottom wins. Ride your bike as if you were riding a horse. Let what's underneath you absorb the shock. Think of skiing—same thing. We bend our knees to absorb the bumps and undulations on the slope. On a mountain bike we can stand up on our pedals, off the saddle (Fig. 10-2). We can grasp the handlebars with our arms slightly bent (Fig. 10-3). We can relax and focus on what's up ahead, pick our line, just as if we're picking the smoothest, most efficient line around the moguls on a ski slope. We can angulate with our knees (Fig. 10-4), depending on which way the slope of the hill is leaning. This allows us to always be over the balance point of our bike. I can't help but feel that the winter skiers and former motorcycle racers in the mountain biking groups have a distinct advantage over other racers in the

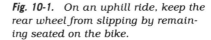
Fig. 10-1. On an uphill ride, keep the rear wheel from slipping by remaining seated on the bike.

Fig. 10-2. On a steep mountain slope, stand up on the pedals, off the saddle.

Fig. 10-3. For control downhill, grasp the handlebars with arms slightly bent.

Fig. 10-4. Shift your weight around by your knees to maintain balance.

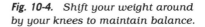

way they handle their bikes, the lines they choose, and the confidence they exhibit at high rates of speed down the hill.

I prefer my handlebars to be around 21–22 inches across. This for me is my shoulder width. Shorter handlebars inhibit my breathing. Wider handlebars feel awkward and unbalanced when descending.

I recommend toe clips. This gives you more power per stroke and prevents your foot from slipping off the pedal. Some beginning riders may feel frightened of the "locked-in" feeling, especially while traveling over technical (author's note: spell that terribly difficult, treacherous terrain) rocky sections. However, the toe clips don't need to be clamped tightly across the foot. I usually ride with mine loose, and secure them only when I know that I will not be dismounting during a course.

Warm-ups Are Important: Warming up properly before a hill climb or downhill is also very important to ensure optimum performance. Generally speaking, the shorter the race, the longer I warm up. For me, it takes a good hour before my body starts responding to fast speeds. I also recommend a good session of stretching or yoga in the morning. Whatever it takes for you to relax and allow only positive energy into your body can only translate into a good race for you. The body is very adaptable, and once it gets into a certain routine, I find mine actually craving it or reminding me if I have neglected certain things, such as stretching.

I remember my first ride on the infamous Slickrock trail in Moab, Utah. I woke up the next morning with my body feeling as if I had just finished a game of football and someone had taken a sledgehammer to my forearms. After much *more* experience and time on my mountain bike, I found that by using the above tips, my body was a much happier unit.

3. The Cross-Country Race

This is my favorite of all races. This is the real test of mountain biking, because a racer must be a good overall bike handler and be in top aerobic shape in order to win. Usually the course is from one starting point to a different finishing area (point to point). Or the race may start and end at the same location—one big loop of any length. The rider never crosses the same part of the course twice, which requires top-notch concentration for the unknown. Always pre-ride a racecourse if possible. Knowing what to expect and how to pace yourself can only help your performance. I also like to have short goals while racing in the backcountry for several hours. For instance, I play games: I tell myself that "I know at the top of this hill, it will be flat and I can recover." Or "If I make it around this corner and up that hill, it's home-free." Just like the Little Train That Could, "I think I can, I think I can." Once the mind starts defeating itself, the body soon follows and performance plummets. Instead of "I think I can," try "I know I can." It really works!

Gearing for the cross-country course depends on the individual rider's strength. Choose gears that allow you to spin efficiently with a relatively high cadence. Pushing hard gears will give you nothing but knee pain down the road. For my smallest gear in front (chainring), I use a 24-tooth. In the rear, I use a 28-tooth cog. This can usually get me up anything in Colorado, and if I need something easier than this, I'm better dismounting and running my bike up the hill. Again, this is all personal preference.

4. The Circuit Race

A circuit race is one where the racers ride around a closed course several times, usually more than 2 miles/lap and less than 10 miles/lap. Since you will be doing a multitude of laps, perhaps it is a good time early on in the race to observe the faster riders ahead of you. What are their weak points? If I notice that some ahead of me are slower on the flats than me, I pick an opportune time to pass them there, try to catch them off guard so that when I go by them it is already too late for them to respond. This is a great trick to pull right before the finish line. It usually demoralizes them so badly that they just give up as I ride by them, trying not to smile too much! Or if a competitor is floundering through a short technical section, try dismounting your bike and running by him. (Remind the author *never* to race against this lady!) I remember one time trying to finesse my way through some shin-deep mudholes back East, when the top male rider ran by me as if I were going backward. From then on, I did the same—even though it meant taking the chance of getting my shoes sucked off in the process.

5. Dual Slalom

Just as in skiing, the rider must negotiate and go around "gates." The rider is usually paired up against another rider in a similar course, side by side. The winner is the first across an imaginary finish line with the least amount of dirt on the body, i.e., no wipeouts. The adrenaline is high when you wait behind the starting gate, hearing the countdown, trying to get out of the start position just a bit faster than your opponent.

I find, though, that it's the one who can be the most level-headed, who handles her bike the smoothest, with the best finesse, who takes the straightest line around the "gates," who is the one who makes it across the finish line with no falls and the quickest time of the day.

The dual slalom not only is a real gas to do but also improves your bike-handling skills tremendously. It teaches you how to take corners at high rates of speed (Fig. 10-5), which translates to other areas of racing, such as in the downhill or cross-country course. I found that by applying a bit more pressure on your back brake and a little less in the front, you can pull off a move called the "brody," which will impress all former BMX racers. This move swings your rear tire around much quicker, rather than having to steer the wheel around.

Some riders like to compete in the dual slalom without toe clips. This enables you to drop your foot to the inside of your turn (Fig. 10-6), thus providing almost a pivot point, something on which to turn. Plus it's a good safety backup in case you feel yourself going down. You may be able to bounce back up and still maintain that clean image we all strive for when we cross that finish line.

6. Observed Trials

This competition is not considered racing—in the aerobic sense, that is. This involves a single rider going over obstacles such as stumps, boulders, and logs, going under logs, hopping over holes in the ground (Fig. 10-

Fig. 10-5. Sara Ballantyne taking a corner at speed.

Fig. 10-6. Without toe clips you can drop your foot to the inside of your turn, and use your foot as a pivot point to avoid a fall.

7). This all happens within a 10–20 yard distance! There is no time involved. There is, rather, a scoring system where the rider accumulates points by "dabbing" or touching the ground with his foot (off his pedal) (Fig. 10-8). There are usually six to ten different sections that the rider

Fig. 10-7. Another trials obstacle is holes in the ground.

Fig. 10-8. A trials participant is charged points each time his foot touches the ground (dabs).

must complete two or three times. The rider moves from one trials section to another with a little scorecard (which always reminds me of playing putt-putt when I was a little kid). Each section has a judge who watches you carefully and lets you know how many points you have accumulated in one section—the maximum being 5 points per section. The rider with the least number of points is declared the winner. Today there are several different observed trials categories to enter:

1. Novice stock bike
2. Intermediate stock bike
3. Expert stock bike

A stock bike has a few criteria to meet, such as a minimum of a 40-inch wheelbase, a rear derailleur with two or more gears, no skid plate (a device that goes under the bottom bracket and allows the bike to roll smoothly over logs instead of the chainring hitting). Other categories include

1. Novice modified bike
2. Intermediate modified bike
3. Expert modified bike

These are the bikes that people call "trials bikes." They generally have a minimum of a 20-inch diameter wheel. Other than that guideline, each "trials" bike could be very different (Fig. 10-9).

The trials rider is not allowed to practice the sections before competing but can walk through the sections to get an idea of what line to ride.

Fig. 10-9. *A bike made for trials events. Note the tiny chainring up front, and the high bottom bracket clearance over the log.*

EQUIPMENT

Equipment used in off-road racing includes:

   1. *Helmet.* Always wear one! To me, not wearing a helmet is the same as not wearing your seat belt while driving a car. There are such lightweight helmets made now that you hardly even notice they are on your head. It only takes one rock against the head to prohibit you from ever riding again. Check to make sure the helmet is ANSI approved. (A standard all racing helmets must pass.) There should be a sticker inside every helmet stating this. I recommend the LT 700 helmet.
   2. *Gloves.* These not only provide extra cushioning for those long, rocky descents but also add protection for the palms of your hands in case of a fall.
   3. *Glasses.* You can choose now between different-colored lenses— and the color does make a difference. I like the orange or yellow lenses when it is partly cloudy. Clear lenses are good for muddy courses or rainy days. Gray or darker lenses are better for bright days where the rider will be out in the open with direct sunlight.
   4. *Shoes.* Most racers nowadays are wearing cleated shoes. These shoes, along with toe clips, provide a tight fit into the pedal, enabling the optimum power from each stroke. Also, a stiffer shoe will provide a better platform to push against, translating into a more efficient, powerful pedal stroke—as opposed to riding in your tennis shoes where more energy is lost due to the excess flexibility in the shoe.

   Remember this, though. My theory has always been that 80 percent of your performance is yourself and 20 percent is the bike! I received my first mountain bike as a Christmas present about four years ago. It was a lower-end model ranging in price around $450. The following spring, we went to Moab, Utah. This is where the bug bit me. I was amazed at what these two-wheeled vehicles could roll over and the constant abuse they took over the sandstone crags. It was incredible what those knobby tires could grip onto, as if we were actually climbing with sticky rubber shoes over and around these prehistoric land sculptures. These bikes were built for this treatment. They were still in one piece after every ride. When I returned to Colorado in May, I decided to enter a local race, feeling very primed from my ventures on Slickrock and other infamous trails in Utah. I was mentally ready and psyched (and a bit nervous) for my first race. It worked! I beat most of the top-level women, who were riding $1,500 bikes, when I was a rank beginner.

TRAINING

Which brings me to another issue in racing, and that is the homework it requires—or rather training. I train with a heart monitor and find it really beneficial. What's even better is to include a VO_2 max test. Usually at universities you can pay to have the test done or be a guinea pig for an exercise physiologist major. This test tells you your maximum heart rate and many other interesting facts about your body that are useful for training correctly and efficiently. The combination of the heart monitor and VO_2 test gives you guidelines on how hard you should be training day to day. The following is a general workout week for me during race season:

Sunday: Race.
Monday: Recovery day. Easy spin. One to one and a half hours. Low
  heart rate.
Tuesday: Intervals. Speed work. High heart rate.
Wednesday: Long distance. 3–5 hours. Medium heart rate.
Thursday: Sprints. Same as Tuesday.
Friday: Easy day. Get body ready, relaxed.
Saturday: Race.

It is important during the days before a race to make sure your body is well hydrated and properly tanked up. Check your urine. Yellow, dark urine is a good indication of being dehydrated—unless you take a lot of vitamins, your urine should be clear when you are well hydrated. On longer races, I take Power Bars, fig bars or dried fruit. I need to eat every couple of hours; otherwise my performance goes downhill and I'm not enjoying life much either. I always race with two full water bottles— unless it's a very short race (less than one hour). The morning of a race, what I eat depends on the length of the course. If it is a hill climb, I tend to eat lighter, like a bowl of cereal with fruit. For a longer cross-country event, I'll eat one to two hours beforehand and eat a bigger breakfast, like pancakes. I begin eating about one hour into the race to keep my blood sugar level high and to avoid "bonking." When your car runs out of gas, it doesn't run, and our bodies are certainly the same!

If you are still fascinated with all this preparation and work, I suggest you ride down to your local bike shop and find a race in your area to enter. Why not? There is nothing to lose and you may even have some fun at it. In fact, I haven't met a rider yet who hasn't enjoyed a first attempt at racing. I guarantee you'll be at the dinner table that same evening sharing tall tales with fellow "mudheads" about the day's adventures. Watch out—it's contagious!

All racers must have a current NORBA license to enter. All shapes and sizes are encouraged to enter. You can obtain an application at the race or write: USCF, 1750 E. Boulder, Colorado Springs, CO 80909, or phone 719-578-4581.

TANDEMS

In my experience of off-road racing, I had the opportunity to ride a 150-mile race in southern California called the Dodge 150 Desert-to-Sea. This was a race open to both single mountain bikes and tandems. We (Gary Fisher and I) opted for the latter, and what a day was in store for us! We rode from Palm Springs to Dana Point, traversing the San Gabriel and Santa Ana Mountains. Granted most of it was on fire roads—thank God—but we did have a short 5-mile section of technical single track, with 90-degree switchback turns and rocky gullies. I must admit this took some creative thinking, since our Fisher tandem did not have a bungy cord in the middle or any other device that would allow the bike to fold itself in half in order to master these abrupt turns. So we planned for me, "the stoker" (person behind the driver), to grab my running shoes (since I was wearing road cleats, not exactly the most comfortable things to run in). Well, I forgot to pick them up at the aid station, and we were well on down the road before we realized this. I'm not quite sure how Gary maneuvered the tandem around the tight turns, but when I threw a quick glimpse over my shoulder, while running comfortably down the rocks, it was a funny sight to see! The rear wheels were bouncing off the ground and Gary was whooping and hollering. Or was that cussing and swearing I heard?

Anyway, tandems can move very fast on the road because of all the momentum you have. Only one person breaks the wind. We were averaging speeds of 45 mph at times on the pavement, with slick tires on pumped up to 100 psi. When we returned to the dirt roads, we pulled over at the designated aid station and changed back to our Fisher FatTracks (knobby off-road tires at 40 to 50 psi).

It is a very different feeling to be the "stoker" and relinquish all control and vision to the person in front. It is just like sitting on the back seat of a motorcycle or a toboggan where you must lean with the driver for a smooth ride to occur.

There aren't many tandems in mountain bike races. Technical terrain plus the long wheelbase of the tandem makes off-road ATB tandeming quite difficult. Tandems operate much better on wide open roads, where tight turns and large obstacles are not encountered. There are, however, ATB races where the courses are outlined specifically for tandems.

A BRIEF HISTORY OF ALL-TERRAIN BICYCLING

This is your author back again. The history of all-terrain bicycling is brief because the sport is so new. When the earliest versions of ATBs hit the road back in 1974 or so, their share of the total bicycle market was virtually nil. Today the comfort, durability and all-round utility of these machines have captured some 70 percent of the market. Each year ATBs capture more of the market, it seems.

All-terrain bicycling in the United States started in the early 1970s when a group of young people in Marin County, California, across the bay from San Francisco, discovered the fun of "bombing" full tilt down the trails and fire roads of Mt. Tamalpais. The bikes they rode were not conventional road-racing bikes, although many of them were bicycle racers and had good 10-speed road bikes. The preferred bike for riding down the 2,500-foot drop of Mt. Tam was the same 60-pound balloon-tire bicycle that was so popular in the early 1930s (Fig. 10-10). In fact, these bicycles became so popular that riders scoured bike shops in the area and picked them up for $5 or so. The most sought after ballooner was the old Schwinn Excelsior (Fig. 10-10). This bike had one speed, a coaster brake (Fig. 10-11), wide, flat handlebars, balloon tires that imitated those that were so popular on cars of that era, and an imitation gas tank, complete with working horn, which also gave the bike overtones of a motorcycle. Kids loved this bike. As a bomber for tearing down the mountain the bike was amazingly quick, had good steering response, comfort and stability. Even its frame, although made of mild carbon steel, held up well.

Eventually the supply of these oldies but goodies ran dry, and those that were left began to break beyond the ability of frame repairers to patch. At about the same time, the mountain riders, who had to bum rides up to the top in pickup trucks, began trying to ride their heavy one-speed steeds to the peak of Mt. Tam. But only the strongest could

Fig. 10-10. Early model Schwinn Excelsior coaster brake model was in demand by trail riders in the early 1970s, before true ATBs were designed and manufactured.

Fig. 10-11. The coaster brakes on the vintage 3-speeds used for trail riding would burn out on just one or two passes down a mountain trail.

make it; even though stripped of the imitation gas tank and the heavy steel rack, the bikes still weighed around 50 pounds. Finally, around 1975, Gary Fisher, a veteran road racer and today a manufacturer of ATBs, got the idea of adding a multispeed derailleur transmission to the clunkers. Now the clunkers could be ridden up to the top by everybody.

As these old frames wore out and fell by the wayside, premier frame builder and bicycle racer Joe Breeze built the first batch of some dozen true ATBs, using high-quality steel but borrowing frame geometry from the Schwinn Excelsior. The bikes were quickly snapped up and the mountain bikers asked for more. This was in 1977, and the all-terrain bicycle, much as we know it today, was off and running. These early bikes weighed between 35 and 40 pounds.

Now that the frames were hi-tech and strong, the problem was what to do about the wheels and tires. It took awhile, but Joe Breeze and others, such as Tom Ritchey, who began to make ATBs in volume persuaded Japanese manufacturers to make aluminum rims to fit the fat tires, cutting 4 more pounds off the ATB. By 1979, the heavy, dead, unresponsive balloon tires of the Excelsior era were replaced by today's light, responsive, skinwall 26-inch tires that cut 2 more pounds off the ATB. Now these bikes were down to around 30 pounds, and racing versions were refined down to around 28 pounds. By 1979 Tom Ritchey was in large-volume production of high-quality ATBs, and by 1980 just about every major bicycle manufacturer, in this country and abroad, began either making them domestically or importing them under their own label from Japan and Taiwan. The rest is history.

Appendix

Alignment: Applies to the bicycle frame. Dropouts should be parallel; fork blades and stays parallel to the top tube; top tube centered between the stays; the head tube parallel to the fork blades; fork blades parallel to each other; stays parallel to each other; seat tube should be parallel to the bottom bracket sides.

Ankling: Technique of pedaling in which the foot follows through nearly 360 degrees of pedal arc.

Bicycle Computer: An electronic version of the mechanical bicycle odometer. The computers measure elapsed mileage for the day and total mileage for the trip, cadence, and miles per hour; some can measure pulse rate.

Binder bolt: Any bolt and nut that hold a part onto a bicycle, such as the binder bolt(s) for saddles, brakes, carriers, lights, generators, computers, derailleurs, cranks and other bolted-on parts.

Bottom bracket assembly: Spindle, bearings, cones, cups and locknut. The crank arms are attached to the spindle.

Bottom bracket hanger: The short round tube containing the bottom bracket assembly and to which the down tube, seat tube and chainstays are attached.

Brake bridge: A tube mounted between the seat stays to which the rear brake is attached. May also hold fender mount and carrier mount.

Brake levers: Handlebar-mounted levers which control the brakes.

Cables: Flexible steel cables connecting brake levers to the brakes and the shift levers to the front and rear derailleurs.

Cadence: Crank revolutions per minute, a measure of how fast the rider can spin the cranks. A good touring cadence would be 70 to 80 crank revolutions per minute for the casual touring cyclist, up to 100 more for the trained racer.

Chain: The articulated drive unit connecting the chainwheel gears to the freewheel gears.

Chainstays: The frame tubing from the bottom bracket to the rear drop-outs.

Chainwheels: The toothed gears attached to the bottom bracket spindle that deliver pedal power to the freewheel gears. Chainwheels may be single, double or triple.

Coaster brakes: A brake mechanism contained in the rear wheel hub, which is actuated by backpedaling.

Cotter Key: A key or pin that holds cottered cranks on the bottom bracket spindle.

Crank Arm: The long shaft that is attached to the bottom bracket spindle and to which the pedals are attached.

Cyclometer: A mechanical odometer for measuring mileage.

Derailleur: From the French meaning "to derail" or "shift." The rear derailleur shifts the chain from one freewheel cog to another; the front derailleur shifts the chain from one chainwheel to another.

Down tube: The frame tube that is connected to the head tube and to the bottom bracket.

Dishing: Describes truing the rear wheel so the rim is centered exactly between the hub axle locknuts. Necessary because of added width of the freewheel. In dishing, the rear wheel rim is more toward the right hub flange, whereas the front wheel rim, which is not dished, is centered between the hub flanges.

Dropouts: Slotted openings into which wheel hub axles fit. Hold front and rear wheels.

Fork: Consists of the fork blades, fork crown, front wheel dropouts, and steering tube.

Head tube: The short tube to which is connected the top and down tubes and which holds the fork with its associated headset bearings, cups, cones and locknut.

Hub: The front and rear wheel units that hold the wheel axle and to which are attached the spokes.

Panniers: Bike packs and bags.

Quick release: A cam-and-lever-actuated mechanism which permits quick and easy removal and installation of a bicycle wheel.

Saddle: The seat.

Seat post: A hollow tube sized to fit into the seat tube, designed to hold and support the saddle. Adjustable so saddle can be tilted and moved closer to or farther away from the handlebars.

Seat stays: Two hollow steel tubes attached at one end of the seat tube and at the other end to each of the rear wheel dropouts. With the chainstays (see above) they form the rear triangle of the bicycle frame.

RESOURCES

Catalogs

Campmor, Box 999, Paramus, NJ 07653-0999. Outside NJ 1-800-526-4784, in NJ 201-445-5000. Wide selection of high-quality camping gear.

L. L. Bean, Freeport, ME 04033. 1-800-221-4221. High-quality camp gear, clothing, bikes. The old standby.

Moss Tent Works, Inc., Mt. Mattie St., Camden, ME 04843. 207-236-8368. Super top-line tents by America's premier tentmaker. For the bike packer.

Palo Alto Bicycles, P.O. Box 1276, Palo Alto, CA 94302. Everything bicycles. Outside CA 1-800-227-8900, in CA 415-328-0128.

Pedal Pushers, 1130 Rogero Rd., Jacksonville, FL 32211-5895. Outside FL 1-800-874-2453, in FL 1-800-342-7320. Good catalog, compiled by cyclists.

Performance Bicycle Shop, P.O Box 2741, Chapel Hill, NC 27514. 1-800-334-5471. A beautifully put together catalog of bicycles, parts, components, accessories, clothing. Much help in parts selection.

Recreation Equipment, Inc., P.O. Box C-88125, Seattle, WA 98188. 1-800-562-4894. For Canada, Hawaii and Alaska, 1-206-575-3287. If you join their benefits program (fee $5) you receive a membership card which, when used with orders, gives you a quite substantial discount. Everything outdoors. Camping gear, bicycles, books, you name it, they have it.

Rhode Gear, 765 Allens Avenue, Providence, RI 02905. 1-800-HOT-GEAR. Excellent panniers and other equipment designed by this firm. Plus lots of parts, clothing and other gear.

The Third Hand, P.O. Box 212, Mt. Shasta, CA 96067. 916-926-2600. The bike tool doesn't exist if it's not in their catalog. Plus small parts unavailable elsewhere.

Custom Bicycles

Breeze Cycles, 18 Meadow Way, Fairfax, CA 94930. 415-454-6536.

Klein Bicycle Corporation, 207B S. Prairie Rd., Chehalis, WA 98532. 1-800-345-5346.

Mezzatesta Custom Cycles, 5 May Ct., Poughkeepsie, NY 12603. 914-462-2340.

Dave Plantagena Custom Cycles, 407 W. Taylor, Kokomo, IN 46901. 317-457-8877.

Romic Cycle Company, 4433 Steffani Lane, Houston, TX 77041. 713-466-7806.

Richard Sachs Cycles, One Main St., Chester, CT 06412. 203-526-2059.

Stephan & Sharp Design Group, 30170 Via De La Mesa, Rancho, CA 92390. 714-676-5861.

Stout Custom Cycles, 3474 S 2300 E, Salt Lake City, UT 84109. 801-278-9875.

Strawberry Cyclesport Inc., 224 NW 10th Ave., Portland, OR 97209. 503-225-0136.

Terry Precision Bicycles for Women, 140 Despatch Dr., East Rochester, NY 14445. 716-385-6398.

Health and Fitness Books

Rafoth, Richard, MD. *Bicycling Fuel: Nutrition for Bicycle Riders.* Bicycle Books, San Francisco, 1988.

Roy, Karen E., and Thurlow Rogers. *Fit & Fast, How to Be a Better Cyclist.* Vitesse Press, Brattleboro, VT, 1989.

Sjogaard, Gisela, et al. *Psychology in Bicycling.* Movement Publications, Ithaca, New York, 1988.

Tandems

Burley Design Cooperative, 4080 Stewart Rd., Eugene, OR 97402. 800-423-8445.

Cannondale Corporation, 9 Brookside Pl., Georgetown, CT 06829. 800-433-6543.

Fisher Mountain Bikes, 140 Mitchell Blvd., San Rafael, CA 94903. 800-354-2247.

Ibis Cycles, P.O. Box 275, Sebastopol, CA 95473. 707-829-5615.

Moots Cycles, Box 2480, Steamboat Springs, CO 80477. 303-879-1675.

Technical Books

Brandt, Jobst. *The Bicycle Wheel.* Avocet, Inc., Menlo Park, CA, 1983.

Burke, Edmund, ed. *Science of Cycling.* Human Kinetics Books, Champaign, IL, 1986.

Hayduk, Douglas. *Bicycle Metallurgy for the Cyclist.* Douglas Hayduk, Boulder, CO, 1987.

Hinault, Bernard. *Memories of the Peloton.* Vitesse Press, Brattleboro, VT, 1989.

Marr, Dick. *Bicycle Gearing: A Practical Guide.* The Mountaineers, Seattle, WA, 1989.

Whitt, Frank Rowland, and David Gordon Wilson. *Bicycling Science.* The MIT Press, Cambridge, MA, 1988.

Sloane, Eugene A. *Sloane's New Bicycle Maintenance Manual.* Simon & Schuster, New York, 1991. How to fix everything on your bicycle. Hubs, wheels, chainwheels, freewheels, brakes, tires, frame alignment are just a few of the subjects covered.

————. *Sloane's Handy Pocket Guide to Bicycle Repair.* Simon & Schuster, New York, 1988. How to make emergency repairs on your bicycle when you are far from a bike shop. Covers brakes, hubs, spoke replacement, freewheel, tire repair and other common on-the-road mechanical problems.

Trail Riding Books

Bunnelle, Hasse, and Shirley Sarvis. *Cooking for Camp and Trail.* The Sierra Club, San Francisco, 1984. An appetizing guide to energy sustaining foods for the trail.

Bunnelle, Hasse, and Thomas, Winnie. *Food for Knapsackers.* The Sierra Club, San Francisco, 1971. A totebook with lots of excellent data on nutrition, meals planning, equipment and recipes. You can get hungry just browsing through this book.

The Complete Guide to America's National Parks. The National Park Foundation, Washington, D.C., 1984. Comprehensive data on all 360 U.S. National Parks, including maps, mailing addresses, phone numbers, directions, permits, fees, facilities, regulations, weather, points of interest and more. At $10 a copy, a real bargain! Cost is tax deductible as a contribution to the nonprofit chartered National Park Foundation, P.O. Box 57473, Washington, D.C., 20037. 1-202-785-4500.

Greenbank, Anthony. *The Complete Book of Survival.* New American Library, New York. Lots of good information on first aid, hypothermia and trail rescue. An excellent sourcebook for anyone preparing for a wilderness trip.

Higley, Don C. *Pocketwise Tips on Use of the Compass, Man-Made and Natural.* Seattle, Self-published, Washington, 1981. This booklet is as short as its title is long, but it does cover the basics, in simplified form, of the use of the compass. Covers topo map reading and some star sighting.

Lobeck, Armin K. *Things Maps Don't Tell Us.* The Macmillan Company, New York, 1956. Kind of a fun book on map reading and interpretation. Not for finding your way about, but an explanation of why land, lake and other natural formations are the way they are. Sort of a phrenological approach to the way the world is shaped today.

Watts, Alan. *Instant Weather Forecasting.* Dodd Mead & Company, New York, 1968. A really great little guide, with color photos of how to interpret local weather phenomena, such as clouds, wind direction and velocity, to predict the weather you'll likely face each day. A practical approach to being your own weather forecaster, wherever you are.

Index

(Page numbers in *italics* refer to illustrations.)